The Innocent Eye,

CHILDHOOD IN
MARK TWAIN'S IMAGINATION

by Albert E. Stone, Jr.

ARCHON BOOKS   1970

SBN: 208 00820 9
Library of Congress Catalog Card Number: 79-103991 √
Printed in the United States of America

He had a wife and family; indeed, random drippings from his gossipy pen rather clearly indicate that he had more than one family; for he often mentions by name "children" of his who must have been illegitimate, since he nowhere gives them the family surname. Among these are two sons whom he is so weakly fond of that he parades them literally without discretion or shame—Huck Finn and Tom Sawyer. In unguarded moments he quotes remarks of theirs which expose the fact that their mothers were of low origin and illiterate.

From "Eddypus," an unpublished manuscript in the Mark Twain Papers, University of California, Berkeley

Preface

FOR A GENERATION nurtured on Freud, Gesell, and Dr. Spock it is difficult to imagine a time when childhood was not considered by Americans the most significant period of life. As readers of literature, too, we accept as a matter of course the present-day preoccupation of writers and dramatists with the world of children. Almost every issue of, say, the *New Yorker* carries a short story in which some precocious child or youth is introduced, painfully at least and perhaps tragically, into maturity. Salinger, Saroyan, Faulkner, Welty, Porter, Grau, Capote—the list is long of the serious writers who have taught us to regard this theme as natural to our time. Moreover, the novelists themselves, as members of a society in which fiction is both self-expression and commodity, reflect by their characteristic subject matter the interests and values of American culture. On the stage, too, the situation is similar. In recent seasons the ambiguously innocent face of evil has been that of a child in *The Bad Seed* and *The Turn of the Screw.* American audiences have witnessed Nazi brutality seen through a young girl's eyes in *The Diary of Anne Frank.* The loneliness of love has for our day received one classic demonstration in *A Member of the Wedding.* In striking ways the modern artist finds the child's mind—innocent, fresh, acute—an appropriate mirror and an ideal mask for his art.

Like other aspects of American culture, this concern has been part of our tradition for longer than we may realize. Its origins lie somewhere in the early years of the nineteenth century

vii

when the Transcendentalist movement began to change modes of thought in New England. As early as 1842, for instance, Emerson was noting wryly in his Journal, "Dr. Bradford said it was a misfortune to be born when children were nothing and live until men were nothing." The Romantic imagination had indeed reversed the traditional Puritan family order of things. Men like Emerson and Bronson Alcott asserted, with Wordsworth, that children, far from being little limbs of Satan, were in fact innately superior to adults, closer to Nature and hence to God, more alive to sensuous, emotional, and moral experience. At the same time—that is, beginning in the 1830's and 40's—the importance of the formative years came to be felt in other areas of American life. Catharine Beecher, Elizabeth Peabody, and Horace Mann in education; Horace Bushnell in theology; Samuel Goodrich and Jacob Abbott in magazine writing; itinerant portrait-painters like Erastus Field and Henry Walton—they are but some of those who reflected, in the decades before the Civil War, the new sympathy and interest. In fiction the first flowers of this development were certain of the sketches and short stories of Nathaniel Hawthorne. "The Gentle Boy" (1832) may be taken as a landmark in a new literary genre.

It was not until after the Civil War, however, that childhood as a theme attracted more than a few writers whom we today call serious artists. All the major novelists of that generation—Howells, James, Twain, and Crane—followed the example of Hawthorne. Within a span of twenty years or so *Tom Sawyer*, *Huckleberry Finn*, "The Pupil," *What Maisie Knew*, *The Awkward Age*, *The Turn of the Screw*, *A Boy's Town*, *The Red Badge of Courage*, and *The Whilomville Stories* were added to the body of American letters. Furthermore, these years saw an equally astonishing efflorescence among less talented writers of works that dealt with "the unwarped primal world" of childhood. Sarah Orne Jewett and B. P. Shillaber in New England;

Edward Eggleston and Edgar W. Howe in the Middle West;
Frances Hodgson Burnett in New York; Joel Chandler Harris
and Kate Chopin in the South, and other less familiar figures
peopled the pages of American magazines and books with a
procession of young boys and girls. A favorite vehicle was the
new childrens' magazine, which in the fifteen years after the
War sprang into prominence and popularity and proved so
formative an influence on a whole generation of Americans like
"Teedie" Roosevelt. *Our Young Folks, The Riverside Magazine*, the *St. Nicholas* pursued the novel policy of soliciting for
the edification of their young readers the work of the best
writers of the day. In this endeavor editors like Mary Mapes
Dodge, John T. Trowbridge, and Horace E. Scudder notably
affected the range and quality of literary expression in the
United States.

At the center of this development in American fiction stands
Mark Twain. To a degree unexcelled by any of the novelists
of his generation, he devoted a career to writing about childhood. Five of his novels, several long novelettes, and a number
of short stories, sketches, and essays depict the world of
adolescents, children, or infants. In the form of a young boy
or girl he gave imaginative life to those heroic roles which in
our culture (child-centered though it is) are normally enacted
by adults—the vagabond, the detective, the political ruler,
the general, and the saint. Indeed, Twain's fascination with
immaturity was so deep-seated and persistent an aspect of his
imagination that many of his fictional adults are conceived
essentially as grown-up children. In *The Mysterious Stranger*
he carried this tendency to its ultimate when he depicted God
in the guise of an omnipotent Bad Boy. As the matter of Europe
was Henry James' grand motif, clearly childhood was the central experience of life and the chief mode of thought for Mark
Twain.

It is to this theme in Twain's fiction that the present book is addressed. One cannot say, of course, that childhood is the hidden figure in the carpet of his prose; three generations and more of common readers have been well aware of his dedication to boyhood, though it may come as a surprise to some to discover how deep was his devotion to young girls. Critics and biographers have pointed out this dimension of Twain's art and thought. Recently, historians have traced the social and intellectual currents in his world which help to account for his and others' passion for youth. Many of these efforts, however, have been in the form of *obiter dicta* in briefs for other clients.

Conceived as the filling-in of one significant gap in American studies, this book was originally written as a doctoral dissertation at Yale University. As such, it inevitably bears marks of many minds besides the author's. Though they are not to be saddled with my shortcomings, much credit for guidance and criticism belongs to the following: Norman Holmes Pearson in particular, the late Stanley T. Williams, the late Charles A. Fenton, Richard W. B. Lewis, John Morton Blum, Walter Blair, Henry Nash Smith, and David M. Potter. I also acknowledge gratefully the financial assistance provided by the Fluid Research Fund of the Yale Graduate School. Publication of this book was assisted by the Ford Foundation.

The following libraries, institutions, and collections were consulted and I owe a debt of gratitude to the obliging members of their staffs: the Mark Twain Papers, University of California, Berkeley (whose librarian, Frederick Anderson, deserves a special citation for helpfulness); the Henry W. and Albert A. Berg Collection, New York Public Library; the Yale Collection of American Literature; the Houghton Library, Harvard University; the Mark Twain Library and Memorial Commission, Hartford; the Watkinson Library of Reference, Trinity College; the Connecticut State Library; the Mark Train Library, West Redding, Connecticut; and the private collections of C. Waller Barrett of New York City and Harold L. Mueller of Redding, Connecticut.

Quotations from the works of Mark Twain appear with the permission of his publishers, Harper and Brothers. To the Duke University Press I am grateful for permission to reprint from *American Literature* most of the material of Chapter 7. Parts of Chapters 1, 3, and 5 were rehearsed in lectures delivered at Amherst College, in 1957, and Stetson University, in the summer of 1960.

Finally I wish to thank three ladies: Mrs. Jane Sherman, Mrs. Grant Robley, and especially my wife, Grace Woodbury Stone. Without their unstinting gifts of time and effort, this book would still be a set of notes.

A. E. S., Jr.

New Haven, Connecticut
August 1960

Contents

1.

Mark Twain and New England

ALL HIS LIFE Mark Twain found it difficult to settle down. For a writer who made a living and a world-wide reputation from the fruits of his travels, establishing permanent roots was a challenge. Early in the fall of 1871, however, he did exactly that, by moving with his family from Buffalo to Connecticut. Twain and his wife had not been happy in Buffalo, and when the chance came to rent a spacious house from John Hooker of Hartford, they accepted at once. It was the most significant move Twain ever made.

Twain had visited Hartford many times before and had long eyed the Connecticut capital as a possible home. On business trips to the American Publishing Company, which had issued *Innocents Abroad* in 1869, he had met many of the writers, editors, and clergymen who gave Hartford the reputation as a New England cultural center not far behind Boston. He had lectured on the Sandwich Islands at Allyn Hall and had been warmly received. "Of all the beautiful towns it has been my fortune to see," he wrote back to the *Alta California* in September 1868, "this is the chief . . . Some of these stately dwellings are almost buried from sight in parks and forests of these noble trees. Everywhere the eye turns it is blessed with a vision of refreshing green. You do not know what beauty is if you have not been here." [1] Privately, too, Twain voiced the convic-

1. *Alta California* (Sept. 6, 1868), reprinted in Henry Darbee, ed.,

1

tion, "I desire to have the respect of this sterling old Puritan community, for their respect is well worth having." [2] Hence his arrival in the city in 1871 fulfilled an ambition the Western humorist had harbored for some time.

The neighborhood to which he brought his wife and infant son was known locally as Nook Farm. Lying in a pleasant wooded plot just to the west of the city, it was a small and decidedly genteel community where many of Twain's new friends had their homes. One such neighbor was Charles Dudley Warner, editor of the *Courant* and soon to collaborate with Twain on *The Gilded Age*. Warner's brother and sister-in-law, George and Lilly Warner, lived a stone's throw away. Lilly Warner was known locally as a writer of children's stories; her close friend and frequent house guest was Mary Mapes Dodge, a little later to found the *St. Nicholas Magazine*, to which Lilly contributed. Other Yankee families in the neighborhood who welcomed the Clemenses were the Hookers, the Gillettes, the Burtons, and the Stowes. The Stowes were the poorest but the most famous of the Nook Farmers. The Reverend Calvin Stowe, a rotund and absent-minded professor of theology, had retired from Andover Seminary to Hartford. His wife Harriet supported the family on the earnings of her numerous books. Her fame, of course, had been made in 1852 with *Uncle Tom's Cabin*, and in 1871 the Nook Farm neighbors were reading and praising her *Little Pussy Willow*, a pleasant and edifying story for girls which had appeared the previous Christmas. Over on Woodland Street, not in Nook Farm but conveniently near to it, lived the Reverend Joseph Twichell, pastor of the Asylum Hill Congregational Church and already

---

Mark Twain in Hartford (Hartford, Mark Twain Library and Memorial Commission, 1958), p. 5.

2. MT to Mrs. A. W. Fairbanks (Jan. 24, 1868), in Dixon Wecter, ed., *Mark Twain to Mrs. Fairbanks* (San Marino, Calif., Huntington Library, 1949), p. 15.

one of Twain's closest cronies. Joe Twichell had helped to marry Twain to Olivia Langdon in Elmira the previous year.

This small and somewhat self-contained settlement of intellectuals by the early 1870's had come to enjoy an enviable reputation in the city. The Hartford *Post* once referred to the "atmosphere of holy domesticity" and "the enkindling intellectuality" of the Hooker home, and this description would equally well have fitted the whole neighborhood; [3] it was universally acknowledged by visitors that Nook Farm had a social, spiritual, and intellectual flavor all its own. Families lived there in close and tolerant conviviality. Doors were seldom locked and neighborhood children and their parents ate and played together in a seemingly endless round of domestic gatherings. When in later years some of the residents grew older and more peculiar, it was not taken amiss for Isabella Hooker to conduct séances in her parlor or for gentle, senile Mrs. Stowe to wander unbidden into the Clemens' house and pick flowers from the conservatory. After all, she had designed the room herself.[4]

Twain's advent soon gave Nook Farm a national as well as local fame. The large brick residence which the Clemenses built in 1874 became a landmark toward which a stream of visitors from all over America and the Continent directed expectant feet. Over the mantlepiece in the library was carved "The ornament of a house is the friends who frequent it," and this sentiment from Emerson's "Domestic Life" aptly described the spirit of the place. Bronson Alcott, William Dean Howells,

3. Quoted in Kenneth S. Andrews, *Nook Farm, Mark Twain's Hartford Circle* (Cambridge, Mass., Harvard University Press, 1950), p. 4.

4. See Andrews, chap. 3. See also Mary Lawton, *A Lifetime with Mark Twain: The Memories of Katy Leary, for Thirty Years His Faithful Servant* (New York, Harcourt, Brace, & Co., 1925), p. 35; Albert B. Paine, *Mark Twain, a Biography. The Personal and Literary Life of Samuel Langhorne Clemens* (3 vols. New York, Harper & Brothers, 1912), *1*, 476 ff.

Thomas Bailey Aldrich, Bret Harte, Matthew Arnold, Moncure D. Conway, George Washington Cable, Joel Chandler Harris—these and many other literary notables were entertained at Nook Farm, usually in the Clemens' palatial home, where the wit and conversation were matched by the wine and food and service. Olivia Clemens, who until her marriage to the author of *Innocents Abroad* had been the pampered and invalid daughter of a wealthy Elmira businessman, had her hands full running a household that in some respects resembled more a diplomat's than a writer's ménage. For almost twenty years Twain's home was the center of a literary circle notable for its combination of private happiness, quiet luxury, and social éclat. In spite of their many activities, Twain and his wife found time to devote to their three daughters. He was adopted by a New England society that was domestic, literary, and expensive. Despite a boisterous Western background— it was several years before Howells and Twichell could get him to abandon his black string tie—he fitted smoothly into Nook Farm. His life likewise became domestic and literary— and very expensive. Together with his neighbors, he spent many hours with his daughters and their young friends. Picnics, walks, charades, plays, and Christmas parties were family affairs at Nook Farm, to be enjoyed by old and young together. Reading, too, was a family ritual. "One of the pleasantest neighborhood customs that grew up in the Hartford home," Twain's brother-in-law later recalled, "was the gathering of an evening, around the library fire while Mr. Clemens read aloud. He liked stirring poetry, which he read admirably, sometimes rousing his little audience to excitement and cheers." [5] On such occasions the novels of Dickens, Cooper, Charlotte Mary Yonge, or Louisa May Alcott were enjoyed. Children's maga-

5. Jervis Langdon, *Samuel Langhorne Clemens—Some Reminiscences and Some Excerpts and Unpublished Manuscripts* (privately printed), reprinted in Darbee, *Mark Twain in Hartford*, p. 14.

zines like the *Youth's Companion* were avidly consumed by the small folk of the neighborhood. The Clemens' library, in common with others at Nook Farm, contained Jacob Abbott's Rollo books, *The Heir of Redclyffe*, *Daddy Darwin's Dovecot*, and numerous other stories written especially for the new and growing audience of the young.

One reason why children's literature was so popular at Nook Farm was that several of the parents had a professional interest in the genre. Mrs. Stowe was making a respectable living from her tales of her own New England girlhood; *The Minister's Wooing* (1859), *The Pearl of Orr's Island* (1862), and *Oldtown Folks* (1869) were for children to read as well as grownups, and children figured prominently in all of them as characters. In a few years Lilly Warner would become a charter contributor to Mrs. Dodge's *St. Nicholas* and Charles Dudley Warner would turn from essays to the writing of *Being a Boy* (1878). When Mark Twain discovered, as he speedily did, that living at Nook Farm cost more than his winter lecturing tour could support, it was only natural for him to consider writing fiction as his neighbors did. The sort of fiction he began to write on his own (after the trial balloon, *The Gilded Age*) modeled itself on local products. It exploited, like theirs, experiences of childhood and domestic life and was written to interest all members of a family audience. *Tom Sawyer*, *The Prince and the Pauper*, and *Huckleberry Finn* were written for a variety of reasons, but one of these was that Mark Twain's Hartford neighbors had shown him that childhood was a lode that would pay.

"The atmosphere of holy domesticity" which the Hartford *Post* detected in a Nook Farm home suggests another element in the New England air of 1871 which acted upon Mark Twain. The Farm was not only child-centered but also church-going; it held liberal Protestant notions about Christian nurture. By this time, the traditional Calvinist belief in children as innately depraved offspring of Satan had been swept away. Hartford was particularly prone to regard children as important and integral members of the religious body because of the presence in the city of liberal Congregationalism's leading theologian. Dr. Horace Bushnell, retired pastor of the North Church in Hartford, was a divine well known in Nook Farm. The author of *Christian Nurture* (1861), Bushnell probably met Twain through the Monday Evening Club. At biweekly meetings of this Club, of which Dr. Bushnell, Calvin Stowe, and J. Hammond Trumbull were founders, a select group of Hartford citizens presented papers and discussed all manner of literary, intellectual, political, and religious topics. Shortly after his arrival in the city Twain was elected and for the next twenty years attended its meetings pretty faithfully when he was at home. To its membership he presented some of his most intimate ideas. *What Is Man?*, his "Gospel" of pessimistic determinism, was first outlined in a paper to this Club as early as 1881. (It was greeted with universal and vehement opposition.)

At these friendly meetings Twain must have become acquainted with Bushnell's advanced ideas on child-rearing. There is no evidence that Twain ever read *Christian Nurture,* and its pious tone would probably have dismayed him if he had. But the young writer greatly respected Bushnell—"that noble old Roman" he called him later in an essay [6]—and doubtless discovered that he shared some of the aged minister's dislike of traditional doctrines. Twain's own religious experiences as a boy in Hannibal had developed in him a fascinated loathing for Calvinist doctrines of sin and damnation.[7] By the

6. "Down the Rhone," in *Europe and Elsewhere: The Writings of Mark Twain,* Definitive Edition (New York, Gabriel Wells, 1922–25), 29, 143. All references, unless otherwise specified, will be to this edition.

7. Dixon Wecter, *Sam Clemens of Hannibal* (Boston, Houghton Mifflin, 1952), pp. 86–90.

6

1870's, in spite of the family pew maintained at Joe Twichell's church (which he jokingly referred to as the "Church of the Holy Speculators"), Twain was privately a skeptic. Infant damnation, in particular, was a dogma repugnant to him. In a paper he wrote at this time he scathingly denounced the Old Testament:

> Its God was strictly proportioned to its dimensions. His sole solicitude was about a handful of truculent nomads . . . He sulked, he cursed, he raged, he grieved, according to his mood and the circumstances, but all to no purpose; his efforts were all vain, he could not govern them. When the fury was on him he was blind to all reason—he not only slaughtered the offender, but even his harmless little children and dumb cattle . . .[8]

Bushnell might have been upset by the tone of his young friend's outburst, but he would have sympathized with Twain's indignation over the "harmless little children." *Christian Nurture* attacked precisely the Calvinist dogma which held that children by birth and nature were totally depraved and stood outside the church until regenerated by an emotional conversion that came only with adulthood. Bushnell's answer was infant baptism. "Never is it too early for good to be communicated," he asserted. "Infancy and childhood are the ages most pliant to good. And who can think it necessary that the plastic nature of childhood must first be hardened into stone . . . before it can become a candidate for Christian character!"[9]

Instead of regarding the young as worthless and depraved, Bushnell believed they should be baptized and reared by their parents in Christian fellowship, so that there might never be a

8. Quoted in Paine, *1*, 412.
9. Horace Bushnell, *Christian Nurture* (New York, Scribner, 1861), p. 22.

time when they felt alienated from parents, church, or God. Such a theological position in the mid-nineteenth century was not a radical but a traditional belief. It represented a return to the seventeenth-century Congregational practice and doctrine that had been submerged during the ascendancy of revivalistic Protestantism of the eighteenth and early nineteenth centuries.[10] To those who still insisted upon a mature conversion experience before admitting a young person to membership Bushnell retorted, "What is the use of a fold, if the lambs are to be kept outside till it is seen whether they can stand the weather?" [11]

Twain remembered with horror his own childish fears of Missouri preachers who had proclaimed the doctrines Bushnell was opposing. Repeatedly in his later writings Twain ridiculed revival meetings and the dogmas pronounced at them. Toward the close of his career when he was writing *The Mysterious Stranger,* set in early Hannibal, he made a note that reveals how strongly he still felt on this issue. In that unfinished version of the story young Satan takes Tom Sawyer and Huck Finn down to Hell one Sunday, where "they wipe the tears of the unbaptised babies roasting on the red hot floors—one is Tom's little niece that he so grieved to lose—still, as she deserves this punishment he is able to bear it." [12] In spite of, indeed because of, his growing skepticism, Twain must have

10. For the seventeenth-century attitude toward children in the church see Edmund S. Morgan, *The Puritan Family* (Boston, The Trustees of the Public Library, 1944), pp. 90–104. A discussion of Bushnell's role in the nineteenth-century revival of older attitudes of Christian nurture is found in Sandford Fleming, *Children and Puritanism* (New Haven, Yale University Press, 1933), pp. 185–208. See also Lewis B. Schenck, *The Presbyterian Doctrine of Children in the Covenant* (New Haven, Yale University Press, 1940), pp. 142–47.

11. Bushnell, *Christian Nurture,* 309.

12. MT, Notebook 32(II) (last date Nov. 11, 1898) Typescript p. 51, in Mark Twain Papers (MTP), University of California, Berkeley. © Mark Twain Company.

found Bushnell's ideas as congenial as he found the old man's character admirable.

Christian Nurture was not the only expression of a new religious attitude toward children which Twain might have picked up at Nook Farm in the early years of his residence there. At neighborhood family gatherings he may well have heard of Catharine Beecher's *Religious Training of Children in the School, the Family, and the Church* (1864). Not only was the author the sister of his neighbor Mrs. Stowe, but she had run a famous female seminary for girls in Hartford many years before and was a well-known figure there. Although she had moved, somewhat fashionably, from the Congregational to the Episcopal Church, Catharine Beecher had done so, as she asserted, because the Anglican Church trained its children "on the assumption that they are lambs of Christ's fold, and that the 'Grace' needful to their successful training for heaven will be bestowed in exact proportion to the faithfulness of parents and children in striving to understand and obey the teachings of Christ." [13]

Twain's antipathy for theology is well known. But even if he never looked inside the covers of *Christian Nurture* or *Religious Training* he could have painlessly absorbed through fiction the liberal ideas they contained. Harriet Beecher Stowe's *Oldtown Folks* appeared just two years before the Clemenses came to Hartford, and we know from a reference in "The Man That Corrupted Hadleyburg" that Twain was familiar enough with this novel of New England village life to mention one of its characters in his own story.[14] Mrs. Stowe, like her older

13. Quoted in Charles Foster, *The Rungless Ladder: Harriet Beecher Stowe and New England Puritanism* (Durham, N.C., Duke University Press, 1954), p. 180.

14. Sam Lawson is the character from *Oldtown Folks* to whom Jack Halliday, "the loafing, good-natured, no-account, irreverent fisherman, hunter, boys' friend, stray-dogs' friend" is compared in "The Man That Corrupted Hadleyburg," 23, 18.

sister, was perturbed by infant damnation; indeed, it appears to have been a live issue in Nook Farm throughout the early years of Twain's life there. Through Ellery Davenport, a dashing young Bostonian, the author voiced her opinions on the subject. "I admit that your catechism," the young Congregationalist remarks to Miss Deborah, a pretty and devout Anglican, "is much better for children than the one I was brought up on."

> I was well drilled in the formulas of the celebrated Assembly of *dry*vines of Westminster, and dry enough I found it. Now it's a true proverb, "Call a man a thief, and he'll steal;" "give a dog a bad name, and he'll bite you;" tell a child that he is "a member of Christ, a child of God, and an inheritor of the kingdom of heaven," and he feels, to say the least, civilly disposed towards religion; tell him "he is under God's wrath and curse, and so liable to all the miseries of this life, to death itself, and the pains of hell forever," because somebody ate an apple five thousand years ago, and his religious associations are not so agreeable,—especially if he has the answers whipped into him, or has to go to bed without his supper for not learning them.[15]

Here are the same ideas of Dr. Bushnell and Catharine Beecher, but expressed in a form more likely to interest and amuse a skeptic who might grow drowsy during theological debates at the Monday Evening Club. Twain probably did not consider important the religious implications of these ideas about children. But it is clear from his writings and from his family life at Nook Farm that he did consider their social implications. Along with his new neighbors, he accepted the organic

15. *Oldtown Folks and Sam Lawson's Oldtown Fireside Stories,* 2 vols. in *The Writings of Harriet Beecher Stowe,* Riverside Edition (Boston and New York, The Riverside Press, 1896), *1,* 360–61.

unity of the Christian family, and he regarded Susy, Clara, Jean, and their friends as full-fledged members of the social body. To accord children this status hardly seems noteworthy today, but in the 1870's it was a necessary prelude to writing fiction for them and about them.

If Nook Farm needed secular justification for its child-centered domestic and literary life, one prime source was the author of the motto over Mark Twain's mantle. Ralph Waldo Emerson was well known in Hartford. He had lectured there in the not-too-distant past. His *Essays* were to be found in every cultured home, including the Clemens'. Twain read Emerson as a matter of course; in 1879 Joe Twichell and he had a long and serious talk in which the implications of Emerson and the *Rubaiyat* were aired.[16] Such attention was only natural in an intellectual community which almost self-consciously considered itself a latter-day Concord.

Dr. Bushnell's liberal views about children may themselves have found inspiration in Emerson. Both thinkers stressed the natural virtues of the young. "To the well-born child all the virtues are natural, and not painfully acquired," Emerson asserted in "The Over-Soul." [17] In the eyes of the Sage of Concord, children were not only morally superior to adults but intellectually more independent and discerning. "The nonchalance of boys who are sure of a dinner," he wrote in "Self Reliance," "and would disdain as much as a lord to do or say aught to conciliate one, is the healthy attitude of human nature. A boy is in the parlor what the pit is in the playhouse; independent, irresponsible, looking out from his corner on such people as pass by, he tries and sentences them on their merits, in the swift, summary way of boys, as good, bad, interesting,

16. Andrews, *Nook Farm,* p. 72.
17. Ralph Waldo Emerson, *Collected Works,* Riverside Edition (Cambridge, Mass., Houghton Mifflin, 1883), 2, 259.

silly, eloquent, troublesome." [18] We may imagine how congenial such an assertion must have sounded to Twain, already the author of some satiric newspaper sketches in which boys behaved exactly as Emerson said, and soon to be the creator of Tom Sawyer and Huck Finn. Moreover, Emerson's pithy language may have opened Twain's eyes: "They know truth from counterfeit as quick as the chemist does," Emerson observes in "Education." "They detect weakness in your eye and behavior a week before you open your mouth, and give you the benefit of their opinion quick as a wink. They make no mistakes, have no pedantry, but entire belief on experience . . . If I can pass with them, I can manage well enough with their fathers." [19]

From the point of view of modern child psychology, it is interesting to compare Emerson and Bushnell in their judgments as to the most significant period in a child's life. For Bushnell it was the very earliest years. Forty years before Freud he observed: "it is made clear, I think, to any judicious and thoughtful person, that the most important age of Christian nurture is the first; that which we have called the age of impressions . . . more, as a general fact, is done, or lost by neglect of doing, on a child's immortality, in the first three years of his life, than in all his years of discipline afterwards." [20] Emerson, on the other hand, in line with Transcendentalist emphasis on process, growth, and change, considered adolescence the "crisis in the life of the man worth studying." In his *Journal* he commented on the age of puberty:

> It is the passage from the Unconscious to the Conscious; from the sleep of the Passions to their rage; from careless receiving to cunning providing; from beauty to use; from omnivorous curiosity to anxious stewardship; from faith

18. Ibid., *2*, 50.
19. Ibid., *10*, 138.
20. Bushnell, *Christian Nurture*, p. 248.

to doubt; from maternal Reason to hard, short-sighted Understanding; from unity to disunion; the progressive influences of poetry, eloquence, love, regeneration, character, truth, sorrow, and of the search for an Aim, and the contest for property.[21]

Though neither Horace Bushnell nor Mark Twain could have read such a comment, similar statements are to be found scattered throughout the *Essays*, especially in "Education" and "Domestic Life." It was through Emerson more than any other writer and lecturer that New Englanders in mid-nineteenth-century America were made aware of the Romantic image of the child as natural saint and natural aristocrat.

To the Transcendentalists, childhood had special value. It was the state most closely in tune with God and the physical world. Consequently, it is hardly surprising to find Emerson enjoining writers of his own generation to investigate this area of life. "You need not write the History of the World," he advised in 1859, "nor the Fall of Man, nor King Arthur, nor Iliad, nor Christianity; but write of hay, or of cattle-shows, or trade sales, or of a ship, or of Ellen [Emerson's small daughter], or of Alcott, or of a couple of schoolboys, if only you can be the fanatic of your subject, and find a fibre reaching from it to the core of your heart, so that all your affection and all your thought can freely play." [22] No more appropriate advice for Twain can be imagined. By the time he had moved to New England the direct influence of Emerson was on the decline, but for the older generation of Twain's Lyceum-going neighbors it was still potent. Nook Farm imitated Concord by respecting Concord's gods. Hence, in the secular realm, Emerson's influence on the Stowes, the Warners, the Twichells, and

21. E. W. Emerson and W. E. Forbes, eds., *Journals of Ralph Waldo Emerson* (Boston, Houghton Mifflin, 1910), 3, 376–77.
22. Ibid., 9, 207.

Twain paralleled and reinforced the religious influence of Horace Bushnell.

Emerson's advice, that writers take for their proper province such near and familiar subjects as a little daughter or "a couple of schoolboys" bore fruit. In his own day there emerged writers who demonstrated convincingly that childhood was both a legitimate and lucrative field for fiction. Stimulated by the international success of Charles Dickens, these New Englanders—men like Nathaniel Hawthorne, Jacob Abbott, and Thomas Bailey Aldrich, and ladies like Louisa May Alcott and Harriet Beecher Stowe—created models and prototypes for stories about children which the Nook Farm practitioners later imitated. Charles Dudley Warner and Lilly Warner were in touch with this tradition—indeed, Mrs. Stowe incarnated it—and when Mark Twain became their neighbor he quite naturally and informally absorbed this cultural environment. Like many masterpieces, *Tom Sawyer* and *Huckleberry Finn* had precedents which, while not all "sources" in the strict sense, help to explain their shape and success.

On June 9, 1870, scarcely a year before the Clemenses arrived at Nook Farm and Twain began to write fiction, Charles Dickens died. News of the event must have touched Twain and his wife. They would recall the January evening in 1868 when Dickens, "in a black velvet coat with a large and glaring red flower in the buttonhole," read the storm scene from *David Copperfield* to a gala audience in New York's Steinway Hall. That audience included Twain and Olivia Langdon, face to face for the first time in her father's box. Like many of their countrymen in 1870, the Clemenses doubtless perceived that a great career had closed. In fact, before Twain himself began to write, the nineteenth century had not produced so successful a novelist of childhood as Charles Dickens.

In the perspective of history, parallels between the works

14

of Dickens and Twain seem obvious and striking: both wrote about children as part of an emotional and literary commitment to unaristocratic life; both were innovators in the use of vernacular English for artistic purposes; each produced masterpieces of first-person singular narrative in which the hero is a boy; the novels of each, characteristically mixtures of humor, acute social criticism and sentimentality, appealed to vast numbers of readers; and posterity has sometimes consigned their works to the children's shelves in libraries. Critics, as well, have noted certain temperamental and biographical similarities.[23]

But the curious fact is that Twain, until his marriage and removal to Hartford, was not particularly a devotee of Dickens. As a young man he read *Oliver Twist* and *Martin Chuzzlewit*, but when he himself began to write in San Francisco he discovered so many colleagues on the newspapers and magazines who "were ambitiously and undisguisedly imitating Dickens" that he was repelled.[24] What put Twain off was the very aspect of Dickens' fiction that made him so successful and invited imitation—his pathos. One such mimic was Bret Harte, on whom Twain wasted little love anyway. "This is the very Bret Harte," he wrote years later, "whose pathetics, imitated from Dickens, used to be a godsend to the farmers of two hemispheres on account of the freshets of tears they compelled."[25]

When Twain became a husband and father, however, his scorn for Dickensian sensationalism and sentimentality abated. Along with Browning, George Macdonald, Charlotte Yonge,

23. Edward Wagenknecht, *Mark Twain: The Man and His Work* (New Haven, Yale University Press, 1935), p. 36. See also Gladys C. Bellamy, *Mark Twain as a Literary Artist* (Norman, Okla., University of Oklahoma Press, 1950), pp. 51–54, and Stephen Leacock, "Two Humorists: Charles Dickens and Mark Twain," *Yale Review*, 24 (1934), 118–22.

24. Bernard DeVoto, ed., *Mark Twain in Eruption* (New York, Harper and Brothers, 1940), pp. 266–67. For Twain's early resistance to the Dickens cult see Wecter, *Sam Clemens of Hannibal*, p. 240.

25. DeVoto, p. 265.

and later Rudyard Kipling, Dickens became at Nook Farm what he was in most literate American homes in those days— a household institution, to be enjoyed aloud in the library, the nursery, and the boudoir. Kate Leary, the Clemens' colorful Irish servant girl, describes this familiar situation, and identifies Dickens as the subject of an adult reading group Twain led during one winter at Nook Farm.[26] Twain's private reading, too, during the 1870's came to include as a favorite *A Tale of Two Cities*. "You know I have always been an admirer of Dickens," he told a friend some time later, "and his 'Tale of Two Cities' I read at least every two years."[27] This may well be Twainian exaggeration, but, as Walter Blair has pointed out, both *Tom Sawyer* and *Huckleberry Finn* were clearly influenced by *A Tale of Two Cities*.[28]

Twain's liking for Dickens' story of the French Revolution does not vitiate any earlier disinterest in the other novels. Even if taken literally, his well-known assertion, "I like history, biography, travels, curious facts and strange happenings, and science. And I detest novels, poetry, and theology"[29] would not prevent him from appreciating what is the least typical and most historical of all Dickens. *A Tale of Two Cities*, besides providing in Jerry Cruncher, Jr., an amusing young scamp who—like the Artful Dodger, Jo, or Rob the Grinder— might readily be turned into an American Bad Boy, deals with a theme dear to Twain's heart. From its opening message, "recalled to life" through the midnight adventures of the resurrection men, the plot in *A Tale of Two Cities* circles around

26. Lawton, *Katy Leary*, pp. 39–40. Katy Leary may have confused Browning and Dickens; on this point see Paine, 2, 846–49, and Clara Clemens, *My Father, Mark Twain* (New York, Harper and Brothers, 1931), p. 25.

27. Henry W. Fisher, *Abroad with Mark Twain and Eugene Field* (New York, N. L. Brown, 1922), p. 60.

28. See *Mark Twain and Huck Finn* (Berkeley and Los Angeles, University of California Press, 1960), pp. 61, 117, 128.

29. Paine, *Mark Twain, 1,* 512.

death and rebirth in a fashion Twain himself was later to explore. This theme, rather than the arraignment of monarchy, aristocracy, and the Church, may explain his special admiration for A Tale of Two Cities. In any case, the novel is the only one of Dickens which the mature Twain singles out for specific comment.

Twain's tie to Dickens, then, was atypical. Unlike many readers of his generation—and, indeed, writers as well—he deprecated the pathos and melodrama which enveloped Little Nell, Paul Dombey, and Oliver Twist and produced tears from Dickens' audiences everywhere. Though Twain, too, was to get at social and historical problems by exploiting in his own novels the "childhood-at-bay" situation, his fictional creatures were to resemble more the Dickensian lower-class ruffians than the saccharine and sickly children of The Old Curiosity Shop or Dombey and Son.

In this respect, as in others, Twain represented a new force in American writing. The "cult of sensibility," which flourished during the early Victorian era in England and led men like Macauley and Thackeray to weep unashamedly over the deaths of Jo or Little Nell, hung on longer in America and was by no means dead in 1871.[30] But the climate was beginning to change, and Twain himself (though he was at times no freer of sentimentality than Bret Harte or Dickens) was one cause of the shift.

One of the reasons Mark Twain could ignore most of Dickens except for A Tale of Two Cities was that he followed earlier writers who had worked their way through the cult of sensibility and by the 1870's had prepared American readers for childish characters different from Little Nell. The first and most ambitious of these predecessors was Nathaniel Hawthorne, who, curiously enough, might never have discovered

30. See George H. Ford, Dickens and His Readers (Princeton, Princeton University Press, 1955), chap. 4.

17

the possibilities of juvenile fiction in the 1830's if it had not been for a native of Hartford, Samuel Goodrich. Under the protective pseudonym of Peter Parley—"Nursery literature had not acquired the respect in the eyes of the world it now enjoys," he confessed later—Goodrich began, as early as 1827, to publish the *Tales of Peter Parley*. Simple didactic stories for and about children proved so immensely popular that by 1850 he had written 170 volumes, of which five million copies are reputed to have been sold.[31] *Peter Parley's Magazine* also proved popular; among its subscribers in the late 1830's was one John Clemens of Florida, Missouri.[32]

Within a few years *Peter Parley's Magazine* was so successful that it had called forth a number of competitors. One of these was the *Youth's Keep-Sake,* an annual magazine for young readers. In the 1835 number appeared "Little Annie's Ramble," an early sketch by Hawthorne. Though not of the quality of "The Gentle Boy," this slight piece illustrates even more purely the kind of children's story which pleased popular taste in post-Calvinist New England. The tiny heroine is the same sweet, wooden figurine Dickens made world-famous in Little Nell a few years later. "Dear little Annie" is conducted on a walk through the Salem streets by a melancholy young man—obviously and ironically Hawthorne himself—who delights in the "sinless child." Annie's cherry innocence evokes spontaneous homage from every passer-by; even the elephants in the traveling menagerie bow down to the child. But her symbolic passage through the adult world is not without its touch of sin and evil, for the midget and the monkeys at the menagerie shock her "pure instinctive delicacy of taste." Hawthorne does not, however, permit his little heroine to be

31. Cornelia Meigs, Anne Eaton, Elizabeth Nesbitt, and Ruth H. Viguers, *A Critical History of Children's Literature* (New York, Macmillan, 1953), pp. 144–45.
32. Paine, *Mark Twain, 1,* 14.

touched or changed by evil. "Well, let us hasten homeward;" he concludes, "and as we go, forget not to thank Heaven, my Annie, that, after wandering a little way into the world, you may return at the first summons, with an untainted and unwearied heart, and be a happy child again." [33]

Here, expressed in elementary form at the beginning of the tradition, is the characteristic formula of American childhood fiction. The confrontation of an innocent with a soiled and soiling adult society, the demonstration of the power of innocence over the experienced world, but, finally, the child's retreat from that contact—this is a pattern later repeated in Hawthorne, Henry James, Stephen Crane and, as we shall see, Mark Twain. In a sense, Annie is the forerunner of Phoebe Pyncheon, Priscilla, Hilda, the Snow Maiden, Pansie—all Hawthorne heroines who in one way or another shrink from adult involvement, as do many of James' girls, Crane's Maggie, and Twain's Joan of Arc and Cathy Alison. The virginal maiden is one typical juvenile character in our fiction, and she may be traced into the twentieth century, though transmogrified, in the young children of Katherine Anne Porter, Eudora Welty, Truman Capote, and others.

"Little Annie's Ramble" illustrates in primitive but representative form the children's story popular during the early years of the nineteenth century. Like his New England successors, Hawthorne was a professional writer who had to sell his stories in order to live. So, when he discovered the formula for successful juvenile magazine pieces, the author of "Little Annie's Ramble" followed with "Little Daffydowndilly," "The Ambitious Guest," "The Old Apple Dealer," and other sketches and tales, each affording readers a sweet and unrealistic image of childhood. This sort of fiction developed into a series of story books—*Grandfather's Chair, Biographical Stories for Children,*

33. *Works of Nathaniel Hawthorne,* Riverside Edition (Cambridge, Mass., Houghton Mifflin, 1883), *1,* 151–52.

The Wonder Book, Tanglewood Tales. The juvenile characters in these tales all bear the family features of Little Annie. They are, as Mark Van Doren has observed, "little men and women, prettily exclaiming and pouting," but they bear faint resemblance to real boys and girls.[34] Their conversation is didactic and stilted. As Hawthorne himself was well aware, they are too exclusively compounds of the "thin air of romance" rather than beings endowed with a robust illusion of life.

Attempting to remedy this defect, Hawthorne began in his *American Notebooks* a "quest for physical reality" in the fictional presentation of children that he could only intermittently achieve in his published stories of the 1840's. Moreover, after the birth of his own children—Una, Julian, and Rose—he recorded in minute detail their appearances, behavior, and personalities. These observations of real children occur side by side with suggestions in the *Notebooks* for stories about children.[35]

Nearly twenty-five years later, Mark Twain, himself the father of three children (though Langdon Clemens had by this time died), began a similar journal. In August 1876, during the first flush of inspiration at beginning *Huckleberry Finn,* he started "A Record of the Small Foolishnesses of Susie & "Bay" Clemens (Infants)." [36] As it turned out, he did not need the inspiration of his own children to impart realism to his fiction. Unlike Hawthorne, his Western background as humor-

34. Mark Van Doren, *Nathaniel Hawthorne* (New York, Viking Press, 1957), p. 107.

35. See Randall Stewart, ed., *The American Notebooks* (New Haven, Yale University Press, 1932), pp. 99, 101, 122, 125, 136, 141.

36. To which title he added "And Mary treasured these sayings in her heart[.] Begun in August at Quarry Farm on the Elmira hills— country residence of Mr. Crane [MT's brother-in-law] [.] Hartford, 1876." The manuscript of this journal, which MT kept for only a few months, is in the Collection of C. Waller Barrett of New York City. © Mark Twain Company.

ist, newspaper writer, lecturer, and raconteur equipped him with richer resources for realism than a family notebook could provide. Only at the close of his career, in "A Horse's Tale," did he incorporate members of his immediate family into his fiction—and then with disastrous results.

Hawthorne, on the contrary, when he turned to writing novels, felt he needed all the help he could get to create more lifelike children. All his later fiction drew upon the *Notebooks*, but none more so than *The Scarlet Letter*. That he modeled Pearl on his daughter Una is well known.[37] Though primarily intended as the "living hieroglyph" of her parents' sin, Pearl, as Randall Stewart points out, closely resembles Una Hawthorne. The changeable temper, manners of play, the disconcerting habit of staring deep into the eyes of adults as if "to embarrass the springs of spiritual life and the movements of the soul"—these are details indicating that Hawthorne intended the girls as alter-egos. Consequently Pearl's bizarre behavior, though in part a reflection of the turmoil in the natures and situation of her parents, was also meant to be as natural and normal as Una's.

Pearl's primary function in *The Scarlet Letter* to be sure, is not as realistic image but as unifying symbol. Her ambiguous innocence, which borders on devilishness and inhumanity, finally brings about the moral redemption of her father. For it is Pearl, not Hester, who confronts her father in the forest with his true sin; it is she who clasps his hand at midnight upon the scaffold and she who later grasps his knees in the final noonday act of expiation. Pearl, the impurely pure child, is a principal instrument of spiritual rebirth in *The Scarlet Letter*.

37. See Julian Hawthorne, "The Making of *The Scarlet Letter*," *The Bookman* (1931), pp. 74, 401–11, and Stewart, *The American Notebooks*, pp. xxiii, xxix–xxx.

In the literary tradition of which Twain was legatee this novel is important for two reasons. In the first place, it shows, at least by intent, Hawthorne's genuine attempt to transcend the romantic stereotype of the sinless child he had felt constrained to manufacture in "Little Annie's Ramble," "The Gentle Boy," and other early pieces. Placed "side by side with nature" in the form of Una Hawthorne, Pearl came alive more vividly than any of the simpering miniature adults of *Grandfather's Chair*. In the second place, Pearl's position at the center of the dramatic and symbolic core of *The Scarlet Letter* proves that, by 1850, at least one major American writer had realized the potentialities of childhood as a serious theme for adult art. Children need necessarily no longer be wooden little figures in instructive tales for the young; Pearl showed they could provide a wholly fresh subject matter and angle of vision into the problems of innocence and experience, appearance and reality, initiation and the preservation of moral integrity. Prior to *The Scarlet Letter* no one had aimed so high.

After 1850 Hawthorne turned to the childlike character in another guise in his later work. Perhaps he was still observing Pearl as she grew into girlhood; at any rate, subsequent novels have as an important figure, near but not usually at the center of the action, a young maiden. Phoebe, Priscilla, Hilda, the Snow Maiden, Alice Vane, and Sylph Etherage are all "on the outer limits of childhood." They are "girls almost women grown" and their significance lies precisely in this thin line which, at least at the beginning of each narrative, separates them from adults. Hawthorne's handling of these maidens constitutes a major thread in his fiction, one that has later repercussions in the novels and stories of Henry James and in Twain's *Joan of Arc*.

Apart from the virginal Phoebe Pyncheon, *The House of the Seven Gables* in particular marks a real advance in Hawthorne's efforts to make children lifelike. "Many passages of this book," he wrote James T. Fields, his publisher, in November 1850, "ought to be finished with the minuteness of a Dutch picture, in order to give them their proper effect." [38] Phoebe only partially answered this need for Flemish realism; too often her creator could not avoid using the same sweetly sentimental language to describe her that Clifford Pyncheon employs. But the lesser figures, especially Ned Higgins, add a breath of much-needed life to the romance. "This square and sturdy little urchin" is depicted with an attention to details of dress and manner that suggests the genre paintings of Eastman Johnson or William Sydney Mount. In his blue apron, wide trousers, chip-hat, and "shoes somewhat out at the toes," Ned moves in an ambience much different from that of Ilbrahim, the Gentle Boy. He helps to give the book, which is not a novel but a romance, its air of social density, its sense of Salem life outside the house of the Pyncheons. Furthermore, Ned plays a minor but significant part in the action. He is the instrument of Hepzibah's introduction into the crass and democratic world of business when he "purchases" the first ginger cookie. Later, Ned is one of the chorus of frightened children who "catch the contagion of a panic terror" from the house where Cousin Jaffrey's corpse sits in silence. This Gothic device of juxtaposing innocence and violent death unites Ned and his playmates with Ilbrahim and Pearl and the little Puritan boy who discovers the first Pyncheon corpse "in the very act of running to climb Colonel Pyncheon's knee." Thus Ned is not just a genre figure imported from the painter's world to give verisimilitude to Hawthorne's story; he is to some degree a cipher in a symbolic drama. As such, he foretells Tom Sawyer, another self-confident boy who has brushes with death.

Still, compared with Tom and other little boys of later American fiction, Ned seems sweet and artificial. In fact, Hawthorne never wholly escaped the conventions of the "cult of

38. Quoted in Van Doren, *Nathaniel Hawthorne,* p. 172.

23

sensibility" in which childhood figured as "the innocent little circle." Expectations of his public, added to a private predilection for symbolic narrative, too often blurred the outlines of the childish characters Hawthorne tried to draw. The results were, by and large, didactic and pictorial stereotypes. For these reasons Hawthorne never created a Bad Boy. In actuality nothing more than a "real human boy" as opposed to romantic stereotypes of innocence, the Bad Boy became, along with the precocious infant and the virginal maiden, a central figure in American fiction after 1850. Hawthorne drew the precocious child brilliantly in Pearl and the maiden in Phoebe, Priscilla, Hilda, and others, but never a Bad Boy. Perhaps, since he relied upon personal observation, Hawthorne found his son Julian less interesting than Una; perhaps it was because the Hawthorne children grew up in such social isolation that the common experiences of boys in gangs did not much figure in the writer's imagination, as it obviously did for Mark Twain. More fundamental a reason, ultimately, was the cast of Hawthorne's mind, which characteristically looked beyond the physical image to the metaphysical or moral verity which that image expressed. The Bad Boy is seldom the product of such an imagination. He is rather the image of an actual, healthy, social animal. Only after the Wordsworthian notion of children as beings from God had lost its force—as it had not done for Hawthorne—could the Bad Boy appear. It was a later generation of writers, reacting against both traditional Calvinism and Transcendental Romanticism, who completed the gallery of juvenile characters in our nineteenth-century fiction.

In common with other and larger developments in American life after the Civil War, the Bad Boy actually had his beginnings before 1860—well back in the 1850's, in fact. Thomas Bailey Aldrich is popularly supposed to have presented the first Bad Boy to American readers, in the January 1869 issue of *Our Young Folks* magazine. *The Story of a Bad Boy* did, of course, make the term a commonplace for both young and old in the Gilded Age. But a gradual humanization of fictional boys had taken place during the 1850's, of whom Hawthorne's Ned Higgins was one instance.

Another New England writer who helped this process along was Jacob Abbott, author of the Rollo books which Susy and Clara Clemens so enjoyed reading. A minister, teacher, and indefatigable producer of juvenile fiction, Abbott wrote one series of delightful novels about boys called the *Franconia Stories*. These appeared from 1850 to 1853 and concerned the lives of various small children growing up in the hill country of New Hampshire. Among the many readers of Abbott's series was one small New York boy, Henry James, who later recalled: "I pored in those days over the freshness of the Franconia Stories of the brothers Abbott, then immediately sequent to the sweet Rollo series and even more admired . . ." [39]

Twain himself was more temperate in his enthusiasm for Abbott. One of the many stories which he worked on but never finished was "A Cat-Tale," written, Paine tells us, in 1880. It is a charming children's piece told in the form of questions by Susy and Clara Clemens and answers by Twain himself. The principal figure is a kitten—Mark Twain, of course, was a lifelong devotee of cats—about whom the following exchange takes place:

> Susy—Why, what beautiful language for such a little thing, *wasn't* it, papa?
> Ah, yes indeed. That was the kind of cat he was— cultivated, you see. He had sat at the feet of Rollo's mother; and in the able "Franconia series" he had not failed to observe how harmoniously gigantic language and a microscopic topic go together. [40]

39. A *Small Boy and Others*, in F. W. Dupee, ed., *Henry James: Autobiography* (New York, Criterion, 1956), p. 139.
40. MT, "Letters From the Earth," p. 181, unpublished MS, MTP. © Mark Twain Company.

Twain is only half joking here when he laughs at the language of the *Franconia* stories, for compared with Abbott's own earlier work or with that of Peter Parley or Hawthorne they surely deserve both James' praise and Twain's grudging adjective.

This superiority is especially evident to modern ears in *Beechnut*, published in 1850 as the fifth volume in the little series. Its ostensible hero is Beechnut, a maddeningly resourceful and mature lad of twelve. But the liveliest of Abbott's characters is Beechnut's six-year-old brother, Phonny. This small boy's vivid conversation, imaginative escapades, and highly realistic outbursts of temper mark him as a great advance over Ned Higgins. Phonny is a wholly credible mixture of deviltry, sense, spirit, and, above all, humor. He is, as his name promises, one of the first *funny* children in American fiction. A typical incident which exhibits Abbott's skill is the episode in which Phonny learns that Beechnut is to be allowed to go on a bear-hunt while he must remain at home:

"She will not let you go then?" said Beechnut, snapping some part of the gun back and forth in his attempt to put it in order.

"No," said Phonny, speaking in a very fretful tone.

"How provoking!" said Beechnut.

"Yes," rejoined Phonny, "it is provoking indeed."

"And how unreasonable!" said Beechnut.

"Yes," responded Phonny.

"If I were you I would not bear it," said Beechnut.

"Why, what would you do?" asked Phonny.

"Oh, I don't know," said Beechnut. "I would do something or other very desperate. I would fret about it all day."

Phonny was silent.

"You will not find another thing so good to fret about in

a twelve-month," continued Beechnut. "It is astonishing what trials and straits innocent boys are put to by hard-hearted mothers. Here now is a boy that his mother will not allow to set off in a company of fifty men, with dogs and guns, to make a tramp of six miles through the woods and mountains hunting a wild beast,—and he bears it, dear little fellow, as patiently as a lamb!"

So saying, Beechnut began to pat Phonny gently on the back.

Phonny seized a leather strap, a part of an old bridle which chanced just then to be lying on the bench, and gave Beechnut a great whack across the shoulders with it, and then ran off out of the shop.[41]

This is, admittedly, tame enough humor when compared with Twain's, but it is certainly far livelier than any story Hawthorne wrote about children. Jacob Abbott actually takes children more seriously by writing humorously about them and their world. Moreover, we may detect in Beechnut's and Phonny's speech, in spite of some stiffness, the authentic sound of real people talking. Neither of these boys actually employs language as "gigantic" as Ned Higgins'.

The happy balance of amusement and mild moralizing which animates Abbott's best work was caught by Thomas Bailey Aldrich in 1869, when he published *The Story of a Bad Boy*. In addition, Aldrich made one very significant modification in Abbott's formula. Though it first appeared as a serial in a juvenile magazine, *The Story of a Bad Boy* is the first of a whole line of boy's books written as much for adults as for the boys themselves. This explains the strong strain of nostalgia which distinguishes it so noticeably from the work of Hawthorne and Abbott. With Aldrich, boyhood for the

41. Jacob Abbott, *Beechnut: A Franconia Story* (New York, Harper and Brothers, 1850), pp. 41–43.

first time is a past, not a present, condition of life to be celebrated. "It is with no ungentle hand," he begins, in evoking
the figures of his own childhood, "I summon them back, for
a moment, from that Past which has closed upon them and
upon me. How pleasantly they live again in my memory!
Happy, magical Past, in whose fairy atmosphere even Conway, mine ancient foe, stands forth transfigured, with a sort
of dreamy glory encircling his bright red hair!" [42] Whittier's
"Snowbound" had three years earlier sounded the same note
about the "happy, magical Past," [43] but before Aldrich few if
any fiction writers had done so.

Aldrich's continual recollection of the "pastness" of his narrative involves him necessarily in a double point of view in
The Story of a Bad Boy. He oscillates between recounting
events in Tom Bailey's own words and commenting upon the
scene in the language of Thomas Bailey Aldrich. This shifting
back and forth between boyish character and adult author becomes actually the underlying theme of the novel. For Aldrich
engages in a constant battle with time by emphasizing the
timeless qualities of Tom Bailey's world. "Poor little Binny
Wallace," he laments over a dead playmate of Tom's. "Always
the same to me. The rest of us have grown up into hard,
worldly men, fighting the fight of life; but you are forever
young, and gentle, and pure; a part of my own childhood that
time cannot wither; always a little boy, always poor little
Binny Wallace!" [44]

42. Thomas Bailey Aldrich, *The Story of a Bad Boy* (Boston, Houghton
Mifflin, 1897), pp. 9–10.
43. "Snowbound," *The Poetical Works of John Greenleaf Whittier*
(Cambridge, Mass., Houghton Mifflin, 1892), 2, 159:
        Yet, haply, in some lull of life,
        Some Truce of God which breaks its strife,
        The worldling's eyes shall gather dew,
        Dreaming in throngful city ways
        Of winter joys his boyhood knew;
44. *Story of a Bad Boy*, pp. 163–64.

Under the guise of the remembering adult, rather than the experiencing boy, Aldrich introduces moralizing into his story as blatantly as Hawthorne or Abbott had done. When, for example, Tom's father fails in business and the boy's complete ignorance of money is revealed, Tom observes: "I supposed—if I supposed anything—that all grown-up people had more or less money, when they wanted it. Whether they inherited it, or whether government supplied them, was not clear to me. A loose idea that my father had a private gold-mine somewhere or other relieved me of all uneasiness. I was not far from right. Every man has within himself a gold-mine whose riches are limited only by his own industry." [45] The shift in perspective between the beginning and the end of this passage is jarringly clear. Years later, in *Roughing It*, "Old Times on the Mississippi," and *Joan of Arc*, Twain was to use far more subtly the technique of the double-narrator, the older man and the young boy.

Because of this separation in point of view, narrative action in *The Story of a Bad Boy* is severed almost completely from the descriptive passages. The boy is in the landscape but the old man tells us what the scene looks like, as in this account of sunrise on the river:

> How calm and lovely the river was! Not a ripple stirred on the glassy surface, broken only by the cutwater of our tiny craft. The sun, as round and red as an August moon, was by this time, peering above the water-line . . . As we neared the mouth of the harbor, a little breeze now and then wrinkled the blue water, shook the spangles from the foliage, and gently lifted the spiral mist-wreaths that still clung along shore. The measured dip of our oars and the drowsy twittering of the birds seemed to mingle with, rather than break, the enchanted silence that reigned above us.

45. Ibid., p. 167.

CHAPTER ONE

The scent of the new clover comes back to me now, as
I recall that delicious morning when we floated away in
a fairy boat down a river like a dream! [46]

Clearly, not a boy but a grown man, aware of the pictorial vocabulary of the Hudson River landscape painters, has
written this description. Such treatment of nature contrasts
markedly, as will be pointed out, with the one Twain employs
in *Tom Sawyer*, *Life on the Mississippi*, and *Huckleberry
Finn*. These works, like *The Story of a Bad Boy*, are also mixtures of adult memoirs and boy's fiction, but their styles serve
better perhaps than Aldrich's to cover up their dual nature.

In spite of his story's structural disunities, however, Tom
Bailey himself emerges as a figure of considerable vitality. "I
may truthfully say I was an amiable, impulsive lad, blessed
with fine digestive powers and no hypocrite," he remarks. "In
short, I was a real human boy, such as you may meet anywhere in New England, and no more like that impossible boy
in a story-book than a sound orange is like one that has been
sucked dry." [47] Tom gets into fights, falls in love, meets death,
tries running away from home—all events hallowed by later
convention. In 1869, however, such events were something of
a fictional novelty. Bemused adults were doubtless struck
more by Aldrich's realistic presentation of village life than by
the sentimental evocation of the "happy, magical Past."

Twain himself first read *The Story of a Bad Boy* while stay-
ing in New Haven on a lecture tour at Christmas time, 1869.
But he was not much impressed. "I have read several books,
lately," he reported dutifully to his absent fiancée in Elmira,
"but none worth marking, & so I have not marked any. I
started to mark the Story of a Bad Boy, but for the life of me
I could not admire the volume much."[48] This was nearly two

46. Ibid., pp. 151–52.
47. Ibid., pp. 7–8.
48. MT to Olivia Langdon, Dec. 27, 1869, in Dixon Wecter, ed.,

years before Twain settled at Nook Farm and became a fast friend of Thomas Bailey Aldrich. In later years, as he grew older and his life bitterer, the nostalgic tone of his friend's paean to boyhood did not bother him so much.

Tom Bailey, in spite of his initially cool reception by Twain, is the immediate ancestor of Tom Sawyer. *The Story of a Bad Boy* connects the Western humorist to a New England tradition that over a period of forty years had established in rudimentary form the characters, themes, and styles of fiction written for and about children. There were, to be sure, other writers than the ones mentioned here who helped to create the precocious child, the virginal maiden, and the Bad Boy. Louisa May Alcott was one. But *Little Men* appeared the very year the Clemenses came to Connecticut, and its didactic, genteel, and somewhat humorless tone doubtless made it even less appealing than *The Story of a Bad Boy* was initially for Mark Twain.

In any case, direct influences are not the object here. What has been intended is a demonstration that a definite tradition

---

The Love Letters of Mark Twain (New York, Harper and Brothers, 1949), p. 132. When, however, Twain picked up *The Story of a Bad Boy* again, in 1893, a great deal of water had gone under the bridge. The letter he wrote this time (Dec. 6, 1893) was to Aldrich himself, by now an old friend. "If I had written you last night when I began the book, I should have written breezily and maybe hilariously; but by the time I had finished it, at 3 in the morning, it had worked its spell & Portsmouth was become the town of my own boyhood—with all which that implies & compels: the bringing back of one's youth, almost the only time of life worth living over again, the only period whose memories are wholly pathetic—pathetic because we see now that we were in heaven then & there was no one able to make us know it, though no doubt many a kindly poor old devil tried to. I enjoyed it all—every line of it; & I wish there had been more." This is the complete text (hitherto published only in part in Wecter, *Sam Clemens of Hannibal*, pp. 63–64), from the Clemens Collection, Houghton Library, Harvard University. © Mark Twain Company.

existed among certain New England writers Mark Twain knew or knew about, a tradition of taking childhood seriously as a subject for stories and novels. Such professionals as Samuel Goodrich, Nathaniel Hawthorne, Jacob Abbott, Thomas Bailey Aldrich, Harriet Beecher Stowe, and Louisa May Alcott made a living at this. They found, or developed, a market for such stories. This market comprised by the early 1870's two audiences. One, of course, was the children themselves; the other, and for Mark Twain much the more significant, was that tapped by Aldrich—adults who for a variety of reasons had become interested in reading about children. This new double audience was a secularized, family public. No longer did it favor dry and didactic tales designed to supplement Sunday School tracts, but by the time Twain had commenced writing had come to ask frankly for amusement. That commodity Twain had in abundance. His background as humorist and lecturer stood him in good stead when in 1874 he began to write *The Adventures of Tom Sawyer*.

As he entered with gusto into the family-centered life of Nook Farm and came to share the values of "this sterling old Puritan community," his literary career was shaped accordingly. In common with his friends and neighbors who were themselves professional writers, he learned to utilize near and familiar subjects in his fiction. Childhood was one of the most popular themes for the other Nook Farm writers, so Twain's own first efforts were naturally influenced in this direction. Yet *Tom Sawyer, The Prince and the Pauper,* and *Huckleberry Finn,* in spite of a multitude of debts to the New England tradition, were quite different books from *Beechnut* and *The Story of a Bad Boy* and *Little Pussy Willow.* Great as was the effect of New England on this Westerner, his own imagination was stronger. The forms which his fiction took answered ultimately to forces that lay deeper within his own mind and past.

32

2.

The Apprenticeship of
"The Moralist of the Main"

"I TRIED A SUNDAY-SCHOOL book once," drawls the Next-Door Neighbor in Charles Dudley Warner's *Backlog Studies*, "but I made the good boy end in the poorhouse, and the bad boy go to Congress; and the publisher said it wouldn't do, the public wouldn't stand that sort of thing." [1] In these joking terms Warner reports his neighbor Mark Twain's first attempt to crash the *Atlantic Monthly*. Among the sketches Twain tried to republish in "the most scrupulously cultivated of our periodicals" [2] was "The Story of the Bad Little Boy"; it had already amused newspaper readers in San Francisco, so Twain had some reasonable expectation it might be fitting for a national audience. The "publisher" did not think so; he rejected it, along with "A Fable For Good Old Boys and Girls." "A little fable like yours," wrote William Dean Howells, the *Atlantic's* young assistant editor, "wouldn't leave it a single Presbyterian, Baptist, Unitarian, Episcopalian, Methodist or Millerite *paying* subscriber—all the dead-heads would stick to it and abuse it in the denominational newspapers." [3] In spite of the light tone,

1. *Backlog Studies: The Complete Writings of Charles Dudley Warner* (Hartford, American Publishing Co., 1904), *1*, 249–50.
2. William Dean Howells, *My Mark Twain* (New York, Harper and Brothers, 1910), p. 19.
3. Mildred Howells, ed., *Life in Letters of William Dean Howells* (2 vols. Garden City, Doubleday, Doran and Co., 1928), *1*, 191.

Howells was not joking. It is amusing and significant that the man who later became one of Twain's closest friends and literary advisers opened that relationship by telling him that his Western sketches were too strong for Eastern tastes. Even more symbolic is the fact that one was an anecdote about boys that defined the difficulties Twain would have in becoming a national success.

From the nice New England viewpoint of the *Atlantic Monthly,* nearly everything Twain had written before he settled in Hartford—except perhaps parts of *Innocents Abroad,* which Howells liked—was crude and vulgar. The numerous letters and newspaper sketches he had composed during his journeyman printer's days in the Middle West and later as reporter in Nevada on the *Territorial Enterprise* and in San Francisco on the *Golden Era* and *Californian* simply were not "literature" by genteel standards. They were burlesques which identified Twain, along with such men as Johnson J. Hooper, B. P. Shillaber, and G. W. Harris, as a "phunny phellow." Howells probably considered "The Story of the Bad Little Boy" typical of this tradition. In any event, whatever his private opinions—and Howells was himself a parvenu from Ohio on Beacon Street—the editor knew that readers of the *Atlantic* preferred the gentle urbanities of an essayist like Warner, say, to the exaggerated humor of the frontier.

By any critical standard, Howells and his readers were right. "The Story of the Bad Little Boy" was written originally in 1865; like its companion piece, "The Story of the Good Little Boy," it makes laborious fun of the pious and, to Twain, misleading morality of Sunday School tracts. "Most bad boys in the Sunday books are named James," Twain begins, "and have sick mothers, who teach them to say, 'Now I lay me down,' etc., and sing them to sleep with sweet, plaintive voices, and then kiss them good night, and kneel down by the bedside and weep. But it was different with this fellow. He was named Jim,

34

and there wasn't anything the matter with his mother—no consumption, nor anything of that kind. She was rather stout than otherwise, and she was not pious; moreover, she was not anxious on Jim's account. She said if he were to break his neck it wouldn't be much loss" (7, 44). Jim's amoral exploits match the unorthodoxy of his mother's affection. By the sketch's end he has become a drunkard, brained his family with an axe, "is the infernalist wickedest scoundrel in his native village, and is universally respected, and belongs to the Legislature" (7, 48).

The gap between literature (Sunday School variety) and life is burlesqued even more baldly in "The Story of the Good Little Boy." Jim's opposite number is Jacob Blivens, whose devout ambition is to earn a hero's spot in a Sunday School text. Jacob realizes such a goal is a dangerous one to pursue. "It made him feel a little uncomfortable sometimes when he reflected that the good little boys always died. He loved to live, you know, and this was the most unpleasant feature about being a Sunday-School book boy. He knew it was not healthy to be good" (7, 51). Jacob's fears are well founded. When he tries to stop some nasty boys from tying nitroglycerine to the tails of several dogs, fate arrives in the guise of Alderman McWelter. The bad boys scatter, "but Jacob Blivens rose in conscious innocence and began one of those stately little Sunday-school book speeches which always commence with 'Oh, sir!' in dead opposition to the fact that no boy, good or bad, ever starts a remark with 'Oh, sir!'" The Alderman's whack across Jacob's innocent ear accomplishes the inevitable, and the Good Little Boy, in company with the dogs, is "apportioned around among four townships . . . You never saw a boy scattered so" (7, 54–55).

Both of these early sketches are simply extended jokes. The humor is forced, the style banal, and no effort is made to delineate character or develop situation for any purpose except to provoke laughs. As potentials for fiction, in fact, both anec-

35

dotes show less promise than the "Thomas Jefferson Snodgrass Papers" which Twain had written several years earlier. These pieces of typical Middle Western newspaper humor appeared in the Keokuk, Iowa, *Daily Post* in 1856 and 1857.[4] They were the first bits of writing for which Twain received pay, and in spite of their exaggerated dialect and comic-strip humor, they suggest an intuitive grasp of the fictional techniques best suited to his imagination.

One such seminal technique is the innocent narrator. In the well-established tradition of Sut Lovingood and Ike Partington, Snodgrass is an uncouth rustic whose adventures on a trip to Cincinnati and Chicago are primarily funny because he is so inexperienced.[5] In one of the letters, for instance, Snodgrass is asked by a young lady to hold her basket for a moment. Presently he discovers he has a mulatto baby on his hands. Taking the infant back to his hotel, he relates his trials in these words: "Then the thing quit hollerin, and I locked the door. Becomin a leetle composed, I tuck the tongs and lifted the cretur out of the basket, so as to get a look at it . . . Sich a yell that skeered animal sot up—shucks! a shivaree warn't nothin longside of it . . . 'Sh-h-h!' says I, tossin the brat, 'there now—ther-e-ere, the-e-ere the-e-ere the-re!—your mother's comin (singing a leetle, occasionally,) 'ocky bye, baby, in a tree top, when the wind blows,—there, now, poor dear little —when the wind blows—Oh, *dern* yer everlastin yaller skin, won't you never dry up?" [6]

4. See Edgar L. Branch, *The Literary Apprenticeship of Mark Twain* (Urbana, University of Illinois Press, 1950), chaps. 1, 2; and Ivan Benson, *Mark Twain's Western Years* (Stanford, Stanford University Press, 1938), pp. 14–17.

5. On the topic of MT and Western humor see Constance Rourke, *American Humor* (Garden City, Doubleday Anchor, 1953), especially pp. 169–75; Walter Blair, *Native American Humor* (New York, American Book Co., 1937), pp. 147–62; and Kenneth S. Lynn, *Mark Twain and Southwestern Humor*, Boston, Little Brown, 1960.

6. Reprinted in Branch, *Literary Apprenticeship*, 225.

In spite of cacography, a hallowed convention in the genre Twain is following, the sketch creates a character of some vitality. This is due principally to Snodgrass' language. Twain's Iowa rube *sounds* like a villager. One may, in fact, detect in his speech and manner something of Huck Finn's softhearted, caustic view of life. "The Story of the Good Little Boy" merely satirizes stilted and unnatural modes of speech, but the "Thomas Jefferson Snodgrass Papers" had already actually demonstrated Twain's ear for realistic dialogue.

Subtlety of structure and diction are notably, and understandably, absent in these first sketches Twain wrote in Iowa and California. But beneath the beginner's clumsiness may be seen emerging several characteristic concerns of the later novelist. One of these, clearly, is the satiric impulse. A second is the apparently natural choice of childish figures as instruments of that satire. In this respect, it is evident that Twain's early work uses children as a subject not primarily to amuse or instruct a juvenile or family audience; his target is adults. In this he differed profoundly from other writers of the 60's who were writing about children back in the East. Finally, Twain's attention to the sounds of authentic spoken language shows the means whereby he characteristically ties together satire, subject, and audience appeal.

The record of his later work in San Francisco exhibits a growing awareness of these techniques and mastery of them. Important to this process was the influence he received from the other writers in the city—Bret Harte, Artemus Ward, Orpheus C. Kerr, Charles Warren Stoddard—but in particular from Charles H. Webb, editor of the *Californian*. Twain began to write for Webb late in 1864, abandoning the more plebian *Golden Era* in favor of "the best weekly literary paper in the United States," as he proudly informed his mother and sister.[7]

7. Albert B. Paine, ed., *Mark Twain's Letters* (2 vols. New York and London, Harper and Brothers, 1917), *1*, 100. See also Franklin Walker,

Under Webb's leadership the *Californian* encouraged satire. Many of the so-called "California values," such as the climate and scenery, the "honest miner" stereotype, even (and this is unusual in wartime) patriotism, were lampooned. Mark Twain's real literary apprenticeship took place under peculiarly favorable circumstances. He was encouraged to write satirically for a paper which, on his own word, circulated "among the highest class of the community." [8] Such freedom of expression to address a proper, genteel audience proved a heady experience. The pattern it set persisted throughout his career, and was attended by a host of tensions and contradictions whose effects are evident in most of his subsequent work.

After the Sunday School book, he leveled upon the patriotic parable, the pietistic story in the tradition of Parson Weems. These fables perpetrated a form of untruth Twain considered just as hypocritical as the tract. "Brief Biographical Sketch of George Washington" and "The Late Benjamin Franklin" are crude and irreverent attacks upon national monuments whose lives children were taught to emulate. "As a boy, he gave no promise of the greatness he was one day to achieve," Twain remarks sarcastically of Washington. "He was ignorant of the commonest accomplishments of youth. He could not even lie." [9] Ben Franklin is handled even more roughly. "With a malice that is without parallel in history," Twain observes, "he would work all day, and then sit up nights, and let on to be studying algebra by the light of a smouldering fire, so that all other boys might have to do that also, or else have Benjamin Franklin thrown up to them." The serious echoes in Twain's humor are unmistakable. "His maxims were full of animosity towards boys. Nowadays a boy cannot follow out a single natural in-

San Francisco's Literary Frontier (New York, A. A. Knopf, 1939), p. 132.

8. Paine, *Letters, 1,* 100.

9. *The Celebrated Jumping Frog of Calaveras County and Other Sketches* (New York, 1867), p. 127.

stinct without tumbling over some of those everlasting apho-
risms and hearing from Franklin on the spot" (7, 189). Without doubt Twain is aiming over children's heads at their parents. The venerable Dr. Franklin is made to epitomize adult
vices, specifically mercenary industry and hypocritical wisdom.
Implicit is the writer's preference for quite opposite virtues,
for the natural qualities—laziness, candor, sincerity—which
boys have and which are later to be celebrated in the Mississippi River stories. All his life Twain made fun of Franklin
on precisely these grounds.

During his California newspaper days he earned a number
of nicknames. In addition to "The Washoe Giant," he was also
called "The Moral Phenomenon" and, most frequently, "The
Moralist of the Main." Such epithets attest not only to Twain's
colorful personality and his popularity but to his audience's
recognition of the serious dimensions of his wit. Twain knew
it, too, for he used his Western nicknames proudly, acknowl-
edging that the purpose of his writings was to flay by laughter
and ridicule human affectation and social evils. If, by chance,
children displayed shortcomings, Twain attacked them as
mercilessly as he did adults. Two instances of this comprehensive indignation are "Those Blasted Children" and "Disgraceful Persecution of a Boy." Both pieces were widely read in
the West and "Those Blasted Children" was reprinted in the
New York *Sunday Mercury* for February 21, 1864. The first of
Mark Twain's work to reach an Eastern—and, hence, a national—audience was a sketch about bad boys.

The boys in "Those Blasted Children" are, however, a far
cry from Jacob Abbott or Aldrich. The gang of young rascals
playing in the hotel corridor outside Twain's door are a cruel
and quarrelsome lot. Their behavior is intended to be both
natural and symbolic; it sounds true to life, and each boy
bears the name of a prominent San Francisco grownup.
Twain's satire is clearly intended for adults.

"You, Bob Miller, you leg go that string—I'll smack you in the eye."

"You will, will you? I'd like to see you try it. You jes' hit me if you dare!"

"You lay your hands on me, 'n' I will hit you."

"Now I've laid my hand on you, why don't you hit?"

"Well, I mean, if you lay 'em on me so's to hurt." . . .

"Sandy Baker, I know what makes your pa's hair kink so; it's 'cause he's a mulatter; I heard my ma say so." . . .

"Hi, boys! here comes a Chinaman." (God pity any Chinaman who chances to come in the way of the boys hereabout, for the eye of the law regardeth him not, and the youth of California in their generation are down on him.) "Now, boys! grab his clothes-basket—take him by the tail!" [10]

This brand of humor, pointedly personal and taking a jaundiced view of childish nature in general, upset genteel San Franciscans. Ada Clare, a lady columnist for the *Golden Era*, took Twain to task on the second count, declaring him "guilty of misunderstanding God's little people." [11] By accepted standards of the day, he did indeed misrepresent childhood. The impression left by most of his sketches is that boys (and girls, too, at times) share with adults a natural capacity for selfishness and cruelty.

One of the social conditions in San Francisco which repeatedly aroused Twain's anger was racial intolerance, in particular the mistreatment of Orientals, and here his unsentimental image of young people stands out most starkly. "Disgraceful Persecution of a Boy," instead of blasting Irish mobs or the city police, calls ironic attention to the arrest of a well-dressed lad, on his way to Sunday School, for stoning

10. Reprinted in Branch, *Literary Apprenticeship*, p. 239.
11. Quoted in Walker, *San Francisco's Literary Frontier*, p. 174.

a Chinaman. "What a commentary is this upon human justice!" Twain remarks, ". . . San Francisco has little right to take credit to herself for her treatment of this poor boy." He goes on to itemize various ways Californians maltreat the Chinese and concludes by exonerating the boy completely. By watching his elders "the boy found out that a Chinaman had no rights that any man was bound to respect; that he had no sorrows that any man was bound to pity; that neither his life nor his liberty was worth the purchase of a penny when a white man needed a scapegoat." With but the change of a single noun, this comment might serve as a note to *Huckleberry Finn*—clear evidence of the continuity, in theme as in fictional techniques, between Twain's apprentice writings and his later novels. With one significant difference: whereas Huck is the moral center of his story, here the Sunday School scholar assuredly is not. Yet Twain does not blame him too severely. "And, therefore, what *could* have been more natural for this sunny-hearted boy, tripping along to Sunday-school, with his mind teeming with freshly-learned incentives to high and virtuous action, to say to himself: 'Ah, there goes a Chinaman! God will not love me if I do not stone him!' " (7, 126–29).

Both of these newspaper sketches are noteworthy from a literary viewpoint for their unusual use of "God's little people" as instruments of social commentary. Moreover, "Those Blasted Children" shows Twain's growing flexibility in the handling of lifelike dialogue. The little Californians playing, arguing, and tormenting the laundryman are presented dramatically through Twain's sense of the right childish phrase and expression. The form he is working toward, of course, is the dramatic monologue, a favorite of Western humorists and raconteurs and not basically different from the "Thomas Jefferson Snodgrass Papers" of a decade earlier. But in a piece like "Fitz Smythe's Horse"—a humorous spoof of a fellow journalist told through the mouth of a remarkably offhand little boy—Twain demonstrates how far he has come from the exaggerated style of the Snodgrass letters. At one point the urchin mentions the gargantuan appetite of Fitz Smythe's horse: "Why, he nipped a little boy, Sunday, which was going home from Sunday school; well, the boy got loose, you know, but that old hoss got his bible and some tracts, and them's as good a thing as *he* wants, being so used to papers, you see. You put anything to eat anywheres, and that old hoss'll shin out and get it . . . He'd climb a tree, he would, if you was to put anything up there for him—cats for instance —he likes cats—he's et up every cat there was here in four blocks—" [12] And the boy goes on piling exaggeration on exaggeration in the innocent, deadpan manner of Simon Wheeler, the narrator of "The Celebrated Jumping Frog of Calaveras County" and "Jim Wolf and the Tom-Cats."

The story of Jim Wolf itself is another humorous monologue, drawled out by old Simon in the meandering style of the Jumping Frog anecdote that made Twain famous. The story actually developed from a childhood experience in Hannibal and Twain deliberately utilizes a reminiscent tone. "We was all boys, then, and didn't care for nothing," Simon begins, "and didn't have no troubles, and didn't worry about nothing only how to shirk school and keep up a revivin' state of devilment all the time. Thish-yar Jim Wolf I was a talking about, was the 'prentice, and he was the best-hearted feller, he was, and the most forgivin' and onselfish I ever see . . ." Jim's qualities, like those of Snodgrass, dimly prefigure Huck Finn's, but Twain makes him the dupe of misfortune, rather than its narrator-observer. When Jim pursues some yowling tom-cats out on a slippery roof at night, the inevitable humorous mishap occurs; he slips and falls "like a yearth-quake in them two dozen sassers of red-hot candy" cooling on the porch below.

Simon Wheeler's narration is an inseparable part of the

12. Reprinted in Branch, p. 134.

story he relates. Though ostensibly an old man, yet in vocabulary, diction, and outlook as soon as he gets into the reminiscence, Wheeler becomes a boy again. "Jim he was a sight. He was gormed with that bilin' hot molasses candy clean down to his heels, and had more busted sassers hangin' to him than if he was an Injun princess—and he come a prancin' up-stairs just a-whoopin' and a cussin', and every jump he give he shed some china, and every squirm he fetched he dripped some candy!" [13] The "Injun princess" simile and the string of verbs at the end convince the reader he is listening to the authentic idiom of a Western boy, so successfully has Twain merged narrator and narrative. Simon's manner is that of an innocent, drawling out absurdities and jokes with the naiveté of a thirteen-year-old.

This masterful control over the dramatic monologue derived much of its charm and authenticity, as Delancey Ferguson has pointed out,[14] from Twain's own success as a storyteller and lecturer. Twain the writer learned much from Twain the talker, and the humor of his newspaper sketches depends chiefly upon the ear, not the eye. Actually, his career as lecturer commenced just at this time. He delivered the famous initial address, whose agonizing preparations are related in *Roughing It*, on October 2, 1866.[15] The same colloquial language, the same studied use of outrageous hyperbole, reversed values, the proper pause, the carefully prepared climax, all of which made him an instantaneous hit on the platform, are to be found in his sketches. Techniques tested by the living listener's laugh have been adapted to the written style. They may, in fact, have been directly transcribed. In later years Twain had a habit of testing the appeal of his fiction by read-

13. Ibid., pp. 269, 270.
14. *Mark Twain: Man and Legend* (Indianapolis and New York, Bobbs-Merrill Co., 1943), p. 113.
15. For MT's acount see *Roughing It*, chap. 37.

ing aloud the day's work to his family and friends. In both cases he developed a natural (though carefully contrived) style and a realistic treatment of character through his ear for the right intonation, the apt word, of the speaking voice. The mature style of *Huckleberry Finn* is implicit in "Fitz Smythe's Horse" or "Jim Wolf and the Tom-Cats."

With characteristic enthusiasm, Bernard DeVoto has asserted what other critics have also pointed out about Twain's apprenticeship work: "All the rest of Mark Twain's books are embryonic in what he had written by December, 1866, when he went east," DeVoto writes. "Washoe and California had finished what the mid-western frontier and the Mississippi had begun. These casual pieces outline the future: the humorist, the social satirist, the pessimist, the novelist of American character, Mark Twain exhilarated, sentimental, cynical, angry, and depressed, are all here. The rest is only development." [16]

Certain persistences DeVoto has failed to mention: two in particular are worth adding to his list. One is the presence, in much of the early work, of children as principal characters. From the very beginning of his writing career Twain's imagination fastened upon boys and girls—chiefly, of course, boys— as legitimate topics for investigation. A second continuing thread is the use he makes of the child, the "innocent eye," as an instrument for social criticism. In a city whose genteel spokesman objected to "Those Blasted Children" as something approaching blasphemy against "God's little people," Twain the satirist discovered a double-edged weapon. His childish figures not only are comments on adult hypocrisy, sentimentality, and cruelty, but stand for a moral norm by which the false values of a Sunday School society are being judged. Twain's boys fight, steal, lie, and throw rocks at Chinese laundrymen. But they are always boisterously natural. They never

16. Bernard DeVoto, *Mark Twain's America* (Boston, Little, Brown, 1932), p. 166.

say "Oh, sir!" but "You, Bob Miller, you leg go that string."

This admixture of malice and naturalness makes Twain's first fictional children "innocent" in a way fundamentally different from the innocence displayed, for example, in "Little Annie's Ramble." His satiric stance establishes innocence, for one thing, as something to laugh at, particularly when, as in the Snodgrass papers or "Jim Wolf and the Tom-Cats," it occurs in adults. Yet innocence, never wholly laughable, is often praiseworthy. In children innocence is relieved of moral blame when the evil that results is obviously imitated from adults. Thus at the outset of his career Twain begins to differentiate between innocence as inexperience, which is funny and ridiculous, and innocence as youthful naturalness and elementary moral integrity, which is laudable. Further exploration of the ambiguous face of innocence occupies him for a lifetime.

When the "Moralist of the Main" came East, therefore, and decided to write fiction, he had already developed the literary tools with which *Tom Sawyer* and *Huckleberry Finn* were to be constructed. Admittedly, he had not refined to a high degree his use of these instruments—Howells as literary critic was quite right in refusing "The Story of the Bad Little Boy"—but Twain had at least discovered the devices and tried them out. Children as characters; adult society as locus; innocence as theme; burlesque, farce, and satire as modes; all bound together and given the necessary illusion of life by authentic speech—these were the tools of his craft Twain first learned to use in Iowa, Nevada, and California. Indeed, "the relations between Mark Twain's Western work and his later writings are remarkably sustained." [17]

On February 2, 1870, in Elmira, Samuel Clemens was married to Olivia Langdon. Four days later, in the handsome house on Buffalo's fashionable Delaware Avenue presented to

17. Bellamy, *Mark Twain as a Literary Artist,* p. 112.

the couple by Mr. Langdon, the benedict—now a celebrated lecturer and author of a best seller—sat down to answer a letter from Will Bowen of Hannibal. Twain's "first & oldest & dearest friend" had evidently waxed sentimental over the bygone days of their boyhood and Twain had been duly touched. "My heart goes out to you just the same as ever," he replied. "Your letter has stirred me to the bottom. The fountains of my great deep are broken up & I have rained reminiscences for four & twenty hours. The old life has swept before me like a panorama; the old days have trooped by in their old glory again; the old faces have looked out of the mists of the past . . ."[18] A spate of memories pours on for several pages, to be interrupted finally by a self-conscious eulogy of his new wife and home. At the very moment of settling down to adult married life, Twain first recorded a vivid impression of his own childhood.

This passionate evocation of the past is the first hint of *The Adventures of Tom Sawyer*. Seven separate episodes mentioned in the letter to Bowen reappear in the novel, as well as several others which find a place in *Life on the Mississippi* and *Huckleberry Finn*. But this single letter, significant though it is as a lode for later fiction, is not the only prefiguration of the Mississippi River stories.

Some time later in the same year, according to DeVoto,[19] Twain began, but never completed, the "Boy's Manuscript." Predating *The Gilded Age* by perhaps three years, this fragment is thus his first venture into full-fledged fiction. For the "Boy's Manuscript" is not a sketch, like the earlier writing; it is a short story, complete with plot. The narrative it relates, in spite of its unfinished state and crude, exaggerated sentiment,

18. Theodore Hornberger, ed., *Mark Twain's Letters to Will Bowen* (Austin, University of Texas Press, 1941), p. 18.
19. Bernard DeVoto, *Mark Twain at Work* (Cambridge, Mass., Harvard University Press, 1942), pp. 5–6. DeVoto admits, however, that the date might be as late as 1872.

bears unmistakable relation to *Tom Sawyer*. Billy Rogers, the young protagonist, is Tom; Amy Lawrence is his sweetheart; the plot deals with their childish infatuation in language closely resembling *Tom Sawyer's*. As Twain's initial image of boyhood, the "Boy's Manuscript" is a central document in the apprenticeship of the ex-"Moralist of the Main."

To one familiar only with *Tom Sawyer*, the most notable feature of the "Boy's Manuscript" is the use of the first-person narrative. Billy tells his own tale through the flimsy and often unconvincing means of a diary. Beginning writers frequently tread familiar paths, but Twain had more convincing reasons than most for using this hackneyed device. His recent, successful California sketches had often been dramatic monologues, a closely allied form. Moreover, he doubtless was influenced by the success of his lecturing tours. The manuscript itself supports this latter supposition: the first page that has been preserved (originally the third, for the first and second pages are missing) bears a marginal note "Put in thing from Boy-Lecture." No trace of a "Boy-Lecture" has yet been discovered, but the notation suggests that Twain had an entire lecture composed of comic anecdotes about boys. Perhaps this recitation was adapted from such Western sketches as "Jim Wolf and the Tom-Cats," "Johnny Greer," and "Fitz Smythe's Horse." If so, Twain had some sort of rough manuscript before him as he sat down to write the "Boy's Manuscript." In such a case, lecturing techniques that had proved popular on the platform would naturally influence the neophyte novelist.

Whatever its parentage, Billy's language often strikes a fresh and amusingly natural note. Suffering the pangs of eight-year-old despised love, he laments: "Here lately, sometimes I feel ever so happy, and then again, dreadful often, too, I feel mighty bad. *Then* I don't take any interest in anything. I don't care for apples, I don't care for molasses candy, swinging on the gate don't do me no good, and even sliding on the cellar door don't seem like it used to did." [20] Straining for comic effect is evident, and yet Billy sometimes expresses childish thoughts accurately enough. On occasion, a striking realism is momentarily achieved, as in Billy's daydream of piratical glory. "But won't it be glorious!" he thinks. "I will be away a long time cruising, and then some Sunday morning I'll step into Sunday School with my long black hair, and my slouch hat with a plume in it, and my long sword and high boots and a splendid belt and red satin doublet and breeches, and my black flag with scull and cross-bones on it, and all the children will say, 'Look—look— that's Rogers the pirate!' " [21] These are believably the words of an eight-year-old.

Several years later when Twain turned to *Tom Sawyer*, he incorporated this passage into the longer work, with some interesting and significant changes. Here are Tom's thoughts on the same theme:

> How gloriously he would go plowing the dancing seas, in his long, low, black-hulled racer, the *Spirit of the Storm*, with his grisly flag flying at the fore! And at the zenith of his fame, how he would suddenly appear at the old village and stalk into church, brown and weather-beaten, in his black velvet doublet and trunks, his great jack-boots, his crimson sash, his belt bristling with horse-pistols, his crime-rusted cutlass at his side, his slouch hat with waving plumes, his black flag unfurled, with the skull and cross-bones on it, and hear with swelling ecstasy the whisperings, "It's Tom Sawyer the Pirate!—the Black Avenger of the Spanish Main!" [18, 75]

"Zenith" and "swelling ecstasy" are patently not in the vocabulary of an eight-year-old, which is the age specifically identified as Billy Rogers' in the "Boy's Manuscript." Tom Sawyer has

20. Ibid., p. 28.
21. Ibid., p. 37.

grown older, much more literary, and, one is tempted to say, less lifelike—not primarily because his language is so bookish but also because Twain's presentation of Tom is less dramatic than that of Billy: having a boy tell his own story was Twain's first impulse as a novelist, and it was to prove a sound one.

Nevertheless, Twain had considerable difficulty maintaining the tone of Billy's story. When the lovesmitten little hero writes to Amy, for instance, the contrived nature of the whole story is only too evident. For the diarist and the writer of love letters are seen to be two quite different boys. One writes: "Darling Amy I take my pen in hand to inform you that I am in good health and hope these fiew lines will find you injoying the same god's blessing. I love you. I cannot live and see you hate me and talk with that Jim riley which I will lick every time I ketch him and have done so already." When the diarist-narrator takes over again, however, any illusion that an eight-year-old is speaking is abruptly destroyed. "I directed it to her," he tells us of the love letter, "and took it and put it under her father's door. Then I looked up at her window for a long time, and prayed that she might be forgiven for what I was going to do—and then cried and kissed the ground where she used to step out at the door, and took a pinch of the dirt and put it next my heart where the candy was, and started away to die.—But I had forgotten to get any poison." [22] The letter might be the work of a little boy, but its romantic sequel could have been conceived only by an adolescent. When Clemens came later to the writing of *Tom Sawyer* he had similar, and even graver, troubles maintaining the tone of his narrative in keeping with the age of his boys. In fact, this problem, inherent in the choice of children as characters and insistent whenever a child is selected as narrator, plagued Twain to the end of his career.

DeVoto called the language Twain puts in Billy's mouth

22. Ibid., pp. 34–35.

"stilted and unreal," [23] and so it usually is. But allowances must be made for Twain's farcical intentions. Billy's love letter is meant to be ludicrous, as are his posturings outside Amy's window. Where the writer betrays inexperience is in putting the two bits of farce incongruously together. This forcing of the tone, this pushing of the joke until its unrealism becomes stridently obvious, is a legacy from Twain's Western humorist predecessors and is everywhere evident in the "Boy's Manuscript." At one point, for instance, Billy's moping lovesickness provokes Mrs. Rogers to indulge in an orgy of home cures. These are described at tedious length:

> So she gave me ipecac, and calomel, and all that sort of stuff and made me awful sick. And I had to go to bed, and she gave me a mug of hot sage tea and a mug of hot saffron tea, and covered me up with blankets and said that would sweat me and bring it to the surface. I suffered . . . Then she said I had bile. And so she gave me some warm salt water and I heaved up everything that was in me. But she wasn't satisfied. She said there wasn't any bile in that. So she gave me two blue mass pills . . .[24]

Dixon Wecter tells us Sam Clemens had himself suffered for years under a maternal enthusiasm for allopathic and hydropathic cures, and Twain the writer must always have considered the situation funny, for he repeated it four times.[25]

23. Ibid., p. 9.
24. Ibid., p. 29.
25. See Wecter, *Sam Clemens of Hannibal*, p. 81. An earlier instance occurs in "Those Blasted Children." Tendering mock medical advice to parents, Twain quips: "In the matter of measles, the idea is to bring it out—bring it to the surface. Take the child and fill it up with saffron tea. Add something to make the patient sleep—say a table-spoonful of arsenic. Don't rock it, it will sleep anyhow." Branch, *Literary Apprenticeship*, p. 240. Tom Sawyer, of course, in the episode of Peter and the Painkiller undergoes similar treatment. In the unfinished fragment "Tom Sawyer's Conspiracy" (see below, Chap. 6), the routine is repeated once again.

What Billy Rogers' story most seriously lacks, however, is not originality of plot or poised restraint in the modulation of the humor. After all, neither of these virtues is especially associated with Mark Twain. The missing ingredients of successful fiction that matter most may be discovered by comparing the "Boy's Manuscript" with what had preceded it and what came after. In many of his Western sketches Twain had come very close to fiction, yet fictional illusion of reality was not what gave these anecdotes their distinctive quality. Rather it was the satiric impulse that connected the newspaper pieces to the real world Twain and his readers lived in. There is no such satiric thrust in the "Boy's Manuscript"; its fun is by turns gentle, mawkish, or crude. The plot, as far as it goes, has no point, except to amuse. More serious still, it is not at all clear what audience Twain had in mind to amuse. The action is too banal for adults; it turns entirely upon the complications of calf love. Yet there are not enough "adventures" to sustain a boy's interest for long. Among other indecisions and false steps of the beginning writer one was the most damaging of all: Twain did not really know for whom he was writing Billy Rogers' story.

It is clear, then, that during these years before he wrote *Tom Sawyer* he had a low opinion of juvenile literature in general. His lukewarm reaction to Aldrich's *The Story of a Bad Boy* is evidence of this animus, particularly when one recalls his later enthusiasm for the same novel. Another reinforcement for the notion that Twain came reluctantly to write specifically for young people is found in a letter he wrote his brother Orion in March 1871. "My Dear Bro:" he began, evidently in response to a request for literary advice, "My opinion of a children's article is wholly worthless, for I never saw one that I thought was worth the ink it was written with, & yet you know & I know that such literature is marvelously popular & worth heaps of money . . . I have no love for children's

51

literature." [26] Since the "Boy's Manuscript" had been started and abandoned only a short while before this letter, it is safe to assume that Twain's opinion of juvenile literature was still low, and consequently that Billy Rogers was not intended exclusively for childish readers. In fact, until he was able to accept *both* children *and* adults for his proper audience Mark Twain would find, as Howells was later to point out, that writing fiction would prove a difficult task.

Another area in which, for readers familiar with *Tom Sawyer,* the "Boy's Manuscript" is a disappointment lies in the almost total absence of that nether world of nightmare, terror, and superstition which fills Tom's mind and that of his friend Huck Finn and makes them infinitely more complex boys that Billy. Admittedly, there is one foreshadowing of Huck's necromancy in the character of Wart Hopkins, "that's his nickname—because he's all over warts," who overtakes Billy in the schoolyard after he has "been out to the cross-roads burying a bean that he'd bloodied with a wart to make them go away . . ." [27] But nothing further develops of these superstitious ties with the spirit world, so important an element in the atmosphere of Mark Twain's other boyhood stories. The result is further impoverishment of a story already weakened by fuzzy definition of its central character, aimless plot development, and indecision as to the intended audience. The "Boy's Manuscript," in spite of its fateful choice of a boyish narrator, is chiefly valuable, as DeVoto has pointed out, because "in these random and clumsy scenes a great novelist first struck the vein that was to produce his finest work. Here for the first time he wrote about the Hannibal of his boyhood." [28]

26. MT to Orion Clemens, Buffalo (March 15, 1871), unpublished letter in MTP. © Mark Twain Company.

27. DeVoto, *Mark Twain at Work,* p. 40.

28. Ibid., p. 8.

Among several possible explanations of why Twain failed
to make much of the supernatural element in the "Boy's Manuscript" is one simple but highly significant fact: there are no
Negroes in the story. The image of boyhood that Mark Twain
has stamped upon the American imagination is so manifestly
a double one that it would be hard to picture Tom Sawyer
or Huck Finn apart from Nigger Jim. Children and Negro
slaves, inseparable figures in the landscape of the Mississippi
river stories, exist separately in Billy Rogers' fragmentary story.
Hence, Twain's first fictional boy is denied that prolific source
of information about ghosts, spells, omens, and black magic
which Sam Clemens himself, along with every other boy who
grew up in antebellum Missouri, acquired from the Negroes.
Never again, in his American fiction, was he to separate the
black shadow from the white.

When next he tried his hand at fiction he did not forget the
Negro. It was during those busy spring weeks of 1873 that
Charles Dudley Warner and his Next-door Neighbor accepted
a dinner-table dare from their wives and dashed off the draft
of a novel. Twain began his share of *The Gilded Age* by
introducing his first black "chile," Uncle Dan'l.[29] That he regarded the Negro essentially as a child, and was not using the
word simply metaphorically, is made plain from the first scenes
in which Uncle Dan'l appears. The Hawkins children and Dan'l
are presented together, bound to one another not only by ties
of dependence and guardianship but by affection and a common cast of mind. Innocence, wonder, and superstition are
traits of children's minds commonly shared, in the face of
which other differences between Negro slave and white child
disappear.

29. For a discussion of the respective portions of *The Gilded Age: A
Tale of Today*, written by MT and Charles Dudley Warner, see E. E.
Leisy, "Mark Twain's Part in *The Gilded Age*," *American Literature*, 8
(1937), 445–47.

This feeling of Twain's about children and Negroes is vividly illustrated by an early scene from *The Gilded Age* in which the Hawkins family first reaches the Mississippi River on their way to a new home in Missouri. A tableau of symbolic significance takes place, one for which Twain carefully sets the stage. "A deep silence pervaded the air," he begins, "and was emphasized, at intervals, rather than broken, by the hooting of an owl, the baying of a dog, or the muffled crash of a caving bank in the distance." Both children and slaves are filled with an identical dread by this portentous stillness of the magnificent river:

> The little company assembled on the log were all children (at least in simplicity and broad and comprehensive ignorance), and the remarks they made about the river were in keeping with the character; and so awed were they by the grandeur and the solemnity of the scene before them, and by their belief that the air was filled with invisible spirits and that the faint zephyrs were caused by their passing wings, that all their talk took to itself a tinge of the supernatural, and their voices were subdued to a low and reverent tone. [5, 20]

Moments later a steamboat rounds the bend, pouring out smoke and spangling the twilight with sparks. Both sorts of children, completely unacquainted with this phenomenon, fall to their knees, convinced that it is "de Almighty" Himself. Uncle Dan'l prays for their deliverance, offering himself as a sacrifice if only his young white charges will be spared. "And deah Lord, good Lord, it ain't like yo' mercy, it ain't like yo' pity, it ain't like yo' long-sufferin' lovin'-kindness for to take dis kind o' 'vantage o' sich chil'en as dese is when dey's so many ornery grown folks chuck full o' cussedness dat wants roastin' down dah. Oh, Lord, spah de little chil'en, don't tar de little chil'en away f'm dey frens, jes' let 'em off jes' dis once, and take

54

it out'n de ole niggah" (5, 22). As the apparition draws abreast of the log and lets out a shriek from its mud-valve, everyone flees, Uncle Dan'l in the lead, a white child under each arm.

Though Clemens is certainly spoofing Dan'l's innocence and timidity—when the slave reaches the deep woods and feels ashamed, he turns to shout (but rather feebly): "Heah I is, Lord, heah I is!"—still he frankly admires the Negro's essential moral fiber. In spite of the flight, the slave's self-sacrificing plea is wholly genuine. It foreshadows loving acts of selflessness by Jim and Roxy, two other Negro slaves in Twain's later novels. Moreover, the innocence of Uncle Dan'l and the Hawkins children establishes, in the opening pages of this corrosive satire on human cupidity, a standard by which all the characters in *The Gilded Age* are later judged.

Included among those implicitly condemned by the child's innocent integrity are the white children themselves when grown to manhood and womanhood. The naiveté of Washington Hawkins, of course, like that of Colonel Sellers himself, is merely ludicrous; there is little that is either morally laudable or reprehensible about it, and Washington remains all his life essentially the simple child he was on the riverbank. But his sister Laura travels a great distance from that moment of simple-hearted terror at the steamboat's shriek. Her subsequent career hovers on the immoral in her affair with Selby, and after his murder she must pay for her sins with her own life. As she sits in her sumptuous Washington drawing room, Laura's thoughts revert to childhood. She "dwelt upon it as the one brief interval in her life that bore no curse. She saw herself again in the budding grace of her twelve years, decked in her dainty pride of ribbons, consorting with the bees and butterflies, believing in fairies, holding confidential converse with the flowers . . . 'If I could only die!' she said. 'If I could only go back, and be as I was then, for one hour—and hold my father's hand in mine again, and see all the household about me as in that old innocent time—and then die!'" (6, 299). After this genuinely moving moment, Laura Hawkins' death-scene descends to pure bathos. She remains seated until the servants burst down the door to find she has expired of "heart disease"!

In spite of this absurd touch, Laura's death explicitly re-affirms the moral standard set in the opening scenes. In this satiric work innocence operates at several levels—among simple backwoods boys and girls like the Hawkinses, in the mind of a black "chile" like Dan'l, in the perennial self-delusions of Sellers and Washington Hawkins, and as the lost dream of Laura Hawkins. Though the relation of these aspects of innocence to the broader satire in the novel are not always made perfectly clear, childhood and the qualities associated with it—integrity, sincerity, sacrifice—are essential elements to a serious reading of the satire Mark Twain and Charles Dudley Warner wrote.

With the "Boy's Manuscript" Twain began, falteringly and crudely, to draw the fictional outlines of his image of boyhood. Billy Rogers' story was, as might be expected of a first try, little more than a series of pranks and sentimental poses. Behind these stereotypes lay the Western sketches. Those newspaper squibs about children are humorous, but they also direct serious moral questions at the adult social world as well as at children themselves. They are something more than jokes. The "Boy's Manuscript" failed to catch this bittersweet tone. In his first true piece of fiction Mark Twain unfortunately separated the boy's world from that of grown-ups. A few years later, in *The Gilded Age*, Twain learned, perhaps by collaborating with his more experienced writer-neighbor Charles Dudley Warner, to relate in a muted but unmistakable manner the world of innocent children to society at large. Furthermore, *The Gilded Age*, through its Negro characters, reveals Twain learning to recognize the significance of the imaginative world of ghosts and dreams inside the childish mind. When, therefore, he came to write *Tom Sawyer,* he was equipped by experience to overcome, in large measure, the deficiencies of his first fragmentary story. Tom's narrative not only uncovers a complex inner world of superstition and terror but relates in a meaningful way the childish sphere of games and tricks to the social order of adults. In this sense, *The Adventures of Tom Sawyer* draws together threads from three sources in Twain's early career—the Western satiric pieces, the "Boy's Manuscript," and *The Gilded Age*—which, together with the incomparable experience in the use of realistic speech he had gained on the lecture platform, form his special apprenticeship for the study of boyhood.

3.

Tom Sawyer and His Cousins

"I FINISHED READING Tom Sawyer a week ago," Howells wrote to its author in Hartford late in November of 1875, "sitting up to one A.M., to get to the end, simply because it was impossible to leave off. It's altogether the best boy's story I ever read. It will be an immense success." [1] Though the editor of the *Atlantic Monthly* was speaking as a friend and not *ex cathedra*, his praise for the manuscript Twain had begun the previous year was an honest measure of the distance Twain had come in the ten years since "Story of the Bad Little Boy." The ex-newspaperman from the West Coast had hit the mark with his generation's most perceptive critic. "The best boy's story I ever read" signals triumphantly the end of Twain's apprenticeship. "Jim Wolf and the Tom-Cats," Billy Rogers' fragmentary saga, and *The Gilded Age* had been successfully assimilated into a novel that started Twain upon the major phase of his career. Henceforth childhood was to be the theme of his best fiction.

The manuscript Howells could not put down unfinished did, however, perplex. Howells felt Twain had written only for adults. "But I think you should treat it explicitly *as* a boy's story," he went on to remark in the same letter. "Grown-ups will enjoy it just as much if you do; and if you should put it

1. H. N. Smith and W. M. Gibson, eds., *Mark Twain–Howells Letters* (Cambridge, Harvard University Press, 1960), *1*, 110.

forth as a study of boy character from the grown-up point of view, you'd give the wrong key to it." Then the editor added, "I have made some corrections and suggestions in faltering pencil, which you'll have to look for. They're almost all in the first third. When you fairly swing off, you had better be left alone." Twain himself had requested Howells' red pencil and welcomed criticism from his friend. But he had felt otherwise about the question of readers. The previous July, when he sent the manuscript to Howells, he had explained, "It is *not* a boy's book, at all. It will only be read by adults. It is only written for adults." [2] Difference of opinion could hardly be sharper, and it is well to remember that Twain had written his draft of Tom's story in accordance with his, not Howells', conviction. Originally, *Tom Sawyer* was definitely not a children's book.

Although this was the fourth full-length work, it was the first novel Twain had written alone. His respect for Howells' judgment was great, and likely to weigh heavily against his own unproven preferences. When, therefore, the manuscript arrived back at Nook Farm bearing a number of careful emendations, Twain, who detested rewriting and never willingly read proof, was delighted. Apparently he capitulated completely. "This was splendid, & swept away all labor . . . I reduced the boy-battle to a curt paragraph; I finally concluded to cut the Sunday-school speech down to the first two sentences, (leaving no suggestion of satire, since the book is for boys & girls; I tamed the various obscenities until I judged that [they] no longer carried offense." [3] The "Moralist of the Main" had decided to softpedal the satiric mode that had been his characteristic manner and ostensibly to join the ranks of Abbott, Aldrich, and Miss Alcott, "since the book is for boys & girls."

Years later, however, as if to register a judgment that would settle his own doubts and past compromises, Twain made a

2. Ibid., p. 91.
3. Ibid., pp. 121–22.

comment in his notebook. "Write a preface:" he declared to himself, "I have never written a book for boys; I write for grown-ups who have *been* boys. If the boys read it & like it, perhaps that is testimony that my boys are real, not artificial. If they are real to the grown-ups, that is proof." [4] By 1902, then, the pendulum had seemingly swung back to the position of 1875, before Howells convinced Twain differently. But that this was a final opinion is much to be doubted: as all his autobiographical writings attest, he constantly rewrote the past to fit the moods and needs of the present; hence these vacillations must be accepted at face value. They indicate merely that Twain was of two minds about the readers for whom he finally published *The Adventures of Tom Sawyer* in 1876. Changes such as he acknowledges making, no matter how extensive, could not completely alter the structure or themes, or the handling of characters in a novel originally intended, like all his previous work, for grown-ups.

That early readers of *Tom Sawyer* agreed with Twain and not with Howells is strongly suggested by the reviewer's reaction in the local paper that reported to Hartford the appearance of their neighbor's new work. "The book is all about boys," the *Courant* observed, "and is said to be written for boys. It is a masterly reproduction of boys' life and feeling, but, at the same time, it is written above boys; that is, the best part of it—the wit, the humor, the genius of it—will fly miles above every boy's head in the country. The boys can appreciate the adventure in it as a mere narrative, but not that which makes the adventure valuable to older readers, who recall their own boyhood in it." [5] The reviewer (probably Warner or Charles

4. Notebook 35 (July 7, 1902), Typescript p. 20, in MTP. © Mark Twain Company.

5. Literary Notice, Hartford *Courant*, Dec. 27, 1876, in W. S. Morse Collection of Mark Twain Memorabilia, Vol. 3, pp. 15–16. Connecticut State Library, Hartford.

Clark, both close friends of Twain's) recognizes the double achievement of *Tom Sawyer:* a boy's adventure tale on one level, an adult work on another.

A reading of Tom's story simply as adventure indicates that Twain began with the notion of writing a spoof of the Good Boy – Bad Boy convention that had proved such a congenial subject in California. In the first seven chapters Tom breaks all the rules, commits every minor pecadillo which the literary Good Boy of the day avoided so piously. He steals, lies, threatens his brother, fights, shows off outrageously in Sunday School, and disrupts a church service that must have been the most important community activity in St. Petersburg. "He was not the Model Boy of the village," Twain remarks dryly. "He knew the model boy very well though—and loathed him" (8, 6).

The Model Boy does, in fact, put in an early appearance. After the gentry, the village belles, and the "oiled and simpering" dandies of the town take their places in church, "last of all came the Model Boy, Willie Mufferson, taking as heedful care of his mother as if she were of cut glass. He always brought his mother to church, and was the pride of all the matrons. The boys all hated him, he was so good" (8, 44). Tom's release of the pinch-bug shows how *he* behaves in church; his clodding of Sid (another Willie), his playing hooky, his smoking and running away from home all carry out the pattern of genial mockery of the proprieties observed in conventional stories about children. To make the satire even more obvious, each escapade is rounded out with a mock moral. After the whitewashing scene, for instance, the author concludes, "Tom said to himself that it was not such a hollow world, after all. He had discovered a great law of human action, without knowing it—namely, that in order to make a man or a boy covet a thing, it is only necessary to make the thing

61

difficult to attain" (8, 18–19). In these early episodes Twain's tongue-in-cheek tone, deliberately anti-Franklin, is broad and genial enough to amuse all ages.

Though Tom Sawyer is a Bad Boy, he is not really bad. Aunt Polly, Tom's surrogate mother and the voice of respectability and authority, defends and defines her rebellious nephew. "He warn't *bad,* so to say—only mischeevous. Only just giddy, and harum-scarum, you know. He warn't any more responsible than a colt" (8, 130). Tom lives up to this description; throughout the story, in spite of outrageous conduct, he does nothing positively evil for which he can be held morally responsible. He simply behaves normally. Like Beechnut and Tom Bailey before him, Tom Sawyer is a Natural Boy. Dickens' Mr. Chadband could have addressed him as he did Jo: "You are a human boy, my young friend. A human boy." [6] B. P. Shillaber, the creator of Ike Partington, could use much the same language—"Lively Boy" would have been his term.

Other writers, too, could supply their own names for Tom's kind. *Tom Sawyer* was but one of a whole series of novels appearing after the Civil War which celebrated boyhood by introducing the Bad Boy as a distinctively American hero of fiction. Thomas Bailey Aldrich's *The Story of a Bad Boy* (1869), Charles Dudley Warner's *Being a Boy* (1878), B. P. Shillaber's *Ike Partington and His Friends* (1879), Edgar W. Howe's *The Story of a Country Town* (1882), Edward Eggleston's *The Hoosier School-Boy* (1883), *Peck's Bad Boy* (1883), William Dean Howells' *A Boy's Town* (1890) and *The Flight of Pony Baker* (1902), Stephen Crane's *Whilomville Stories* (1899)— all are works linked by a common thread. Taking the boy Peter Parley did not know as their center of focus and moving freely from this center toward autobiography, farce, satire, social history, and even the beginnings of the psychological novel,

6. *Bleak House,* Centenary Edition of the Works of Charles Dickens (London, Chapman and Hall, 1911), *1,* 327.

these writers established, quite unconsciously in some cases, a tradition which has had wide repercussions in modern American fiction. The potentialities of childhood as theme and comic realism as basic technique have attracted some of the best writers of the twentieth century. Anderson, Hemingway, Faulkner, and Salinger are each, in differing ways and to varying degrees, legatees of these early creators of Bad Boys.

Mark Twain's *Tom Sawyer* and *Huckleberry Finn* stand at the head of this stream. Because its author tried so consciously to make *Tom Sawyer* like the others—"my book is intended mainly for the entertainment of boys and girls" runs the final preface—there is an especially close link between Tom Sawyer and his literary cousins: Aldrich's Tom Bailey, Howe's Ned Westlock, Warner's John, Howells' "my boy," Shillaber's Ike Partington, and the others. Comparing Tom with his fellow anti-prigs uncovers some striking parallels as well as differences equally significant. Tom's pre-eminent position in the roster of the Bad Boys of the late nineteenth century emerges clearly. For one thing, he is no stereotype of the Bad Boy, the Natural Boy, the Lively Boy, or the Human Boy. He is himself, an individual with distinctive traits of speech, mind, and personality. Moreover, the ties uniting him to the life of St. Petersburg are more deep-rooted and complex than is the case with the other village boys. Tom's adventures, unlike those of his fellows, constitute, in spite of a veneer of farcical humor, the serious process by which Twain's boy is initiated into maturity. As a result, *Tom Sawyer* is more than a nostalgic re-creation of Mississippi River life before the War, though it is this, too. Mark Twain pays boyhood the ultimate compliment by using Tom as the vehicle for a full-dress study of personality, community, and the anatomy of social evil.

Although *Tom Sawyer* originated in Twain's imagination as a burlesque aimed chiefly at bemused adults, the novel develops, after the opening chapters, into something far more ambitious than a lampoon of Good Boys and Bad Boys. Tom himself as a person, the village of St. Petersburg and the values by which it lives, the interaction of boy and adults—these considerations speedily engross the novelist's attention. The result is a movement away from farce toward the classic concerns of the novel, namely the relation of individual to the community, to social class, and to money.

It is difficult to reconstruct the process by which Twain moved from one realm to another, for the shift is at times unconscious and incomplete; but certain factors seem to be operating. For one thing, the Good Boy – Bad Boy satire was a limited literary form, best suited to short sketches and incapable of sustaining narrative for the full length of a novel. Furthermore, the Bad Boy story, with its classic plot of boyish rebellion and victory over adult restrictions, had not, in 1874–75, developed fully. Jacob Abbott, Louisa May Alcott, and Thomas Bailey Aldrich were the chief practitioners (apart from Western humorists Twain had read in newspapers), and in fact *The Story of a Bad Boy* was his principal prototype. The first seven chapters of *Tom Sawyer* compress most of the typical pranks of the Bad Boy story into little more than a third of the narrative. In these chapters Twain had begun to draw upon his rich reservoir of recollections of Hannibal life. Also, Tom himself had grown into an interesting and independent character. Hence, Twain, who always admitted to aimlessness and impulse as guiding literary principles, found himself following his boy hero as he moved through the landscape of a past now vividly remembered.

No one was less disturbed by the apparent ambiguity and aimlessness of *Tom Sawyer* than its author. Even before he incorporated Howells' changes, he had written his friend, "I am going to take into serious consideration all you have said,

& then make up my mind by & by. Since there is no plot to the thing, it is likely to follow its own drift, & so is as likely to drift into manhood as anywhere—I won't interpose." [7]

Despite this confession, the novel as completed and revised has a natural structure that encompasses its diverse origins and intentions. Its structural center is, of course, Tom himself. Beginning as a standard Bad Boy, Tom Sawyer, though he does not narrate his own story, nevertheless asserts marked individuality and a distinctive way of looking at the world and reacting to its challenges and opportunities. A more mature character than Billy Rogers, Tom—as his dream of piratical glory reveals—is more graphic and literary in speech, is much better attuned to the adult world, and has an imaginative flair his predecessor never achieves. While Billy is content to awe the Sunday School children, Tom dreams of stalking into church at the zenith of his fame to impress the whole village. Billy contemplates suicide by poison, but Tom leads his cronies to Jackson's Island, watches the steamboat searching for their bodies, and grandly attends his own funeral.

One distinguishing mark of Tom Sawyer's personality is the literary cast to his speech and, as Twain reports it, his thought. When he and Joe Harper play Robin Hood in the woods, they "talk by the book," under Tom's prompting. The dream of "the Black Avenger of the Spanish Main!" bristles with literary clichés—the "black-hulled" racer is "plowing the dancing seas," the "grisly" flag flies, and the "crime-rusted" cutless dully gleams. This bookishness Tom Sawyer shares with (and possibly inherited from) Aldrich's Tom Bailey. Bailey's speech, like Sawyer's, is livelier and more natural than the descriptive passages of *The Story of a Bad Boy*, but it resembles more a boys' magazine version of British public-school lingo than the idiom of an American boy. When, for example, Tom and his crony

7. *Mark Twain–Howells Letters*, 1, 87–88.

Pepper Whitcomb meet in the Rivermouth cemetery, where
Tom is moping in unrequited love of his nineteen-year-old mis-
tress, the following exchange takes place:

"Look here, Tom Bailey," said Pepper, shying a piece of
clam-shell indignantly at the *Hic jacet* on a neighboring
gravestone, "you are just going to the dogs! Can't you tell
a fellow what in thunder ails you, instead of prowling
around among the tombs like a jolly old vampire?"

"Pepper," I replied, solemnly, "don't ask me. All is not
well here,"—touching my breast mysteriously . . .

Pepper stared at me.

"Earthly happiness," I continued, "is a delusion and a
snare. You will never be happy, Pepper, until you are a
cherub." . . .

Having delivered myself of these gloomy remarks, I
arose languidly from the grass and moved away, leaving
Pepper staring after me in mute astonishment. I was
Hamlet and Werter and the late Lord Byron all in one.[8]

The style recalls Billy Rogers outside Amy's window. By the
time Twain came to write *Tom Sawyer* he had largely outgrown such arch clumsiness. Vestiges remain in the author's
comments, but when Tom himself speaks, the vitality and
freshness are unmistakable. As a result, the graveyard scene
in *Tom Sawyer* contrasts strikingly with that in Aldrich's novel.
Twain's boys inhabit a different world.

A faint wind moaned through the trees, and Tom feared
it might be the spirits of the dead, complaining of being
disturbed. The boys talked little, and only under their
breath, for the time and the place and the pervading
solemnity and silence oppressed their spirits . . .

"Hucky, do you believe the dead people like it for us
to be here?"

8. *Story of a Bad Boy*, pp. 230–32.

Huckleberry whispered:

"I wisht I knowed. It's awful solemn like, *ain't* it?" . . .

"Say, Hucky—do you reckon Hoss Williams hears us talking?"

"O' course he does. Least his sperrit does."

Tom, after a pause:

"I wish I'd said *Mister* Williams. But I never meant any harm. Everybody calls him Hoss." [8, 81–82]

Aldrich and Twain are each after a comic effect that is achieved. But the superior skill with which Twain mixes humor and the atmosphere of terror cannot simply be attributed to, say, an unconscious debt to *A Tale of Two Cities*. Twain may have had an echo of young Jerry Cruncher in mind, but any specific literary source has been kept firmly in the background. Fidelity to the authentic spoken voice serves Twain better than adherence to a literary tradition.

Where he surpassed his contemporaries is in his knack of dramatizing the imagination of his young protagonist. In spite of his decision not to employ the first-person narrative, he gets inside his characters better than any of the other boyhood enthusiasts of his generation. Edgar W. Howe, for instance, in *The Story of a Country Town,* has not even accepted Aldrich's advantage of telling Ned Westlake's story through the boy's own mouth. As a result, his narrative of a boy's experiences growing up in a Kansas prairie town is presented flatly and matter of factly. Ned is a small child when the novel begins, but Howe is less concerned with maturation than with using Ned as an innocent eye to record the life of Twin Mounds. Placed, for instance, in the presence of death, Ned reacts with characteristic emotionlessness. "When I was yet a very little boy," he reminisces, "I occasionally went with my father to toll the bell when news came that someone was dead, for we lived nearer the place than any of the others, and when the strokes ran up to forty or fifty it was very dreary work, and I sat alone in the church wondering who would ring for me, and how many strokes could be counted by those who were shivering at home in their beds." [9] Ned shares some of Tom's mood in the St. Petersburg graveyard, but Howe has made no attempt to bring that mood alive by dialogue or appropriate description. Ned's emotions are reported from the distance of the author's weary maturity.[10] Unfortunately, the freshness has departed together with the dramatic immediacy. Thus entire reaches of boyish life in a small town are dismissed by Howe in a sentence or two, where Twain will spend chapters. "Soon after my introduction into the office," Ned relates when he is a fifteen-year-old printer's apprentice,

> I had learned to ink the forms so acceptably with a hand roller that I was forced to keep at it, for a suitable successor could not be found, but at last we found a young man who had a passion for art (it was none other than my old enemy, Shorty Wilkinson; I fought him regularly every week during the first year of my residence in town, but we finally agreed to become friends) . . . Sometimes we invented startling things at night, and spent the time given us in wandering through the woods like idle boys, bathing and fishing in the streams in summer, and visiting the sugar-camps in early spring, where we heard many tales of adventure which afterwards appeared in print under great headings.[11]

Mark Twain, too, was a newspaperman, but he had learned the vital difference between a sketch and a novel. Ned Westlake is an accurate reflecting mirror of the life of his village, but little more.

9. Edgar W. Howe, *The Story of a Country Town* (New York, Albert and Charles Boni, 1926), p. 4.
10. Ibid., preface, p. i.
11. Ibid., p. 172.

68

Twain read *The Story of a Country Town* and recognized Howe's particular qualities. "Your pictures of that arid village life, & the insides & outsides of its people, are vivid, & what is more, true; I know, for I have seen it all, lived it all," he wrote Howe in 1884.[12] Charity alone must have prompted Twain to praise Howe's skill in portraying the "insides" of his boys, so far inferior is *The Story of a Country Town* in this, and every other respect, to *Tom Sawyer* and *Huckleberry Finn*.

Howe was not the only writer of Twain's generation whose failure to grasp the distinction between memoir and fiction resulted in one-dimensional pictures of boyhood. Both of Twain's close friends, Warner and Howells, fell into this trap. *Being a Boy*, which followed *Tom Sawyer* by less than two years, bears close resemblance to Warner's other collections of essays. The fictional veneer is woefully thin. Not only does it lack plot but Warner's boy, John, a generalized image of the author growing up in the Berkshires of Western Massachusetts, is a pallid figure indeed compared with Tom or Huck. The reason is not hard to discover; "There was no attempt at the biography of any particular boy," Twain's next-door neighbor asserts in the preface. "I invented nothing,—not an adventure, not a scene, not an emotion. I know from observation how difficult it is for an adult to write about childhood. Invention is apt to supply details that memory does not carry. The knowledge of the man insensibly inflates the boyhood limitations." [13] Given such antifictional tendencies, Warner's probings into the private life of his John inevitably are superficial. The twelve-year-old farm boy has daydreams that are highly conventional; they run to "a cave full of diamonds, and lots of nail-kegs full of gold-pieces and Spanish dollars, with a

12. Quoted in C. E. Schorer, "Mark Twain's Criticism of *The Story of a Country Town*," *American Literature*, 27 (1955), 110.
13. *Being a Boy*, Illustrated Edition (Boston, Houghton Mifflin, 1897), pp. viii–ix.

pretty little girl living in the cave, and two beautifully caparisoned horses, upon which, taking the jewels and money, they would have ridden off together, he did not know where." [14] Tom Sawyer, on the contrary, always knows in detail the itinerary of his imaginary voyages, and instead of "a cave full of diamonds" his travels around St. Petersburg lead him to a real cave where eventually death leaves actual knife-marks at its door.

Warner was essentially an essayist, and his limitations in respect to fictionalizing boyhood proved finally as disappointing as Howe's pedestrian newspaper reporting. But William Dean Howells was a professional novelist as well as a critic who had helped polish up numerous boyhood stories before he himself entered the field in 1890 with *A Boy's Town*. Moreover, when Howells composed his first eulogy to boyhood he knew precisely what audience he intended to reach. *A Boy's Town* (like *The Flight of Pony Baker* twelve years later) is carefully directed at boys and girls, specifically for the readers of *Harper's Young People* magazine. As a consequence, both of Howells' stories, whatever their shortcomings, maintain a unity of tone that *Tom Sawyer* lacks.

The protagonist (he is no hero) of *A Boy's Town* has no name, and this is fair indication of his fictional limitations. Like Ned Westlake, "my boy" serves Howells as cub reporter to the village life and customs of Hamilton, Ohio, in the 1840's. As passive observer rather than actor, "my boy's" own private imagination is treated exactly like other items in a reminiscence. Swimming in the canal, stealing watermelons, and gathering chinquapin acorns in the woods are boyish pastimes precisely as significant, apparently, as the interior dream-world that Howells calls his small boy's "real self." "My boy" has a mind whose depths are "all vague and vast" to Howells. "While he was joyfully sharing the wild sports and conforming to the

14. Ibid., p. 75.

savage usages of the boy's world about him," the author says, "he was dwelling in a wholly different world within him, whose wonders no one else knew. I could not tell now these wonders any more than he could have told them then; but it was a world of dreams, of hopes, of purposes, which he would have been more ashamed to avow for himself than I should be to avow for him." [15]

Such voluntary chaining of the imagination reduces "my boy" to a shadowy figure. Though Pony Baker, a vagabond modeled evidently on Huck Finn, fares better, both of Howells' lads are prevented from blossoming as distinctive personalities by their creator's astonishing conviction that all boys are much alike. "They do not wish to be so," he points out, "but they could not help it. They did not even know they were alike; and my boy used to suffer in ways that he believed no boy had ever suffered before . . ." Then, turning to his audience of *Harper's Young People:* "The first thing you have to learn here below is that in essentials you are just like everyone else, and that you are different from others only in what is not so much worth while." [16] This little sermon, curiously reminiscent in tone of the early Hawthorne or Jacob Abbott of the Rollo books, is exactly what Mark Twain is turning upside down in *Tom Sawyer.* Furthermore, Howells' dictum destroys his art. If, as he asserts, individuality consists chiefly in naughtiness, which is unacceptable as a theme for stories written for children, then it is no wonder "my boy" is a flat figure. His friend Twain had a firmer grasp on the fictional possibilities of boyhood because he was willing to portray "what is not so much worth while" in his characters as well as their admirable sides. The results were not only funnier but also produced a richer and deeper exploration of boyish character.

Naughtiness, no matter how vitalizing for Twain's image of

15. *A Boy's Town* (New York, Harper and Brothers, 1890), p. 171.
16. Ibid., p. 205.

boyhood as contrasted with Howells' or Warner's, has, nevertheless, distinct limits in *Tom Sawyer*. Tom's days are spent tormenting the bewigged schoolmaster and the primary-class picnic, but his creator has not equated—as is often the case, for instance, with Shillaber and Peck—realistic adolescent behavior with out-and-out cruelty. *Tom Sawyer's* running battle of boys with grown-ups is good-natured and produces less actual suffering or pain than either *Ike Partington and His Friends* or *Peck's Bad Boy*. Each of these later novels exploits so extravagantly the discomforts adults are made to suffer at the hands of mischievous boys that modern readers are tempted to consider Shillaber and Peck purveyors of thinly disguised sadism. *Peck's Bad Boy*, in particular, rings all the changes on this situation, which by the 1890's had developed into a widely popular convention with the invention of the comic strip characters called the Katzenjammer Kids. There is cruelty enough in Mark Twain's boyhood stories, but it is usually dignified with a meaning deeper than practical joking.

In respect to crude language, too, Twain "tamed the various obscenities" in his original story so successfully that *Tom Sawyer's* final tone is scarcely rougher than the novels of Howe or Aldrich, though it is everywhere more vigorous than the gentle flow of *Being a Boy* or *A Boy's Town*. DeVoto has shown in *Mark Twain at Work* just how mild Twain's obscenities actually were and how easy it was to curb his cruder tendencies. For instance, Howells convinced his friend to modify Huck Finn's expression "they combed me all to hell"; so natural was Twain's reaching for the living shape of language he must not have realized how coarse this would sound to genteel juvenile ears. Similarly, Twain rewrote his description of the church service Tom disrupts because Howells thought the sentence "the poodle went sailing down the aisle with his tail shut down like a hasp" sounded "awfully good but a little too dirty." [17]

Some of Twain's modifications in the direction of propriety were more significant than simply cutting out an inadvertent "hell" or an overly graphic "hasp." His pruning of the scene in the schoolhouse between Tom and Becky makes one such profound alteration in the fabric of *Tom Sawyer*. When Tom surprises his sweetheart peeking in Mr. Dobbins' anatomy book with its "handsomely engraved and colored frontispiece —a human figure, stark naked," Becky tears the page. In her fear and shame she berates Tom and flings out of the room. "What a curious kind of fool a girl is," Tom muses to himself. "Never been licked in school! Shucks. What's a licking!" (8, 172). The episode thus turns into an innocuous comment upon the different ways boys and girls regard corporal punishment. Originally, however, quite another meaning had been intended. Following Becky's mortified departure, Tom had first ruminated, "But that picture—is—well, now it ain't so curious she feels bad about that. No . . . No, I reckon it ain't. Suppose she was Mary and Alf Temple had caught her looking at such a picture as that and went around telling. She'd feel—well, I'd lick him. I bet I would." [18] Howell's comment at this point was, "I should be afraid of this picture incident," and Twain killed his realistic impulse to refer, even so obliquely, to a child's sexual curiosity, although as DeVoto points out the episode as written had survived the Elmira eye of Olivia Clemens. This is the only hint of sex in *Tom Sawyer*, indeed in all of Mark Twain's boyhood stories, though Twain had made one passing comment in the "Boy's Manuscript" to the contents of Billy Rogers' pocket, which included, among other boyish paraphernalia, a picture of "Adam and Eve without

17. Quoted in *Mark Twain at Work*, pp. 13–14.
18. Ibid., p. 14.

a rag." Consequently, Tom Sawyer's mind, originally conceived as having a normal interest in such matters as a girl's reaction to sex, is cleared of this complexity and Twain's young hero reverts to the bland presexual pattern of his literary cousins.

Of course, the creator of *Tom Sawyer* was a prude. As a writer Twain was hypersensitive both to his readers' timidities and to his own. Consequently, sex as a motive for human conduct in children, adolescents, or adults is almost entirely absent from his fiction; Roxy in *Pudd'nhead Wilson* is perhaps the sole significant exception. On this point Twain needed no editorial restraints by Howells or Olivia Clemens. Even in his unpublished writings he exhibited unusual myopia in regard to the sexual impulse. "There was the utmost liberty among young people—" he recalled of his own Hannibal boyhood in the manuscript "Villagers of 1840–43," "but no young girl was ever insulted, or seduced, or even scandalously gossiped about. Such things were not even dreamed of in that society, much less spoken of and referred to as possibilities." [19] This is indeed an astonishing recollection of a Mississippi River town. Even if the strict town ordinances of Hannibal had succeeded in outlawing the organized vice that flourished elsewhere along the river, Sam Clemens' town could hardly have been free of private sin.

In other moods, Twain privately recognized the sexual element in his image of boyhood. During the final revision of *Tom Sawyer,* in the summer of 1876, he wrote an acidly sarcastic note to his old friend Will Bowen, the same childhood crony whose letter had stirred Twain's depths six years earlier. Bowen's saccharine references to their common memories of bygone days evidently disgusted rather than delighted Twain this time: "As to the past, there is but one good thing about it," he replied, "& that is that it *is* the past—we don't have to

19. Quoted in Wecter, *Sam Clemens of Hannibal,* p. 173.

see it again. There is nothing in it worth pickling for present or future use." Then he grew even more barbed. "What is the secret of your eternal youth?—not that I want to try it; far from it—I only ask out of curiosity . . . for more than twenty years you have stood dead still in the midst of the dreaminess, the melancholy, the romance, the heroics, of sweet but sappy sixteen. Man, do you know that this is simply mental & moral masturbation? It belongs eminently to the period usually devoted to *physical* masturbation, & should be left there & outgrown." [20] Twain was perfectly aware of sexual realities; this letter, as well as "1601," "Some Thoughts on the Science of Onanism," and other unofficial pieces of mild pornography, proves that. But as father, Nook Farm neighbor, and professional writer he put such knowledge almost completely out of his mind.

The extent to which he acted as his own censor, exceeding even Howells and his own wife in tiptoeing around the matter of sex, is suggested by a letter he wrote Howells urging that the two friends collaborate in turning *Tom Sawyer* into a play. "I would help in the work, most cheerfully, after you had arranged the plot," he confesses, and then adds, "I have my eye upon two young girls who can play 'Tom' & 'Huck.' I believe a good deal of drama can be made of it." [21] If Tom were acted by a girl, the scene in the schoolroom between "himself" and Becky—if by any chance it were incorporated into the script at all—would certainly lose most of its sexual overtones. That Twain could seriously make such a suggestion—and it must have been serious for he started not one but several stage versions of *Tom Sawyer* and in a notebook entry in 1884 even named Ada Rehan as an actress who could play one of his boys—argues a blindness to one side of boyhood that is complete. For all practical purposes, his impression of

20. *Mark Twain's Letters to Will Bowen,* pp. 23–24.
21. *Mark Twain-Howells Letters, 1,* 95.

Tom is as infant Adam living, as DeVoto has put it, "in an eternal summer before the Fall." In this Tom Sawyer differs little from Tom Bailey, John, "my boy," and the other innocent Bad Boys.

One reason Twain, in common with his contemporaries, shied away from the fact of sex in the lives of Tom Sawyer and his playmates stems from a deep-seated ambivalence he felt in respect to time and change. Sexual curiosity implied adolescence, growth toward adulthood. Turning his back upon such an implication, he took pains never to specify Tom's age, as he had done for Billy Rogers and as his fellow writers always did in their boyhood novels. From the first, Tom and Huck were conceived as children of indefinite years, whose presexual innocence absolved Twain from confronting certain problems of maturity, in particular physical love and marriage, which neither his abilties nor his predilections equipped him to develop satisfactorily. The negative evidence is clear: none of Twain's three major novels which deal chiefly with adults—*The Gilded Age, A Connecticut Yankee in King Arthur's Court,* and *Pudd'nhead Wilson*—defines realistically the nature of married love as successfully as the weakest novel of Howells or Henry James. Boyhood was a safer and more congenial area of human experience. There Twain could focus upon an indefinite, timeless moment, in late childhood or early adolescence perhaps, in which a boy, poised between infancy and manhood, could face forward to certain problems grown-ups had to confront and yet backward to a state before puberty. The conclusion to *Tom Sawyer* states as explicitly as Twain was able this precarious position: "So endeth this chronicle. It being strictly a history of a *boy,* it must stop here; the story could not go much further without becoming the history of a *man.* When one writes a novel about grown people, he knows exactly where to stop—that is, with a marriage; but when he writes of juveniles, he must stop where he best can."

Tom Sawyer is punctuated with fleeting vignettes embodying this quality of arrested time. Many involve Cardiff Hill, that "Delectable Land, dreamy, reposeful, and inviting" which is the natural backdrop to Tom's adventures, as the Mississippi is to Huck's. One such symbolic moment occurs as Tom sits at his school desk.

> It seemed to him that the noon recess would never come. The air was utterly dead. There was not a breath stirring. It was the sleepiest of sleepy days. The drowsing murmur of the five and twenty studying scholars soothed the soul like the spell that is in the murmur of bees. Away off in the flaming sunshine, Cardiff Hill lifted its soft green sides through a shimmering veil of heat, tinted with the purple of distance; a few birds floated on lazy wing high in the air; no other living thing was visible but some cows, and they were asleep. Tom's heart ached to be free, or else to have something of interest to do to pass the dreary time.
> [8, 65]

Balanced here against each other are the static state of boy-hood, nostalgically clothed in the same language Aldrich or Howells would employ, and the active presence of Tom Sawyer himself, one particular boy yearning to escape back into time.

This hesitation in Twain's allegiance to the lost past of child-hood is yet another mark of Tom Sawyer's distinctness from his cousins. Whereas Tom Bailey, "my boy," and the others are preserved eternally in the fond memories of their creators, Tom Sawyer moves in an atmosphere only partially golden. Though one of Twain's purposes in his first boyhood novel was "to try to pleasantly remind adults of what they once were themselves, and of how they felt and thought and talked, and what queer enterprises they sometimes engaged in," he did not wholly glorify the past. Thus *Tom Sawyer* contains no such image of the lost peace and happiness of childhood as Howells creates in the opening pages of *A Boy's Town*. There Twain's friend and mentor dwells lovingly upon a certain blue broadcloth cape worn by the father of "my boy": "To get under its border, and hold by his father's hand in the warmth and dark it made around him was something that the boy thought a great privilege, and that brought him a sense of mystery and security at once that nothing else could ever give." [22]

The sense of the mystery and security of boyhood recollected long after—this is the thinly disguised theme of all the writers who have been mentioned here. Some of them, like Howe and Warner, make but a feeble effort to catch the mysterious quality lurking in a young boy's vivid imagination. Others—Aldrich and Howells in particular—are aware of the mystery but try to render harmless any terrors contained therein by bathing the past in nostalgia and an atmosphere of security. In *Tom Sawyer* Twain conjures up a vivid sense of the mystery, terror, and excitement behind the innocent eye of boyhood. But the golden patina of his memory, though in places as striking as any of his friends, is nevertheless dulled by an awareness of Tom's insecurity in a world partly violent and evil. After all, Tom Sawyer has no father under whose broadcloth cape he can retreat. Hence, Twain's boy, whose imagination and language are already so much closer to adult experience than his cousins, lives on a see-saw that constantly dips him in the direction of involvement in the village, rather than escape to Cardiff Hill, into time rather than outside it, toward adolescence and maturity rather than back into the changeless world of childhood.

There are dimensions to *Tom Sawyer* other than the vividly realized individuality of its young hero which render the novel a more complex work of fiction than those of Twain's friends and contemporaries. As James Cox has pointed out, one of the most significant of these facets is the careful manner in which

22. *A Boy's Town*, p. 5.

the plot is structured so that the pranks and adventures of Tom's immediate world are related to the doings of the larger life of St. Petersburg.[23] In a way quite unlike Aldrich, Warner, Howe, or Howells, events in Tom's boy-world predict or repeat occurrences in the adult realm. Thus, on the night after Tom and Joe Harper play Robin Hood and pretend to kill each other Tom witnesses the actual murder of Doc Robinson by real robbers in the graveyard. Similarly, Tom and Becky escape from the same cave, which they visit on a children's picnic, where Injun Joe meets a grim death, whittling futilely with his Bowie knife at the doorframe. And, at a less serious level, Tom and Huck's discovery of the treasure causes every haunted house in the vicinity to be "dissected, plank by plank, and its foundations dug up and ransacked for hidden treasure—and not by boys, but men—pretty grave, unromantic men, too, some of them" (8, 285).

The link between the child's and the adult world is Tom Sawyer. Joe Harper plays Robin Hood and Huck watches the murder, but only Tom does both. Participating in both worlds and perceiving gradually the cruelties, cupidities, and responsibilities of adulthood constitutes the meaning of Tom's summer which emerges from beneath the spoofing of the early chapters. No longer a Natural Boy, Tom Sawyer becomes one particular boy learning some unsavory facts of life.

In the process of Tom's initiation, the village of St. Petersburg itself assumes a larger role than that played by the locales of the stories already discussed here—Aldrich's Rivermouth, Howe's Twin Mounds, or the Boy's Town of Howells. The town in *Tom Sawyer* is more than a setting for an idyll, an Eden in the prelapsarian world before the War; it sits to Mark Twain for its portrait, one of the first in our fiction, of the social life of an American community. People of all sorts and classes

23. See James M. Cox, "Remarks on the Sad Initiation of Huckleberry Finn," *Sewanee Review*, 62 (1954), 390.

inhabit Twain's town—lawyers and drunkards, boys, girls, and schoolmasters, old maids and half-breeds, Negro slaves and gentry. His intention is to suggest the total social reality of a typical river village, as he had already sketched its neighbors Obedstown and Cattleville in *The Gilded Age* and as he was later to do for Hadleyburg, Dawson's Landing, and Eseldorf.

The items of Twain's social history of St. Petersburg make an impressive tally: a Sunday School exercise, a church service, the village school, an informal inquest, a funeral, "Examination Day," a murder trial, a manhunt, and a reception. Senator Benton's Fourth of July speech disappoints Tom, as does the revival, but the circus does not. The inclusiveness of the catalogue may go unnoted simply because each event is presented as part of Tom's daily life. Always the dramatic focus, his personality unfolds as these manifold social forces act upon him. Tom Sawyer is, for all his imagination, essentially a passive character.[24] True to the observed nature of childhood, Twain has made his hero, in spite of occasional smashing victories over adults, subservient in the main to the adult schedule of events.

This social aspect of Tom Sawyer's daily life has been called "the idyll of Hannibal." To do so without also seeing the pervasive presence of evil in St. Petersburg is to miss the point of Twain's novel.[25] It is hardly necessary to cite the deeds and threats of Injun Joe, the half-breed, to show that violence as well as hypocrisy and pettiness are very much of the fabric of Tom's town. Mr. Dobbins' life of noisy desperation in the schoolhouse climaxes in the boys' graduation prank that robs

24. Ibid., p. 390.
25. "This village," wrote Bernard DeVoto, "though violence underlies its tranquillity as it underlies most dreams of beauty, is withdrawn from the pettiness, the greed, the cruelty, the spiritual squalor, the human worthlessness that Huck Finn was to travel through ten years later, that are the fabric of Hadleyburg and Dawson's Landing" (*Mark Twain at Work*, p. 23).

him of wig and self-respect; no wonder, then, that in one of the play versions of *Tom Sawyer* it was a whiskey bottle and not an anatomy book hidden in his desk. The innkeeper of the Temperance Tavern turns out to be a bootlegger on the side. The villagers are at first afraid to bring Injun Joe to trial; later, several of the "sappy women" petition the governor to pardon the murderer. Muff Potter, archetype of the village drunk and genial forerunner to Pap Finn, is alternately tolerated, laughed at, persecuted, and fondled. "But that sort of conduct is to the world's credit; therefore it is not well to find fault with it," Twain wryly remarks (8, 198). The greed for money infecting most of the adults finally impinges on Tom and Huck, whose entrance to "respectable" society comes only after they are rich with the treasure.

On the other hand, it would be equally astigmatic to view St. Petersburg through the Jamesian eyes of Van Wyck Brooks. "Think of those villages Mark Twain himself has pictured for us," Brooks exclaimed, "with their shabby, unpainted shacks, dropping with decay, the broken fences, the litter of rusty cans, the mud, the weeds, the dust! Human nature was scarcely responsible for this débris of a too unequal combat with circumstance, nor could human nature rise very far above it. 'Gambling, drinking and murder,' we are told, were the diversions of the capital city of Nevada, in the days of the gold rush. It was not very different in normal times along the Mississippi." [26] As commentary on Tom Sawyer's community, Brooks' denunciation overstates the case as badly as does DeVoto's encomium. St. Petersburg, though by no means withdrawn from "spiritual squalor," is no sty, and if the separate instances of evil that befall Tom are dissected, it will be seen Twain has taken pains that good shall come out of evil, that the appearance of disaster rather than catastrophe itself is all that hangs

26. *The Ordeal of Mark Twain* (New York, Meridian Books, 1955), p. 40.

over a boy's life, that the ending of each escapade is conventionally happy.

Death, for example, is never far from the pages of Tom's story. Yet the boy's own death—once by drowning in the river, once by the rotten step in the haunted house, and once in the cave—is invariably averted. Tom's "play-deaths" divert attention from, at the same moment that they accent, the pair of real deaths—Doc Robinson's and Injun Joe's—which are treated simultaneously as grisly events and out-and-out melodrama.

Even more significant than the ritual death of Injun Joe is the symbolic nature of Tom's twice-repeated return to life. When the boys attend their own funerals, what begins as a prank on sentimental townspeople is suddenly transformed into a deeply moving scene. As the "dead" boys troop down from the church gallery, St. Petersburg, instead of reacting like parents in a Bad Boy plot, asserts quite genuinely its sense of community. The scene as Twain describes it carries scarcely a trace of satire:

> Aunt Polly, Mary, and the Harpers threw themselves upon their restored ones, smothered them with kisses and poured out thanksgivings, while poor Huck stood abashed and uncomfortable, not knowing exactly what to do or where to hide from so many unwelcoming eyes. He wavered, and started to slink away, but Tom seized him and said:
>
> "Aunt Polly, it ain't fair. Somebody's got to be glad to see Huck."
>
> "And so they shall. *I'm* glad to see him, poor motherless thing!" . . .
>
> Suddenly the minister shouted at the top of his voice: "Praise God from whom all blessings flow—SING!—and put your hearts in it!"

82

And they did. Old Hundred swelled up with a triumphant burst, and while it shook the rafters Tom Sawyer the Pirate looked around upon the envying juveniles about him and confessed in his heart that this was the proudest moment of his life.

As the "sold" congregation trooped out they said they would almost be willing to be made ridiculous again to hear Old Hundred sung like that once more. [8, 152–53]

Though Tom himself only dimly appreciates what he has done, his act has opened the town's "unwelcoming eyes" to a revelation of love and social solidarity. A boy's prank, which in Shillaber or Peck would be treated simply as a hilarious instance of juvenile oneupmanship, becomes in Twain's hands the dramatization of something fundamental in the emotional relations of children and grown-ups.

Though Tom's second return to life is less dramatic than the first, his escape from the cave with Becky and his subsequent discovery of the treasure also have important effects on the community. The Widow's reception is the scene of this reconciliation. Tom again steals the limelight from Huck, who is the real guest of honor for his part in saving the Widow's life. When Tom pours "the mass of yellow coin" out on the table a great change comes over the village, one diametrically opposite to that felt in the church. Now Tom and Huck are "courted, admired, stared at" by the grown-ups. The boys' wealth was "simply prodigious . . . It was just what the minister got—no, it was what he was promised—he generally couldn't collect it," Twain observes. Only superficially a joke, this account of the boys' reception into polite society lays bare St. Petersburg's real attitude toward money. Hadleyburg's will not differ greatly. A theme first adumbrated in *The Gilded Age* is touched upon, lightly but unmistakably, in Twain's boyhood idyll.

Because *Tom Sawyer* chronicles not merely timeless but shifting relations, humorous and otherwise, between a Missouri town and one of its younger citizens, Twain's version of the Bad Boy story inevitably moves beyond parody and social history. Since the focus is always on Tom himself, and because the events characterizing life in his village are ironic and tragic as well as funny, a change takes place in Twain's perceptive hero. Tom learns, through witnessing death and through the sudden access of wealth, something of what it means to be an adult. *Tom Sawyer* is the study of one kind of initiation.

Now initiation implies understanding. In each of the incidents that have been mentioned Tom's recognition of the moral or social truth involved is incomplete. At the funeral scene it is still "Tom Sawyer the Pirate" who acknowledges the admiring glances of the other children while the Doxology is being sung. The reader cannot be sure how much Tom has really comprehended of the moment's meaning. Similarly, the uncovering of the treasure discloses some unsavory facts about St. Petersburg's pecuniary passions. Huck speedily learns what these are, but Tom apparently does not. The latter embraces the respectability purchased by the gold coins, giving no indication that the adulation of his elders is anything but pleasing to his ego. At the story's end, in fact, he is busy convincing Huck of the advantages of monied status and threatening Huck with excommunication from the gang. Of this about-face Walter Blair has written,

> though in chapter xiii Huck in rags was eligible for piratehood and even as late as chapter xxxiii his savagery has not been mentioned as a bar to his joining the robbers, now, to lure the boy back to the Widow's, Tom insists that Huck the Red-Handed will have to live with the good woman and be "respectable" if he is to be allowed to join

the gang. Something has happened to Tom. He is talking more like an adult than like an unsocial child. He has, it appears, gone over to the side of the enemy.[27]

The key insight here is Tom's "talking more like an adult than like an unsocial child," for the undeniable outcome of Tom's adventures during this eventful summer is his acceptance of a grown-up's compromising connection to society. Moreover, nothing Tom does in *Adventures of Huckleberry Finn* will alter this fundamental commitment.

Though neither the Jackson's Island escapade nor the discovery of treasure completes Tom's understanding of the way of the world, his experience in the cave with Becky and Injun Joe comes a great deal closer. Before their harrowing experience underground, Tom and his sweetheart have, like Billy Rogers and Amy, merely been playing at puppy love. But when the two children are lost in the cave's darkness they discover something truer to the nature of human love and companionship than the confessions, spats, and trysts of the schoolyard. When the awful thought dawns upon them that they are lost, something happens to their relationship.

"Tom, Tom, we're lost! We're lost! We never can get out of this awful place! Oh, why *did* we ever leave the others!"

She sank to the ground and burst into such a frenzy of crying that Tom was appalled with the idea that she might die, or lose her reason. He sat down by her and put his arms around her; she buried her face in his bosom, she clung to him, she poured out her terrors, her unavailing regrets, and the far echoes turned them all to jeering laughter. Tom begged her to pluck up hope again, and she said she could not. He fell to blaming and abusing

27. Walter Blair, "On the Structure of *Tom Sawyer*," *Modern Philology*, 37 (1939), 88.

himself for getting her into this miserable situation; this had a better effect. She said she would try to hope again, she would get up and follow wherever he might lead if only he would not talk like that any more. For he was no more to blame than she, she said.   [8, 255]

Tom and Becky demonstrate here and in the scenes which follow a totally new awareness of consideration, loyalty, remorse, trust—qualities just as significant as sex in defining mature love. The two children have left the others in more ways than one. Hence, when the pair emerges from the cave —reborn a second time in Tom's case—it is with a new knowledge of human emotions. They are, in essence, no longer children, but are in the way of becoming like adults, for they have learned to behave as adults.

In the same manner, the death of Injun Joe signals a change in Tom Sawyer. What begins as a "play adventure" for the boy in the graveyard mushrooms into melodrama and turns, finally, into a moral crisis. For the significant event here is not Tom's witnessing of murder, nor even his brush with death in the haunted house, but his decision to testify at Muff Potter's trial. The torment Tom undergoes before he brings himself to risk death issues in a triumphant vindication of Aunt Polly's belief in Tom's essential goodness.

Certain critics, notably DeVoto, charge Twain with passing over the inner struggle preceding Tom's decision in favor of the melodramatic climax in the courtroom.[28] Such a judgment ignores the text. No fewer than seven specific references to the boy's private torment are scattered through the pages de-

28. "Is a boy's mind no wider and no deeper than Tom's? Where are the brutalities, the sternnesses, the strengths, the perceptions, and the failures that will eventually make a man? Well, in part Mark's will was to ignore such things, as when he denies us the entire struggle of fear, pity, and horror out of which Tom's decision to reveal what he has seen in the graveyard issues, in order to give us the simple melodrama of the revelation" (*Mark Twain at Work*, p. 21).

scribing the denouement. At first, the "dreadful secret of the murder was a chronic misery" to Tom, "a very cancer for permanency and pain." When the rest of the town gets religion at the revival Tom creeps home to bed "realizing that he alone of all the town was lost forever and forever." Then, at night, the thunderstorm fills him with "a horror of suspense for his doom." Next day, he wanders about the village, "companionless and forlorn." Every mention of the trial sends "a shudder to his heart," and when Tom and Huck visit poor Muff in jail the latter's gratitude cuts deep into their hearts. That night, Tom retires again full of misery, his dreams full of horror.

With such care does Twain trace Tom's unchildlike wrestling with his moral dilemma that any reader except DeVoto is well satisfied not to have Tom's midnight trip to the lawyer spelled out. Certainly, Twain *has* dramatized the struggle his boy goes through to overcome his dread of the half-breed killer. Even more importantly, he makes clear Tom's realization of true sympathy for Injun Joe trapped at the door of the cave. "Oh, Judge, Injun Joe's in the cave!" Tom cries, and when the murderer's corpse is found, "Tom was touched, for he knew by his own experience how this wretch had suffered." Tom Sawyer had evinced no such feeling for Aunt Polly as he lay hidden beneath her bed and listened to her tears and prayers for her lost boy. The Bad Boy has begun to grow up, and Injun Joe, a stereotyped villain introduced to curdle the blood of juvenile readers, becomes the instrument of a boy's awakening to something approaching moral maturity.

Mark Twain's reactions to his first boyhood story suggest that *The Adventures of Tom Sawyer* turned out not precisely as he had hoped. The novel that began as a satire for adults, trimmed its acerbities to appeal to children, developed into a full-scale social study of a town, and finally emerged as the moral and psychological report of a boy's tentative initiation into manhood was often regarded uneasily by its author. Certainly Twain showed a lordly indifference to the original manuscript he sent up to Howells. "Just send Sawyer to me by Express—" he wrote his friend who had taken such pains to redefine the novel's nature and audience, "I enclose money for it. If it should get lost it will be no great matter." [29] The joking tone of this remark is of a piece with the illusion of formlessness that the novel itself presents. Actually, as completed and revised, *Tom Sawyer* has a natural structure that encompasses the forces pulling it in diverse directions. By keeping the center of attention focused always on Tom, Twain has unified the humorous, satiric, social, and moral dimensions of his Bad Boy story in a fashion unattempted by any of his friends and colleagues working within the same genre. Except in the opening scenes, these themes are interwoven in a manner that makes *Tom Sawyer* readable from start to finish for both of Twain's audiences, children and adults. Howells' influence— limited largely to the first section of the story—did little more than curb the grosser outbursts of the "Moralist of the Main" who had never before written for children.

In spite of *Tom Sawyer's* enduring popular success (it proved second only to *Huckleberry Finn* as a money-maker during Twain's lifetime and has been in the twentieth century the most popular of all his works),[30] its author was never wholly satisfied with it as a study of boyhood. Even before publication Twain was planning a sequel. "By & by I shall take a boy of twelve & run him on through life (in the first person),"

29. *Mark Twain–Howells Letters, 1,* 113. Smith and Gibson comment: "Clemens is indifferent to the risk of loss of the MS in transit because he has another copy of it" (*1,* 114), but this does not entirely take into account Howells' valued marginalia.

30. See Frank L. Mott, *Golden Multitudes* (New York, Macmillan, 1947), pp. 156–57.

he wrote Howells in that busy summer of 1875, "but not Tom Sawyer—he would not be a good character for it."[31] This smacks of disillusion, perhaps with technique, or with structure, or with audience. It may, however, betray deeper disenchantments. One may have been Twain's realization that boyhood as he recalled and recreated it in *Tom Sawyer* was not such a convenient escape from controversial topics as he had hoped; instead, childhood was deceptively nostalgic and appealing, an ambiguous realm filled with unexpected emotional and literary pitfalls. Manhood, too, in Tom's particular case would hold similar disappointments. These mixed feelings are reflected in a note Twain made across the first page of the manuscript of *Tom Sawyer* now preserved in the Riggs Memorial Library of Georgetown University. Evidently the skeleton for a tale of later adventures, the comment runs: "1. Boyhood & youth; 2, y & early manh[ood]; 3 the battle of Life in many lands; 4, (age 37 to 46,) return & meet grown babies & toothless old drivelers who were the grandees of his boyhood. The Adored Unknown & faded old maid & full of rasping, puritanical vinegar piety." Such a sequel—clearly autobiographical in inspiration, for Twain did revisit Hannibal in 1882 when he was 46—was hardly a pleasant prospect. Neither was Tom Sawyer as a grown man; "If I went on now and took him into manhood, he would just lie like all the one-horse men in literature and the reader would conceive a hearty contempt for him," he explained to Howells.[32] This comment admits of two interpretations: either it registers a jaundiced suspicion that "all the one-horse men in literature" include most grownups and hence would include Tom, too, or, more likely, Twain became disenchanted with Tom Sawyer in particular—after all, Tom is one image of Sam Clemens himself. Tom's easy

31. *Mark Twain–Howells Letters*, 1, 92.
32. Ibid., p. 91.

Passport to Propriety

A WORLD-FAMOUS WRITER and lecturer who traveled as widely as any American of his generation, Mark Twain was constantly receiving letters from old friends. By the time the Clemenses had lived at Nook Farm for ten years—a period punctuated by several lecture tours and no less than four trips abroad—they had accumulated so many acquaintances in distant parts that a daily avalanche of mail descended on 351 Farmington Avenue. Twain's career as a writer was now in full swing; he had published five major books and his voluminous correspondence included much friendly (though unsolicited) literary advice.

In October 1881 he received such a letter from Fresno, California. It was from Joe Goodman, one-time owner of the Virginia City *Territorial Enterprise* and his boon companion from San Francisco days. Though now in semiretirement on a small ranch, Joe still kept up with the world of letters and read with avidity and discernment all his friend's books as they appeared. "I see mentions of your forthcoming, 'Prince and Pauper,'" wrote Goodman, "stating that it is a story of remote English life. I'm very impatient to see it, for of all things I have been anxious that you should try your hand at another novel. But what could have sent you groping among the drift-wood of the Deluge for a topic when you would have been so much more at home in the wash of today? I shall discover, I suppose." [1] Goodman did not have long to wait for the answer. Two months later *The Prince and the Pauper* appeared, just in time for the Christmas trade, for which it was elaborately decked out in heavily embossed green covers and crowded with 192 illustrations. By the publishing standards of the Gilded Age, it looked very handsome.

In many respects, the new novel "of remote English life" was indeed a curious sequel to *Innocents Abroad* and *A Tramp Abroad,* Twain's pair of European travel satires, and to *Roughing It* and *Tom Sawyer,* his narratives of the American West. Many readers noted the fresh tack he had taken. The reviewer in the *Atlantic Monthly*—where Twain was *persona grata* since the success of "Old Times on the Mississippi"—registered polite surprise; to him *The Prince and the Pauper* was "certainly not by the Twain we have known for a dozen or more years as the boisterous and rollicking humorist, whose chief function has been to diffuse hilarity with mirth in its most demonstrative forms." [2]

Even superficially, the new departures were many. Not in the least autobiographical in origin, Twain's story of Prince Edward of England and Tom Canty of London's Offal Court seemed an uneasy compromise between romance and history book. Prefaced by a facsimile of the official letter by the Bishop of Worcester announcing Edward VI's birth, and closing with sixteen footnotes citing various books and documents, *The Prince and the Pauper* made claims as history which its wildly improbable plot could not fail to undercut. What, too, was the reader to think of the dialogue? With echoes of Scotty Briggs' or Colonel Sellers' or Tom Sawyer's or Huck Finn's rich American idiom in mind, any reader must wonder at Twain's attempt

1. Joseph Goodman to MT (Oct. 24, 1881), in MTP. © Mark Twain Company.
2. Quoted in Philip S. Foner, *Mark Twain: Social Critic* (New York, International Publishers, 1958), p. 45.

to imitate the English of the sixteenth century, making a country judge speak in these accents: "'Tis a poor ignorant lad, and mayhap was driven hard by hunger, for these be grievous times for the unfortunate; mark you, he hath not an evil face —but when hunger driveth—Good woman! dost know that when one steals a thing above the value of thirteen pence ha'penny the law saith he shall *hang* for it?" (*11*, 189).

Nor did the tone of Twain's romance much resemble the edged, ironic humor or extravagant burlesque of the earlier works. For a hard-shelled Western newspaperman who had jibed at Bret Harte and Charles Dickens for their "pathetics," the final sentences of *The Prince and the Pauper* struck a strange note.

> Yes, King Edward VI lived only a few years, poor boy, but he lived them worthily. More than once, when some great dignitary, some gilded vassal of the crown, made argument against his leniency, and urged that some law which he was bent upon amending was gentle enough for its purpose, and wrought no suffering or oppression which any one need mightily mind, the young king turned the mournful eloquence of his great compassionate eyes upon him and answered: "What dost *thou* know of suffering and oppression? I and my people know, but not thou."
> [*11*, 274]

These radical shifts from Twain's previous subject matter, treatment, and tone were, in spite of Joe Goodman's anticipatory alarm, of little concern to most of the readers for whom *The Prince and the Pauper* had actually been written. The new book was manifestly for the uncritical audience of boys and girls, a "yarn for youth" as its author called it in a letter to Howells, and this was by no means the least significant change in Mark Twain's approach to fiction. Dedicated "To those well-mannered and amiable children, Susy and Clara

Clemens," the story had a plot, turning upon the tried-and-true device of switched identities, that was calculated to attract the rapidly growing juvenile market in England and America. Hence literary considerations of possible interest to grown-ups had evidently been waived by the writer who, for the first time in his career, was trying from the outset to produce fiction of the same sort as his neighbors, Mrs. Stowe and Lilly Warner.

Twain did not consider, however, that in turning finally to juvenile fiction he had lowered himself. Quite the contrary. When in 1878 his old friend from *Quaker City* days, Mrs. Fairbanks of Cleveland, wrote to ask what her younger protégé was writing, Twain replied, quite seriously, "A historical tale, of 300 years ago, simply for the love of it—for it will appear without my name—such grave & stately work being considered by the world above my proper level." Then Twain went on to explain how the novel was being composed. "I have been studying for it, off & on, for a year & a half. I swear the Young Girls' Club to secresy [sic] & read the MS to them, half a dozen chapters at a time, at their meetings. They profess to be very much fascinated with it; so do Livy & Susie Warner. If you & Mollie will come, I will try to wring some compliments from you, too." [3] Mrs. Fairbanks, as it turned out, did come to Nook Farm. She was delighted that the famous friend she had taken under her wing on the *Quaker City*, and whose grosser (as she thought) excesses in taste and deportment she had gently curbed, was writing such a book. She had enjoyed *Innocents Abroad* and *Tom Sawyer*, but her literary ambitions for Twain were not satisfied. "The time has come for your *best book*," she wrote some time later, after she knew *The Prince and the Pauper* was on the ways. "I do not mean your most taking book, with the most money in it, I mean your best contribution to American literature." [4]

3. Wecter, *Mark Twain to Mrs. Fairbanks*, p. 218.
4. Quoted in Andrews, *Nook Farm*, p. 190.

"Mother" Fairbanks (the nickname indicates how genially Twain accepted his role as foster son) was not the only well-wisher who wrote to Nook Farm urging Twain to write something finer than he had done so far. Nor was she the first to note the role money played in shaping his literary career. In a Christmas note of 1880 Dr. Edwin Parker, one of the older and most revered ministers of Hartford, concurred. "I want you to do something!" the old man wrote. "Your rank as a writer of humorous things is high enough—but, do you know —Clemens—that it is in you to do some first-class serious or sober work." Then he continued:

> Now let me say *to* you what I have repeatedly said *of* you—that I know no American writer of your generation, who is capable of writing such forcible, racy English as you. You are abundantly capable of turning out some work that shall bear the stamp of your individuality plainly enough, and at the same time have a sober character and a solid worth & a permanent value.
>
> It might not pay in "shekels", but it would do you vast honor, and give your friends vast pleasure.
>
> Am I too bold? Pardon me, but I wish I had your opportunity & your genius. "*Blow, bugle blow* set the wild echoes flying"! [5]

The Prince and the Pauper was precisely the book Mrs. Fairbanks and Dr. Parker wanted. It was written not, as were Twain's previous literary ventures, primarily to make "shekels," but to please his friends and family. It was designed to satisfy that part of the American public Twain had not yet reached, those genteel (Joe Goodman might even say stuffy) readers who honored "sober character," "solid worth," and "permanent value" above the slapstick humor usually associated with the

5. E. P. Parker to MT (Dec. 22, 1880), in MTP. Quoted in part in Andrews, p. 190.

name Mark Twain. *The Prince and the Pauper* was Twain's literary passport to propriety.

Even before he began writing it, Twain had sensed that one sure-fire way to appeal to a genteel audience was with a children's book, and since he had never really written one he went to considerable lengths to test his writing out on its future public. As his letter to Mrs. Fairbanks shows, he read aloud the manuscript of *The Prince and the Pauper* to nearly everyone in Nook Farm who would listen. "I recall the little audiences of a year ago," Mrs. Fairbanks later reminisced. "Livy on one side of the fire, and those honest little critics, Susie and Clara perched on your arm-chair." [6] In addition to the immediate circle, he entertained each Saturday morning a bevy of well-bred young Hartford maidens, from fifteen to twenty years of age, who composed the Saturday Morning Club. Sworn to silence, they listened raptly to his reading of the weekly stint. The Parker, Twichell, and Warner families were also pressed into service. "I must go warily seeing this is such a wide departure from my accustomed line," he confided to Dr. Parker. "Will you, too, take the manuscript and read it, either to yourself, or, still better, aloud to your family? Twichell has promised me a similar service. I hoped to get criticisms from Howells's children but evidently he spared them, which was carrying charity too far!" [7]

More than any novel Twain wrote, *The Prince and the Pauper* was the product of community collaboration. Howells may have spared his children, but he himself carefully criticized his friend's manuscript. At his insistence, "The Whipping Boy's Story," a humorous incident adapted from Sut Lovingood and involving "a boy, a bull, and some bees," was scratched out because, as Howells thought, "it lowers its dig-

6. Wecter, *Mark Twain to Mrs. Fairbanks,* p. 245 n.
7. Quoted in Andrews, pp. 191–92.

nity." [8] One bit, however, Twain refused pointblank to delete. When Tom Canty, masquerading as the King, is told that Henry VIII's burial will not take place for several weeks, he remarks, " 'Tis a strange folly—Will he keep?" Neither Twichell nor Parker could convince Twain this was not funny.

When, some time late in 1880, *The Prince and the Pauper* was finished to the satisfaction of its author, a large number of Connecticut children, and many adults, it was only natural to think, in addition to the intended Chrismas edition, of serial publication in a children's magazine. Though a number of such periodicals were in the field—the *Youth's Companion* had, in fact, been in circulation since 1827—there was really only one choice for Nook Farmers. That was the *Saint Nicholas Magazine for Boys and Girls*. Its editor, Mrs. Mary Mapes Dodge, was a fairly frequent visitor in the neighborhood and a close friend of Lilly Warner's. Perhaps, therefore, it was the George Warners who suggested writing to Mrs. Dodge, in November 1880, to see if she would accept Twain's new work for serial publication. Mrs. Dodge replied at once, " 'St. Nicholas' happens to be fully supplied with serial stories for 1881," but added, "for all that, we shall be glad to see the opening chapters which you kindly offer to show. If the story should prove to be one that St. Nicholas *must* have (crowded or not) I do not doubt that the publishers and yourself would agree, as to terms." [9]

Two days later, however, after a talk with his publisher, Twain had thought better of his proposal. He wrote to explain:

> My publisher contends that such as wanted the story would go to St. Nicholas for it; & that this would cut our

8. Ibid., p. 192.
9. Mrs. Dodge to MT (Nov. 17, 1880), in MTP.

sales down by 30 or 40,000 copies when we came to issue the thing in book form. I am afraid he is right. One formidable argument or another has always intruded itself to bar me from the pleasure of publishing serially, & now it has happened again; & this time it hurts—for Mrs. Clemens & Mrs. Warner have decided that this particular tale comes under the head of that sort which St. Nicholas "*must* have"—a verdict which makes up for all the dispraise which they have lavished upon some other of my "works." [10]

In spite of all protestations, Twain was, after all, concerned about money, and shekels did stand in the way of presenting *The Prince and the Pauper* to young readers of the Genteel Age in their favorite magazine. But it is worth noting that Mrs. Dodge did not reject Twain's "yarn for youth." All the evidence points to a remarkable congruity between *The Prince and the Pauper* and the requirements of children's magazines of its day.

The novel the cultivated folk of Nook Farm had helped to write was an historical romance, the reconstruction of a remote period in England's past. As such, it was a thorough mixture of the real and the fanciful. Twain, turning away from the American West, heretofore his cachet, had imagined a story in the Dickensian manner, one which, though uncomfortably realistic in its treatment of certain social conditions, spread in general an aura of sentiment over the English past. Furthermore, its picture of family life—one aspect of boyhood Twain had not much treated in *The Adventures of Tom Sawyer*—was also a mixture of uncomfortable truthfulness and reassuring moralism. In addition, the speech of the nobler characters in Twain's story was pure and conventional, as befitted prose meant for

10. MT to Mrs. Dodge (Nov. 19, 1880), in Berg Collection, New York Public Library. © Mark Twain Company.

childish ears; that of the low characters was not coarse, but resembled somewhat the more innocuous parts of Shakespeare. All in all, the *St. Nicholas* could scarcely have discovered a more "must have" item for its bright and sunny pages than *The Prince and the Pauper.*

Just at this time, too, it was much to Mrs. Dodge's advantage for her—and for her colleagues who edited other juvenile journals like the *Youth's Companion* and *Harper's Young People*—to find and publish stories like *The Prince and the Pauper* which were sure to prove solid successes with youthful readers. For this new audience of boys and girls developing during the decade or so after the Civil War was being offered other literary blandishments than *St. Nicholas.* Chief among them was the dime novel. While parents, educators, and genteel publishing people politely tore their hair, the House of Beadle and Adams was deluging the American market with this enticing form of juvenile fiction. Beadle and Adams' Dime Novels by the mid 1870's were selling so well that they were joined by the New Dime Novels, Starr's American Novels, the Boys' Books of Romance and Adventure, the Half-Dime Library, and a host of others.[11] In spite of a fervent protestation that "they (Beadle & Co.) do not allow anything that is impure or immoral in their pages, and, therefore, even boys and girls may read what they publish, with pleasure and profit," [12] the dime novel was anathema to most proper parents in the Gilded Age. In a manner prefiguring the battle that went on over comic books in many literate homes two generations later, the forces of gentility drew together in an effort to stamp out this vulgar literary intruder. There ensued a Battle of the Books which lasted on into the twentieth century. *The Prince and the*

11. See Albert Johannsen, *The House of Beadle and Adams and Its Dime and Nickel Novels* (2 vols. Norman, Okla., University of Oklahoma Press, 1950), *1,* 57–62.
12. Ibid., p. 60.

Pauper, in common with the later *Tom Sawyer Abroad* (which *was* published in *St. Nicholas*), represents Twain's contribution to the forces of conservatism in the controversy. This is, to be sure, not all that Twain's first novel for children amounts to, but considerations of its formal and thematic problems may profitably be viewed from the perspective of the fight between high-brow and low-brow that was raging in many American homes at the very moment *The Prince and the Pauper* appeared.

In April 1875 a fourteen-year-old newsboy by the name of Jesse Pomeroy lay in Boston's Suffolk jail accused of murdering three children and torturing countless others. One afternoon the celebrated Boston publisher James T. Fields, who a generation before had received Hawthorne's letter about *The House of the Seven Gables,* visited Jesse in his cell. Fields' purpose was to question the boy criminal about his childhood. "I see, sir, that you come from no morbid curiosity," young Pomeroy remarked, and there followed this exchange:

> "What kind of books did you first begin to read?"
> "Oh, blood and thunder stories!"
> "Were the books small ones?"
> "Yes, most Beadle's dime novels."
> "How many of Beadle's dime novels do you think you read from nine years old upward?"
> "Well, I can't remember exactly, but I should think sixty." . . .
> "What were the books about?"
> "Killing and scalping injuns and so forth, and running away with women; a good many of the scenes were out on the plains."
> "Were there any pictures in the books?"
> "Yes, sir, plenty of them, blood and thunder pictures, tomahawking and scalping." . . .

"Do you think these books were an injury to you, and excited you to commit the acts you have done?"

"Yes, sir, I have thought it all over, and it seems to me now they did."

"Would you earnestly advise the other boys not to read these books you have read?"

"Indeed, sir, I should." [13]

Pomeroy was the most notorious juvenile delinquent of the age and his testimony left a deeply painful impression on the aging bookman. Fields' discovery that the young criminal "had a mania for literary poison above any of his fellows, had secretly indulged his taste" weighed heavily upon both Fields and his wife.

If James Fields, on one of his many lecture tours in the West, had chanced to visit the tiny Minnesota village of Osage he might there have met a lad whose consumption of Beadle's dime novels surpassed even that of the murderous newsboy of Boston. Hamlin Garland relates that during the first year of his stay in town he devoured "nearly one hundred dime novels, little paper-bound volumes filled with stories of Indians and wild horsemen and dukes and duchesses and men in iron masks . . ." Copies of *Mad Matt the Trailer, The Quaker Sleuth,* or *Jack Harkaway* cost Garland ten cents "when new, but you could return them and get a nickel in credit for another,—provided your own was in good condition." [14]

For all his immersion in fictional gore, the sturdy farm boy, later to become a writer, does not seem to have been much depraved. "Apparently it had very little effect of any sort

13. Mrs. James T. Fields, *James T. Fields: Biographical Notes and Personal Sketches* (Boston, Houghton Mifflin, 1881), pp. 224–26. See also J. N. Makris, *Boston Murders* (New York, Duell, Sloane, and Pearce, 1948), pp. 8–9.

14. Garland, *A Son of the Middle Border* (New York, Macmillan, 1917), p. 186.

other than to make the borderland a great deal more exciting than the farm, and yet so far as I can discover, I had no keen desire to go West and fight Indians and I showed no disposition to rob or murder in the manner of my heroes." [15]

The juvenile literature that commanded such loyalty from Jesse Pomeroy and Hamlin Garland and excited the worst suspicions of James T. Fields had, by the mid-1870's, developed into a major field of American publishing. Though its numerous series were also designed to appeal to semiliterate adults, the House of Beadle and Adams aimed particularly to please children. The dime novels' original plain yellow backs of the Fifties and Sixties were replaced at this time by lurid "illuminated" covers, while the size of certain of the series was altered so as to fit conveniently inside the covers of the new, larger geography books in use in schools. At this time, too, the nature and quality of many dime novels substantially changed. Instead of the pioneer and Indian tales which both Pomeroy and Garland mention, new plots and new heroes appeared. "Bad men" replaced Indian scouts, detective stories replaced historical romances, and bootblacks and vagabond boys began to appear as heroes of adventure stories now often set in urban surroundings.[16]

The Half-Dime Library's opening number of October 1877 carried an archetypal story of this newer sort. Edward L. Wheeler's "Deadwood Dick; The Prince of the Road" created a character whose lawless career spanned thirty-three issues, with ninety-seven more episodes built around his son, Deadwood Dick, Jr. The original Deadwood Dick set the pattern for a generation of fictional "bad men."

> He was a youth of an age somewhere between sixteen and twenty, trim and compactly built, with a preponderance

15. Ibid., pp. 186–87.
16. See Johannsen, *The House of Beadle and Adams, 1*, 58–60.

of muscular development and animal spirits; broad and deep of chest, with square iron-cast shoulders . . . His form was clothed in a tight-fitting habit of buckskin, which was colored a jetty black . . . he wore a thick black vail [sic] over the upper portion of his face, through the eye-holes of which there gleamed a pair of orbs of piercing intensity.[17]

Deadwood Dick and his fellows had a profound effect upon the American family, upon parents as well as boys and girls. Children, of course, were carried away by their hero's exploits, but to older people these bad men and vagabond boys represented a standing threat to law and authority. In a literary style infinitely cruder than *Peck's Bad Boy*, dime novels played all the changes on the theme of adolescent rebellion against family, school, and society in general.

An anti-Beadle campaign began, and one of its spokesmen came from an unlikely place. The celebrated Yale professor of political economy (and later of sociology) William Graham Sumner raised his voice in the March 1878 issue of *Scribner's Monthly*. In a long and alarming article on "What Our Boys Are Reading" Sumner attacked dime novels wholesale. "These periodicals," he asserted, "contain stories, songs, mock speeches, and negro minstrel dialogues,—and nothing else. The literary material is either intensely stupid, or spiced to the highest degree with sensation. . . . The dialogue is short, sharp, and continuous. It is broken by a minimum of description and by no preaching." Describing the plot of one typical story, Sumner observed, "there is not a decent good boy in the story. There is not even the old type of sneaking good boy." One dime-novel hero Sumner particularly detested was the rich, idle city boy whose career consisted in bilking his father of money. "In this class of stories, fathers and sons are represented

17. Ibid., 2, 297.

103

as natural enemies, and the true position for the son is that of suspicion and armed peace."

Respectable family life, the Professor noted, never appeared in dime novels. Invariably, fathers were made to appear niggardly and foolish. In the dime-novel world only two ills were recognized—physical pain and lack of money. "These papers poison boys' minds," Sumner concluded, "with views of life which are so base and false as to destroy all manliness and all chances of true success." While not exactly profane or obscene, the dime novel in his opinion was "indescribably vulgar." [18]

Many agreed with Sumner and a counter-reformation began. It is no coincidence that between 1865 and 1879, at the height of Beadle and Adams' success, four children's magazines— *Our Young Folks* (1865), *The Riverside Magazine for Young People* (1867), *The Saint Nicholas* (1873), and *Harper's Young People* (1879)—were launched. There were several others, but these were the most popular. Unquestionably, the leader in the field was the *St. Nicholas,* which under the imaginative editorship of Mrs. Dodge published an astonishing array of first-class writers. Such men as Tennyson, Longfellow, Bryant, Holmes, Bret Harte, Warner, Rudyard Kipling, and Mark Twain were cajoled by Mrs. Dodge into contributing, for it was her conviction that children merited just as serious literary consideration as adults; otherwise they would read trash.

Children's needs as magazine readers, however, were different from grown-ups', and Mrs. Dodge felt that publishers had not sufficiently realized this fact. The result had been Beadle and Adams. She intended *St. Nicholas* not as "a milk and water variety of the adult periodical" but as a special kind of magazine. In an introductory article in *Scribner's* she described what she hoped to make of *St. Nicholas:* "the chil-

18. *Scribner's Monthly, 15* (1878), 681–83.

dren's magazine needs to be stronger, truer, bolder, more uncompromising than [adult periodicals]. Its cheer must be the
cheer of the bird-song . . . Let there be no sermonizing either,
no wearisome spinning out of facts, no rattling of the dry
bones of history . . . The ideal children's magazine, we must
remember, is a pleasure-ground." [19]

This article was both a challenge to Beadle and Adams and
an invitation to colleagues in more respectable publishing
circles. One man who accepted the opportunity to rescue
American children from the clutches of Deadwood Dick was
Horace Elisha Scudder, who as early as 1867 started the *Riverside Magazine* and after its demise in the depression of 1873
went on to Houghton, Mifflin Company to edit the Riverside
Literature Series for Young People. Scudder eventually inherited Howells' chair as editor of the *Atlantic,* but before
moving into adult realms he performed signal service in the
battle against juvenile low-browism. From his vantage point
at Houghton Mifflin he introduced to a wide audience such
works as Whittier's *Child Life, A Collection of Poems,* the
Maine stories of Sarah Orne Jewett, and the tales of Hans
Christian Andersen. He even studied Danish in order to be
certain Andersen's works were properly translated.[20] In his
own right as well, Scudder contributed to the ever-increasing
body of juvenile fiction with the "Bodley Books," *Dream Children, Seven Little People and Their Friends,* and *Stories from
my Attic.* If Mary Mapes Dodge was the leading woman in

19. "Children's Magazines," *Scribner's Monthly, 6* (1873), 352–54.
See William W. Ellsworth, *A Golden Age of Authors* (Boston and New
York, Houghton Mifflin, 1919), pp. 88–89, for identification of Mrs.
Dodge's responsibility for this anonymous article.

20. See Meigs, *A Critical History of Children's Literature,* pp. 276–77;
also J. Hersholt and W. Westergaard, eds., *The Andersen-Scudder Letters;
Hans Christian Andersen's Correspondence with Horace Elisha Scudder,*
Berkeley, University of California Press, 1949.

the counterattack on dime novels, Horace Scudder was its principal trousered spokesman.

Near the end of the century Scudder brought together his opinions on the whole topic in a book which is the first work in American criticism to discuss childhood as a serious theme in writing. *Childhood in Literature and Art* was published in 1895, but its dedication, to Scudder's own daughter, suggests a much earlier date of composition.[21] Its message is announced in the introduction: "The child has been added to the *dramatis personae* of modern literature." After surveying the treatment of children in Greek, Hebrew, Roman, Medieval, English, French, and German literature, he devoted the final chapters of his book to "American literary art," assessing the contemporary situation in terms echoing Fields, Sumner, and Mrs. Dodge. On this new development, the child in American letters, he was spokesman for his age and class.

Horace Scudder believed a fundamental change had occurred during the nineteenth century, resulting in a wholly novel conception of childhood. Where before boys and girls had been exclusively seen in relation to others—particularly their parents—now for the first time they were observed in relation to themselves. As he saw it, "it was the child as possessed of consciousness, as isolated, as disclosing a nature capable of independent action, thought, and feeling, that now came forward into the world's view . . ." This shift, an outgrowth of Romanticism, had, in Scudder's eyes, reached an "abnormal" stage in America. Here to an alarming degree the child had been almost totally liberated. "The sixteenth amendment to the Constitution reads," Scudder remarked ironically, " 'The rights and caprices of children in the United States shall not be denied or abridged on account of age, sex, or formal condition of tutelage,' and this amendment has been rec-

21. "To S.C.S. Who Was a Child When This Book Was Written." Boston and New York, Houghton Mifflin, 1895.

ognized in literature, as in life, while waiting its legal adoption." [22]

What most upset him was not so much the new sense of aggressive independence American children felt as the way in which American writers had responded to the situation. "It is here, in the books for young people, that one may discover the most flagrant illustration of that spurious individuality in childhood which I have maintained to be conspicuous in our country." Except for one novelist Scudder identified cryptically as "our keenest social satirist"—and there was no hint from this conservative Bostonian that he was referring to Mark Twain,[23] whose name never appears in *Childhood in Literature and Art*—he found writers "of great literature" completely silent. Instead, cheap novels by the scores flooded the American market and tempted the American boy or girl with bad ideas and worse writing. For Scudder the most disturbing of the dime novels had to do with family relations. "Anyone who has been compelled to make the acquaintance of this literature must have observed how little parents and guardians figure in it, and how completely children are separated from their elders. The most popular books for the young are those which represent boys and girls as seeking their fortune, working out their own schemes, driving railway trains and steamboats it may be . . . This is the general spectacle to be observed . . . and the parent or two, now and then visible, is as much in the background as the child was in earlier literature."

Scudder, like William Graham Sumner, was aware of the threat to the family implicit in the popular dime novel, the

22. Ibid., p. 235.
23. Possibly Scudder had Howells in mind. There is no evidence it was Henry James. In fact, there is doubt whether Scudder could have identified "great literature" in this field at all; in 1891, as editor of the *Atlantic*, he received "The Pupil" from James and turned it down; see Leon Edel, ed., *The Selected Letters of Henry James* (New York, Doubleday Anchor Books, 1960), p. 92.

comic book of the Gilded Age. But while Sumner, the sociologist, was content to fulminate against dime novels as the cause of this deterioration in the status of families, Scudder saw the novels as one result of widespread social sickness: "This very ephemeral literature is symptomatic of a condition of things, rather than causative. . . . The disintegration of the family, through a feeble sense of the sacredness of marriage, is an evil which is not to be remedied by any specific of law or literature, but so long as it goes on it inevitably affects literature."[24]

The author of *Childhood in Literature and Art* had a program for reform. "Consider if it be not possible," he advised writers, "to report the activity and comradery of the young in closer and more generous association with the life of their elders. The spectacle of a healthy family life, in which children move freely and joyously, is not so rare as to make models hard to be found . . ." Another suggestion was for writers to forget the distinction between adult and juvenile fiction and to produce "classic Literature" which could be read by young and old alike. In fact, Scudder urged a return to the "simple habit of reading aloud" as a good way the American family could recapture some of its lost unity. This plea in 1895 indicates a withering away of the practice which the Clemens family and their Nook Farm neighbors took very seriously in the 1870's and which had produced *The Prince and the Pauper.*

The success of the battle against dime novels which Mrs. Dodge, Professor Sumner, and Horace Scudder led at this time cannot easily be assessed. The steadily increasing popularity of *St. Nicholas* is one indication, while the declining sale of Beadle's books at the turn of the century was in the face of competition from Nick Carter and Frank Merriwell. More significant, perhaps, is an incident that took place some time in 1892. As the story goes, a sixteen-year-old youth wandered

24. *Childhood in Literature and Art,* pp. 239–40.

into the Oakland public library and casually leafed through a back issue of *St. Nicholas.* His eye caught the title of a story by F. M. White, "The Cruise of the Moonraker." Soon he was deep in the tale of young Harry Bronson who, falling under the sinister spell of trashy novels, ran away from a good home and took up with a gang of wharf-rats cruising New York harbor in a stolen yacht. Harry's father finally tracked down his errant son and, before the astonished eyes of the crew, administered such a thrashing that Harry recognized his lawlessness and reformed on the spot. Jack London was apparently so taken with White's story and its personal implications that he abandoned at once the life of an oyster pirate. Joining the state fish-patrol, he turned toward his future career as a writer. London's first two stories that saw print did so in *St. Nicholas.* One of them, "The Cruise of the Dazzler," had a hero by the name of Joe Bronson.[25]

While Jesse Pomeroy, the boy murderer, languished fifty years in prison (forty-one of them in solitary) thanks to the influence of Beadle and Adams, Jack London was rescued from a life of crime by Mrs. Dodge's cheery magazine. As the first member, too, of the *St. Nicholas* League, he was set on the road to literary fame. The highbrow tradition, which stood for law, justice, authority, and friendliness in family and society alike, had lost the first casualty but by its own account had won the last skirmish.

The Prince and the Pauper was composed at Nook Farm from 1878 to 1880, just at the height of this controversy. If it had not been for the scruples of Twain's publisher, the novel might have figured directly in the campaign; as it stands, the story of Prince Edward and Tom Canty fits the genteel pattern

25. See Harold French, "The Cruises of 'Bay-Pirate Jack,'" *St. Nicholas, 44* (1917), 848–50, and Sam S. Baskett, "Jack London on the Oakland Waterfront," *American Literature, 27* (1955), 363–71.

laid down by Mrs. Dodge and Horace Scudder. Here is no "rattling of the dry bones of history" but a fast-moving story that provides children with a vivid sense of past events. Although overt "sermonizing" is held to a minimum, Twain's version of history is presented with a "stronger, truer, bolder, more uncompromising" simplicity than most adult romances would exhibit. Its author has taken pains to place the childish figures in a close and "generous association" with at least some of their elders. Moreover, though Twain has not especially painted portraits of "healthy family life," he has created some model fathers and ideal mothers. Finally, *The Prince and the Pauper*, while it may not be "classic literature" by universal standards, does at least try to bridge the gap between juvenile and adult fiction. Judging by the fond reception at Nook Farm, anyway, it was certainly a book to be read aloud together; hence it may have served to cement social ties in families torn by literary strife over other forms of fiction.

It is possible, on the other hand, that if the final manuscript of *The Prince and the Pauper* had been sent off to Mrs. Dodge, it would not have passed scrutiny. For in each of the respects in which this novel typifies its age and social milieu there exists an undercurrent of conflict and contradiction. In Twain's treatment of the past, in his handling of antique narrative and dialogue techniques, and in the moral overtones of his story of these two boys, evidences of an internal struggle may be detected. His acceptance of the respectable standards of his adopted environment contends at several points against the natural vigor and satiric honesty of his mind and temperament; the result is at times an uneasy alliance. The forms these tensions create are worth following, for they point to subterranean complexities by no means typical of children's novels in 1881.

The blending of historical truth and fanciful imagination in *The Prince and the Pauper* is one obvious area in which Twain's compromise with his genteel, juvenile readers can be traced. In the first place, the selection of a segment of English history as the vehicle for his story marked his awareness of a growing Anglophilia that swept over the upper reaches of American society during the last decades of the nineteenth century. This novel, like its later imitator *Little Lord Fauntleroy*,[26] was, perhaps unconsciously, part of this fashionable zest for things British which manifested itself, apart from books, in such various forms as international marriages, High Churchism, and the establishment of boarding schools like Groton and St. Mark's.[27] But Twain's choice of an English setting was motivated also by another and opposite American attitude toward the mother country. For his intention in *The Prince and the Pauper* was to show how unjust and undemocratic English life actually was in the sixteenth century. Twisting the lion's tail was as popular in the United States as admiring the English class system, and Twain's book played upon both feelings.

His iconoclasm had its limits, however, for the particular period of medieval British experience chosen to be dramatized was one which his reading led him to consider as not entirely cruel and severe in its laws. "My idea," he explained to Howells, "is to afford a realizing sense of the exceeding severity of the laws of that day by inflicting some of their penalties upon the King himself & allowing him a chance to see the rest of them applied to others—all of which is to account for certain mildnesses which distinguished Edward VI's reign from those that preceded & followed it." [28] Thus he consciously blunted

26. See Paine, *Letters,* 2, 814. According to his Notebook, Twain had copies of *The Prince and the Pauper* sent, most appropriately, to Lilly Warner, Frances Hodgson Burnett, and (through Moncure D. Conway) to Charlotte M. Yonge. Notebook 15, July 26 – December 10, 1880, Typescript, p. 17, in MTP.
27. See Dixon Wecter, *The Saga of American Society* (New York, C. Scribner's Sons, 1937), pp. 241, 402–27, 475–80.
28. *Mark Twain–Howells Letters, 1,* 291–92.

his own satiric point by choosing a time in British history which could legitimately be portrayed as something of an oasis in a general wasteland of undemocratic injustice.

As his letter to Mrs. Fairbanks suggests, he made a careful though unsystematic study of British history in order to ground his narrative solidly in historical fact.[29] Some of the fruits of that labor—which was a labor of love because he always enjoyed reading about the past—are displayed in the notes at the back of his book. They indicate a comprehensive debt to his friend and Hartford neighbor J. Hammond Trumbull, who in 1876 published *The True-Blue Laws of Connecticut and New Haven and the False Blue Laws*. Trumbull's work was a patriotic attempt to prove English laws, of Tudor times and long after, far more severe and unjust than the so-called Blue Laws of his native state. Twain agreed wholeheartedly with Trumbull. The same theme is stated implicitly throughout *The Prince and the Pauper* and explicitly at the end of the book. "There has never been a time—under the Blue Laws or any other—when above FOURTEEN crimes were punishable by death in Connecticut. But in England, within the memory of men who are still hale in body and mind, TWO HUNDRED AND TWENTY-THREE crimes were punishable by death! These facts are worth knowing—and worth thinking about, too." So runs the General Note on which Twain closes. Its tone suggests that the author wished to rest the pendulum of his mind on the iconoclastic side.

In addition to using Trumbull and other historians to ex-

29. See Leon Dickinson, "The Sources of *The Prince and the Pauper*," *Modern Language Notes*, 44 (1949), 103–6. Wagenknecht suggests a plausible reason why Twain, in a romance for children, should take such care to be (as he thought) historically precise. According to a view Twain expressed several times in his novels, fiction based squarely on facts was superior to purely imaginative writing. This attitude, Wagenknecht believes, was a common Middlewestern literary opinion. See *Mark Twain: The Man and His Work*, p. 49.

pose legal injustice, Twain's democratic impulse lead him to focus attention on the lower reaches of Tudor society. Here he found exploitable an old seventeenth-century history of vagabonds, criminals, and gypsies, *The English Rogue* by Richard Head and Francis Kirkman. His debt to this volume is as comprehensive as to Trumbull. He lifted bodily from it colloquial expressions, bits of actual dialogue, ideas for scenes, and even descriptive passages. The practice paid off in many of the novel's most effective episodes. The meeting of the vagabonds in the barn, culminating in the mock crowning of the real King, is handled with imaginative vigor as well as scrupulous regard for the rogues' idiom. Likewise the burning of the two women heretics, the coronation scenes in London, and several other events where he employs "the quaint wording of a chronicler" are both true to history and lively fiction as well.

When he narrows his focus down to individual actors and forsakes the general historical setting for private doings of his characters, however, a shift occurs in the tone of *The Prince and the Pauper,* away from historical realism and toward sentimentality. The modulation is often swift, as in this description of the death by fire of the two Anabaptists:

> The women bowed their heads, and covered their faces with their hands; the yellow flames began to climb upward among the snapping and crackling fagots, and wreaths of blue smoke to stream away on the wind; the clergyman lifted his hands and began a prayer—just then two young girls came flying through the great gate, uttering piercing screams, and threw themselves upon the women at the stake. . . . Both the girls screamed continually, and fought for freedom; but suddenly this tumult was drowned under a volley of heart-piercing shrieks of mortal agony. The king glanced from the frantic girls to the stake, then turned away and leaned his ashen face

against the wall and looked no more. He said, "That which I have seen, in that one little moment, will never go out from my memory, but will abide there; and I shall see it all the days, and dreams of it all the nights, till I die. Would God I had been blind!"   [*11*, 221–22]

This is strong medicine for children, especially *St. Nicholas* readers. It is as graphic, in fact, as any of the similar scenes of death by burning in *Connecticut Yankee* and *Joan of Arc*. Yet in such clumsy circumlocutions as "clergyman"—where the apt historical word surely would be "priest"—and in the young King's speech at the end, so reminiscent in its antiphonal phraseology of the King James Bible, the description strikes a stilted and artificial note at the end markedly different from that of the beginning. An inexperienced writer is being pulled stylistically as well as emotionally in two directions at once.

In this particular scene, as in many others, *The Prince and the Pauper* exudes a faintly religious aroma. Neither Trumbull nor *The English Rogue* provided Twain a precedent, nor did his own skeptical temperament. But another amateur historian did—one Twain does not mention in his notes but whose presence can be felt at several points in his romance. Charlotte M. Yonge was an English writer well known in the Clemens household, particularly in the nursery. Author of *The Heir of Redclyffe, The Prince and the Page,* and *The Little Duke,* all three of which were among Susy and Clara's books, Miss Yonge was perhaps the favorite British juvenile writer of her age. In the summer of 1877 Twain read his daughters' copy of *The Prince and the Page* at Quarry Farm in Elmira and caught the germ for his own romance. "The thought came to me from the outside—suggested by that pleasant and picturesque little history-book, Charlotte M. Yonge's 'Little Duke,'" he recalled years later, and although the old man has confused *The Little*

Duke with *The Prince and the Page,* the link between his own work and Miss Yonge's is clear.[30]

Though as Paine properly suggests, "there is no point of resemblance between *The Prince and the Pauper* and the tale that inspired it," Twain obviously borrowed from Miss Yonge the generic device of a person of noble rank changing places with a beggar. Furthermore, *The Little Duke* may also have helped Twain; it tells a story of the diminutive son of William of Normandy involved in the Crusades, thus giving Twain grounds for confusion and a possible inspiration for introducing a royal boy to adventures outside the confines of his Court. Also, both of Miss Yonge's stories take pains to document historical incidents by footnotes in the back of the book, for she considered herself both novelist and historian.

On the historical side, too, Charlotte Yonge may have influenced Twain while he was writing *The Prince and the Pauper.* In the Clemens family library were copies of her *Young Folks History of England* (1879) and *Cameos from English History* (1871), both of which he must have read. Although the latter volume deals with the England of an earlier era—King Richard II and the times of Wat Tyler's Rebellion —one of its themes is the treatment of serfs in the late fourteenth century. Writing of Richard's vetoing of Parliamentary restriction on villeins, Miss Yonge points out that certain of the cruel statutes enacted at this time (1391) "have never been repealed." Twain was struck by this, for in his copy he made two significant marginal comments. "Slavery still exists by (obsolete) law in England" he wrote with evident satisfaction next to this passage. But he also made a contrary comment. "Southern slavery. Slavery. we 500 yrs behind England both

30. Paine, *Letters,* 2, 813. See also Paine, *Mark Twain,* 2, 596–97. *The Heir of Redclyffe* was in Clara Clemens Samoussoud's library when it was sold at auction April 10, 1951 (Item O4, signature Olivia L. Clemens, *Mark Twain Library Auction Catalogue* in MTP).

in slavery and official corruption." [31] Twain's double reaction to this comment on the mistreatment of common folk is of a piece with his own view of British history as everywhere expressed in *The Prince and the Pauper*.

In spite of these links between Charlotte Yonge's and Mark Twain's historicism, the Englishwoman's influence upon Twain's story was no more than general. A fervent member of the Oxford Movement, Miss Yonge stressed in her books ecclesiastical reforms and social kindnesses in medieval England more than political and legal injustice. Twain was no Anglo-Catholic and was not much interested in church affairs. To be sure, his Prince evinces at times a Christian saintliness (visible in the heretic-burning episode) that may owe something to Miss Yonge, but in general her version of the English past was too feminine and antiseptic for the American writer. For instance, her picture of Edward VI in *Young Folks History of England* is vastly different from Twain's. "The little son of Henry VIII and Jane Seymour," she relates, "of course reigned after him as Edward VI. He was a quiet, gentle boy, exceedingly fond of learning and study, and there were great expectations of him . . . He had never been strong, and he had learnt and worked much more than was good for him. He wrote a journal, and though he never says he grieved for his uncles [executed by Henry VIII], most likely he did, for he had few near him who really loved or cared for him, and he was fast falling into a decline, so that it became quite plain that he was not likely ever to be a grown-up king." [32] This image of Edward as sickly and bookish, doomed to an unhappy life and an early death, is one Twain had little sympathy

31. Marginalia in Twain's copy of Charlotte M. Yonge, *Cameos from English History* (New York and London, Macmillan, 1871), p. 134, in Collection of Harold Mueller, Redding, Connecticut. © Mark Twain Company.

32. *Young Folks' History of England* (Cincinnati and New York, 1879), p. 220.

for. On the contrary, his Prince is an athletic lad who can, when necessary, trounce a vagabond in a cudgel fight. In spite of the novel's sentimental final sentences, Twain wastes surprisingly little emotion on the fact of Edward's early death. He is far more concerned with the Prince's active life among the riffraff of his realm.

Another way he adjudicated between his juvenile audience's expectations and his own private sense of historical and psychological verisimilitude was in the delineation of the characters of his two boy heroes. There was, first of all, the problem of their ages. Since one of his boys was an historical personage, whose dates were known, it became necessary, if that boy was to do and say and see all the things assigned to him in the plot, to pretend he was much older than Edward VI had actually been. This is precisely what Twain has done. In a letter to his publisher he explained himself as follows: "Please let the artist always picture the Prince & Tom Canty as lads of 13 or 14 years old. I know I was making them too wise & knowing for their *real* age, so I studiously avoided mentioning any dates which would remind the reader that they were under 10 years old. Perhaps I mention the date of Henry VIIIs death, but I don't mention the date of Prince Edward's birth." [33] Tom Canty, too, while he needs no suppression of historical fact to do so, is made to act much older than is likely for a boy born on the same day as the Prince. He learns to read Latin from kindly Father Andrew, and at Offal Court behaves in a manner so "curiously ceremonious and courtly" that even adults recognize his maturity and bring their perplexities to Tom for solution.

The result of these compromises is a pair of boyish figures who not only act much older and wiser than their years but look very much more dainty than the real boys Twain was

33. MT to Mr. Anthony (March 9, [1881]), in MTP. © Mark Twain Company.

used to picturing. The unreality of their appearance is strikingly apparent in the book's many illustrations. These pen-and-ink drawings depict both the Prince and his lower-class alter ego as slender, effeminate striplings. This is just what Twain intended. "Merrill probably thinks he *originated* his exquisite boys himself," he wrote his publishers, "but I was ahead of him there!—in these pictures they look & dress exactly as I used to see them in my mind two years ago. It is a vast pleasure to see them cast in the flesh, so to speak—they were of but perishable dream-stuff, before." [34]

Their speech, too, in common with that of everyone in this story of the sixteenth century, sounds in general like an unconvincing compound of *The English Rogue*, the Bible, and Elizabethan drama, as in this characteristic exchange between the two boys:

> "What is thy name, lad?"
> "Tom Canty, an it please thee, sir."
> " 'Tis an odd one. Where dost live?"
> "In the city, please thee, sir. Offal Court, out of Pudding Lane."
> "Offal Court! Truly, 'tis another odd one. Hast parents?"
> "Parents have I, sir, and a grandam likewise that is but indifferently precious to me, God forgive me if it be offense to say it—also twin sisters, Nan and Bet."
> "Then is thy grandam not overkind to thee, I take it."
> "Neither to any other is she, so please your worship. She hath a wicked heart, and worketh evil all her days."
> [*11*, 13]

It is possible, of course, that Twain thought in writing dialogue like this that he was reproducing the actual language of sixteenth-century Englishmen. He knew Shakespeare well

34. MT to B. T. Ticknor (Aug. 14, 1881), in Yale Collection of American Literature. © Mark Twain Company.

enough to be a Baconian and may have read other Elizabethan and Jacobean playwrights during the year and a half he spent working up *The Prince and the Pauper*. "I was reading ancient English books with the purpose of saturating myself with archaic English to a degree which would enable me to do plausible imitations of it in a fairly easy and unlabored way," he recalled in *Mark Twain in Eruption*.[35] At about this time, too, he composed his celebrated piece of bawdry, "1601, or Fireside Conversation in the Time of Queen Elizabeth." This gently spiced anecdote is narrated ostensibly by the Queen's cupbearer in an idiom even more archaic than Prince Edward's or Tom's: "Then conversed they of religion & mightie worke ye olde dead Luther did doe by ye grace of God. Then next about poetry, and Master Shaxpur did read a part of his King Henrie IV, the which it seemeth unto mee is not of the value of an arseful of ashes, yet they praised it bravely, one and all." [36] As approximation of real speech, this is not greatly different except in vocabulary from most conversations in *The Prince and the Pauper*. One of the ways, clearly, by which Twain tries to give his youthful readers a sense of the past is to sprinkle "methinks" and "mayhaps" liberally through his narrative. Yet strictly as style, apart from the often sentimental burden of the sentences, the dialogue convention of *The Prince and the Pauper* was intended to imitate, as realistically as could be expected of a partly educated and insecure writer, the speech of Englishmen long dead. Hence it is unfair to compare the results with his prose reproducing the speech of live Americans.

The perplexities of writing a genteel historical romance for children were, indeed, many for a man of Twain's predilections and background. The most delicate topic of all was family life. As the remarks of Sumner, Scudder, and the others indicate,

35. *Mark Twain in Eruption,* p. 206.
36. Privately printed (1921), p. 20.

this was the area of juvenile experience on which the writer was expected to be as affirmative as possible. For reasons Twain himself never made clear, he had skirted the heart of the matter in *Tom Sawyer* by making Aunt Polly into a stereotype of the Bad Boy's mother. In fact, not wholly trusting himself to project his own mother into fiction, he had freely borrowed characteristics of Shillaber's Mrs. Partington for Tom's mother-substitute.[37] Even more significantly, Tom Sawyer had no father at all. Most likely Twain was unwilling to exhibit, in his very first novel, the animus that he had secretly felt as a child against John Clemens and that was sure to come out in any portrait of Tom Sawyer's father.[38] Brotherly relations in *Tom Sawyer*, on the other hand, receive overt and more honest attention, though Twain's tendency here was to take refuge in the simplified Good Boy – Bad Boy pattern that Tom and Sid exemplify. Sister-brother ties, too, were stylized in Tom Sawyer's world. The result was a more subtle delineation of Tom's relation to the whole village than to his own immediate family.

When he came to compose *The Prince and the Pauper*, Twain must have felt great social pressure to idealize family relationships, but he did not wholly succumb. Both in the Palace and in Offal Court an honest and in general unsavory picture is painted of the interaction of fathers and offspring. Tom Canty and his sisters are regularly beaten by a drunken, thieving father and, even more astonishingly, by their old grandmother. John Canty finally commits murder and his punishment at the novel's end is complete oblivion. At the Court, the Prince and his royal sisters, Elizabeth and Mary, fare somewhat better, though Henry VIII is invariably pictured as a gouty old tyrant—until safely dead. Then, the little Prince gets a lump in his throat, "for the grim tyrant who had

37. See Blair, *Native American Humor*, pp. 151–53.
38. See Wecter, *Sam Clemens of Hannibal*, pp. 67–68, 91–92.

had been such a terror to others had always been gentle with him" (*11*, 76).

Yet in spite of cruel and domineering fathers, neither Tom Canty nor Edward lacks for kind, fatherly love and protection. Tom is befriended by Father Andrew (the title is significant). The "good old priest" teaches him Latin, tells stories, and lends him books just as any interested Nook Farm parent would have done. The Prince, too, on his journey of initiation through the lower reaches of his kingdom has a father-surrogate. Miles Hendon is a small boy's dream of a father-protector. His sword rescues the little King from the London rabble, and at one point Miles even undergoes the whip in place of his young friend. Consequently, the affectionate ties between Miles and the Prince are entirely idealized. This is as true of the man's affection for the boy as vice versa. When, for instance, Edward is kidnapped, Hendon sets out at once to find him with this thought in mind:

> Would the search for him be difficult, or long? No, it was likely to be easy and brief. He would not hunt for the boy, he would hunt for a crowd; in the center of a big crowd or a little one, sooner or later, he should find his poor little friend, sure; and the mangy mob would be entertaining itself with pestering and aggravating the boy, who would be proclaiming himself king, as usual. Then Miles Hendon would cripple some of those people, and carry off his little ward, and comfort and cheer him with loving words, and the two would never be separated any more. [*11*, 261-62]

Hero worship—which in *The Prince and the Pauper* replaces the puppy love of *Tom Sawyer* as boyish emotional expression —works both ways.

Blood fathers in *The Prince and the Pauper* require and receive idealized substitutes. Mothers, on the other hand, need

121

none; they are wholly sentimentalized from the beginning. Thus Tom's starving mother in Offal Court "would slip to him stealthily with any miserable scrap or crust she had been able to save for him by going hungry herself," and was often beaten for her devotion. The peasant mothers whom the Prince encounters on his tour of the underworld are likewise invariably loving and self-sacrificing. They are all waxen figurines; nor does any realistic touch intrude that might impair their status as idols.

Tom Canty's mother, however, plays a more functional role in the plot of *The Prince and the Pauper* than simply the Ideal Mother. She precipitates the moral crisis of the story. When she darts out from the coronation crowd and recognizes her son dressed in the robes of a king, Tom spurns her with the remark, "I do not know you, woman!" Unheard in the tumult, Tom's words recall Peter's denial of Christ, and they bring home dramatically to Twain's young readers that a double process of moral initiation has been unobtrusively taking place in the story. While Prince Edward has been learning at first hand the severities of the laws of his kingdom, his street-urchin substitute has been moving imperceptibly in the opposite direction. As the Prince learns sympathy through suffering the commoner's lot, Tom Canty gradually learns how pleasant it is to enjoy absolute power. Frequently, of course, he employs that power for good, as when he pardons the Duke of Norfolk and disproves the superstitious accusations against a witch. But in spite of worthy deeds Tom slips readily into the role of Prince (Father Andrew's Latin comes in handy here) and is quite prepared to have himself consecrated King. The spurning of his mother climaxes this subtle process of moral disintegration. The act awakens Tom to awareness of the depths of his pride and callousness; "whilst the crowd was swallowing her from his sight, she seemed so wounded, so broken-hearted, that a shame fell upon him which consumed

his pride to ashes, and withered his stolen royalty. His gran-
deurs were stricken valueless; they seemed to fall away from
him like rotten rags" (*11*, 242). When the chips are down, Tom
proves a worthy son to his beatific mother by recognizing his
own hubris.

This drama of Tom's moral fall and rise is closely related to
the larger theme of *The Prince and the Pauper*. As spelled out
by Twain, that theme has two horns: the superiority of democ-
racy to monarchy, and the molding force exerted on an individual by his environment. Both boys exemplify both points.
When Tom repudiates his mother, he symbolizes thereby the
corrupting power of princedoms. Back in Offal Court he had
been a moral paragon, studying hard with Father Andrew and
settling the disputes of adults by his superior wisdom. But this
passion for probity begins to wither as soon as it is withdrawn
from its roots in the life of common folk. Pride, selfishness, and
callous indifference are the garments Tom puts on with those
of the Prince, and the meeting with his mother merely drama-
tizes a moral collapse that the palace environment has brought
about.

The reverse process occurs in the life of the Prince who dons
pauper's clothing. Though Edward is spared actual physical
punishment (Miles Hendon volunteering to play Whipping
Boy) he learns how the common people fare. Like Tom, the
Prince is an imposter among the rabble. Almost against his
royal will, he assimilates the humility, courage, and fellow feeling of the poor folk he encounters. Environment makes Prince
Edward kind as it makes Tom Canty proud.

This democratic moral was later to be elaborated by Twain
more caustically and comprehensively in *A Connecticut Yankee
in King Arthur's Court*. The exchange of identities, with similar moral results, recurs in *Pudd'nhead Wilson*. But the sarcastic and pessimistic overtones so evident in the later novels
are in large measure missing from *The Prince and the Pauper*.

This is not so much because Twain ignores the pessimistic implications of his environmental explanation of behavior as that he submerges such conclusions beneath the triumphant figures of his two boys in command of the adult world.

For the final image of boyhood that emerges from *The Prince and the Pauper* is that of the child as wise ruler. Long before he changes clothes with Prince Edward, Tom Canty plays this role in Offal Court; and "with a child's facility in accommodating itself to circumstances" he quickly learns to do the same at Westminster. Prince Edward even more justifiably is the archetypal Child King, worthy in all respects—as Tom is not—of the deference of the adults who are his courtiers. As Tom Canty's alert common sense surpasses that of grown-ups, so Edward's compassion outstrips Tom's. The symbolic suggestion at the story's end is thus almost that of a boy Christ and a boy Peter who have jointly inherited the kingdom of the earth. But behind this reassuring image hovers the shadow of a Darwinian explanation of human conduct that is later to grow and to engulf Twain's rosy image of childhood.

It is in such terms that *The Prince and the Pauper* rehearses for its childish audience themes and figures of Twain's other, more adult, fiction. In spite of community pressure, friendly and welcomed as it was, he wrote his own kind of story. Though feeling the necessity of blunting his satiric impulse and curbing his taste for realistic detail, he was able to make this historical romance a *relatively* honest picture of Tudor life. The dialogue is conventionally quaint, perhaps, yet it was intended to sound authentic, so that the prime medium of his literary realism has not been entirely compromised. Moreover, his picture of family life in the sixteenth century is a convincing mixture of unpleasant and ideal relationships. Bad fathers are definitely there, but they have worthy stand-ins; mothers require no substitutes. Children in this story are by no means separated from their elders; even though they are smarter and

more compassionate than grown-ups, both get along well together—as long as the children rule. In the process Twain
has appropriated many of the dime novel's characteristic and
popular features, but by having his boys win through goodness
instead of deviltry, he has pleased parents as well as children.

Horace Scudder's formula, then, was in ample measure fulfilled in *The Prince and the Pauper,* although the proper
Bostonian never hinted at this in *Childhood in Literature and
Art.* A writer of "great literature" had created an imaginative
world for children in a romance of the English past purified
of grosser unpleasantnesses. It was the sort of book the whole
family could enjoy reading together around the library table.
In short, *The Prince and the Pauper* was in all fundamentals
acceptable as a passport into the province of genteel letters.
This social achievement, however, did not prevent the writer
from exploring certain areas of human conduct that ordinarily
lay outside the scope of a children's story. The story of Tom
Canty and the young Prince was written primarily to please
small readers and their parents; it also uncovered a number of
basic moral problems about a "world made wrong" and suggested quite seriously the part boys might play in righting that
world.

5.

Huckleberry Finn and the Modes of Escape

THE PRINCE AND THE PAUPER is the expression of Mark Twain's momentary integration with one dominant literary tradition of his age. Inspired by Charlotte Yonge, admired by Harriet Beecher Stowe and the whole of Nook Farm, and imitated by Frances Hodgson Burnett, Twain's historical romance soon took its place on family book shelves alongside *Little Men, Little Lord Fauntleroy*, and the bound volumes of *St. Nicholas*. Except for *Joan of Arc*, it was Twain's only novel to enjoy complete social respectability.

But it did not sell very well. The $17,000 it reportedly earned its author was scarcely more than one-sixth of the Clemens' family expenditures for the year in which it was published.[1] One of the ironies of Twain's career was that the one book he wrote for Nook Farm did not earn enough money to allow him to meet the cost of living there.

By the early eighties he was finding that the idyllic family life of Hartford extracted from him an increasingly heavy toll of time and money. Though an admiring friend in 1884 might write "yours is one of the few *restful* homes in which intelligence, culture, luxury, and company combine to the compounding of a pleasure which every visitor longs to taste again," [2] Twain

---

1. See Paine, *Mark Twain, 2,* 723–31; DeVoto, *Mark Twain in Eruption,* p. 158; and Samuel C. Webster, *Mark Twain, Businessman* (Boston, Little, Brown, 1946), p. 182.

2. Quoted in Andrews, *Nook Farm,* p. 94.

himself somewhat ruefully quipped that the bus company ought to run a line from the railroad station to his house for the use of his friends. He confided privately to Howells that "a life of don't-care-a-damn in a boarding house is what I have asked for in many a secret prayer." [3] This fatiguing social pace had doubtless been one reason for the Clemenses' extended escape to Europe in 1878–79.

The constant round of entertaining, the literary dinners, the family charades and whist parties, the Monday Evening Club, the Saturday Morning Club, and the Browning Club consumed more and more of the author's time. "Work?—one can't you know, to any purpose," he wrote an old California friend, "I don't really get anything done worth speaking of, except during the three or four months that we are away in the Summer. I keep three or four books on the stocks all the time, but I seldom add a satisfactory chapter to one of them at home . . . Maybe you think I am not happy? the very thing that gravels me is that I am." [4]

One does not need to endorse fully *The Ordeal of Mark Twain* to see that the social and financial pressures of genteel living had a profound effect on Twain's method of writing and on what he wrote. The well-known habit, for instance, of composing under the inspiration of the moment and then putting the manuscript aside when that original impulse slackened was in part accommodation to this social pattern. With only the summers entirely free for concentrated labor, it is not surprising he wrote by fits and starts. As an amanuensis, he had to defer to the caprice not only of *his* daemon but to those of his house guests.

The effects of this situation can be observed at the very inception of *Adventures of Huckleberry Finn*. In the summer of 1876 Howells received this note from his friend: "The double-

3. Smith and Gibson, *Mark Twain–Howells Letters, 1,* 389.
4. Paine, *Letters, 1,* 405.

barreled novel lies torpid . . . I may take it up again next winter, but cannot tell yet. I waited & waited to see if my interest in it would not revive, but gave it up a month ago & began another boy's book—more to be at work than anything else. I have written 400 pages on it—therefore it is very nearly half done. It is Huck Finn's Autobiography. I like it only tolerably well, as far as I have got, & may possibly pigeonhole or burn the MS when it is done." [5] If we are to credit the report of its author, *Huckleberry Finn* was conceived in a weary season.

Nearly seven years and four books later Twain addressed Howells on the same subject but in another mood. "I wrote 4,000 words today," he exulted. "I have finished one small book, & am away along in a big one that I half-finished two or three years ago. I expect to complete it in a month or six weeks or two months more. And *I* shall *like* it, whether anybody else does or not. It's a kind of companion to Tom Sawyer." [6]

In between 1876 and 1883 Twain had probably worked at the book that was to be his masterpiece two or three times. [7] But during this stretch, too, he was expensively preoccupied with business speculations—in the manner of the business barons trying to make a financial killing by investing in one invention after another—and with piecing together several other books. [8] As the Paige typesetter ate up his capital, he laboriously ground out *A Tramp Abroad* (1880), *The Stolen White Elephant* (1882), and the later chapters of *Life on the Mississippi*, which appeared in 1883. Though outwardly on the crest of social and literary popularity, he more than once admitted to dissatisfaction and disenchantment. On one occasion, having attended a travelogue at which the lecturer de-

5. *Mark Twain–Howells Letters, 1,* 144.

6. Ibid., p. 435.

7. See Walter Blair, "When Was *Huckleberry Finn* Written?", *American Literature, 30* (1958), 1–25.

8. See Webster, *Mark Twain, Business Man,* pp. 171 ff.

scribed "how retired tradesmen and farmers in Holland load
a lazy scow with the family and household effects, and then
loaf along the water-ways of the Low Countries all the summer
long," he confessed his envy to Howells. "If you had hired such
a boat and sent for us we should have a couple of satisfactory
books ready for the press now with no marks of interruption,
vexatious wearinesses, and other hellishnesses visible upon
them anywhere." [9] Prophetic indeed was this catalogue, for
the novel Twain was to complete within five months was to
show, just beneath the surface of its infectious gaiety, visible
marks of the literary ills he mentions. One indisputable reason
for the differences between *Tom Sawyer* and its sequel was the
change in tempo of their creator's private and public life.

When in 1884 *Huckleberry Finn* was finally ready for the
presses, Twain bent every effort to ensure that his new book
would not flop, as *The Prince and the Pauper* had done. He
wrote his agent, *"The book is to be issued when a big edition
has been sold—& not before. . . .* There is *no date* for the book.
It can issue the 1st of December if 40,000 have been sold. It
must wait till they *are* sold, if it is seven years." [10] But seven
years were not necessary. With the most extensive advance
publicity of any of his books, *Huckleberry Finn* was sold by
subscription up and down the land. Package arrangements
with *Tom Sawyer* and *The Prince and the Pauper* (emphasizing its nature as "another boy's book") were offered young
readers. Over a quarter of it ran serially in Richard Watson
Gilder's *Century Magazine.*[11] On a lecture tour with George
Washington Cable, Twain himself read extracts to delighted
audiences. These efforts paid off, for the 40,000 copies Twain
insisted upon were sold before publication, and upon its ap-

9. *Mark Twain–Howells Letters, 1,* 426.
10. Webster, p. 248.
11. With some interesting results: see A. L. Scott, "The *Century
Magazine* Edits *Huckleberry Finn,* 1884–1885," *American Literature,* 27
(1955), 356–62.

pearance in February 1885 the book was an immediate success. "No other book of mine has sold so many copies within 2 months after issue as this one has done," he wrote his sister in April 1885.[12] Within the year, if we can credit Twain's own words, *Huckleberry Finn* had earned its enterprising author $54,500, over three times what he had received from *The Prince and the Pauper*.[13] For the next two decades or so, "Huck Finn's Autobiography" continued to be Mark Twain's best-paying book.[14]

Though a resounding commercial success from the start, it was a dismal failure with the critics. The two opposite reactions were apparently related. The principal event which boosted its popular appeal was, of course, the banning by the Concord Library Committee. "They have expelled Huck from their library as 'trash and suitable only for the slums'. That will sell 25,000 copies for us, sure," Twain exclaimed to Charles Webster, his business manager.[15] He was probably exaggerating, but there is little doubt that as the guardians of taste in the magazines and newspapers united in damning Twain's latest display of gross humor, *Huckleberry Finn's* sales went up. And, conversely, the book's very success seemed to convince critics that in condemning it as "the veriest trash" they were right.

The Springfield *Republican* was particularly emphatic. "It is time that this influential pseudonym should cease to carry into homes and libraries unworthy productions," pontificated the reviewer. "Mr. Clemens is a genuine and powerful humorist . . . but in certain of his works degenerates into a gross trifling with every fine feeling. His notorious speech at an Atlantic dinner, marshalling Longfellow and Emerson and

12. Webster, p. 317.
13. DeVoto, *Mark Twain in Eruption*, p. 169. See also Paine, *Mark Twain*, 2, 793.
14. Mott, *Golden Multitudes*, pp. 156–57.
15. Paine, *Letters*, 2, 452–53.

Whittier in vulgar parodies in a Western miner's cabin, illustrates this, but not in much more relief than the 'Adventures of Tom Sawyer' did, or these Huckleberry Finn stories do . . ." Then this arbiter of provincial propriety made a final and, to him devastating, comparison. "They are no better in tone than the dime novels which flood the blood-and-thunder reading population." [16]

Even T. S. Perry, who wrote in the *Century* the only favorable review that reached a wide audience, was uneasy in his enthusiasm. Though he praised Twain for creating "a vivid picture of Western life of forty or fifty years ago," he wrote guardedly of Huck himself as little more than "an incarnation of the better side of the ruffianism that is one result of the independence of Americans." [17] Even to enthusiasts, Twain's new book bore unmistakable traces of Beadle and Adams vulgarity.

Some years after these first reactions the genteel world of New England letters passed its generation's final judgment on Mark Twain's masterpiece. Fittingly enough, it was one of the editors of the *Youth's Companion* who did so. Charles Miner Thompson was a colleague of Mrs. Dodge and Horace Scudder, and his article surveying Twain's literary achievement appeared in the *Atlantic Monthly* in 1897. The tone of his highly critical judgments indicate that William Dean Howells, who had been trying for twenty years to convince respectable Americans that his friend Twain was a fine writer, had made little headway.

Thompson's dislike of Twain's fiction centered, as might be expected from his magazine job, on the childish characters. In his eyes, Tom Sawyer, for example, was only one more representation "of the general idea—boy" and, in fact, an inferior

16. Quoted in A. L. Vogelback, "The Publication and Reception of *Huckleberry Finn* in America," *American Literature, 11* (1939), 270–71.
17. Ibid., p. 267.

literary creation to the Bad Boy of Thomas Bailey Aldrich. As for Tom's comrade, "what Huck really is . . . is simply the usual vagabond boy, with his expected shrewdness and cunning, his rags, his sharp humor, his practical philosophy. The only difference between him and his type would be found in his essential honesty, his strong and struggling moral nature, so notably Anglo-Saxon." [18] To this refined Easterner, Tom and Huck seemed "the typical American in little," boyish representations of the Westerner who, compounded from the image of Herndon's Abraham Lincoln and the comic-strip character of Uncle Sam, was "a sort of composite personality" known to everyone. The lineaments of this typical American were likewise those of Mark Twain himself: "a shrewd, ready, practical, irreverent, humorous, uncultivated man, who is apt to jeer at art and the civilization of Europe, but for whom you have, nevertheless, a large affection and a high respect, partly because he has, to a striking degree, such excellent qualities as essential seriousness of character, self-reliance, courage, kindliness, honesty, and simplicity of heart, the domestic virtues . . ." [19]

In spite of these redeeming features of Twain and his fictional offspring, Thompson could not stomach the bad taste, the lack of formal discipline, the humor, and the frivolous postures. All these were manifestations of that "shifting and evanescent semi-civilization," the frontier. He summed up: "The society of the West is not yet settled into its final form, as that of the East may be considered to be; but already it, and we who know it, have traveled far from the possibility of appreciating its special humor. A few years more, and most of its fun will seem to all, as it seems to many now, the merest extravagance, as hard to

18. Charles M. Thompson, "Mark Twain as an Interpreter of American Character," *Atlantic Monthly,* 79 (1897), 443–50; reprinted in A. L. Scott, *Mark Twain: Selected Criticism* (Dallas, Southern Methodist University Press, 1955), pp. 58–59.
19. Scott, p. 63.

understand as the spirit which prompted the gargoyle on the mediaeval church." [20]

Charles Thompson's reaction in 1897 to Twain—and it was typical of many literate Americans'—stemmed not simply from Eastern inability to appreciate irreverent frontier humor but also from his tie with conventional juvenile fiction. As editor of *Youth's Companion,* the oldest boy's magazine in America, he could not help judging *Huckleberry Finn* in terms of *The Prince and the Pauper.* Against this background, *Huckleberry Finn* did betray a formlessness, a low taste for burlesque humor, and a stereotyped Ruffian or Vagabond Boy as hero, which made pigeon-holing it easy. That was in a slot right next to the yellow-backed copies of the Half-Dime Library.

Thompson's age and class failed in large measure to appreciate *Huckleberry Finn* because they could not fit it to the pattern of boys' stories in the genteel magazines. On the other hand, thousands of common readers of that age and after were able to enjoy Twain's novel because they found in its western locale, the picaresque adventures of its raffish characters, and the strongly subversive stance of its vagabond hero a pleasing and familiar package. Neither group, to be sure, bothered to discover in the literary form of "Huck Finn's Autobiography" those themes and patterns which today delight and puzzle professors and poets.

Conceivably, all three groups of admirers possessed partial and distorted images. For as the recent controversy over the novel's ending suggests, Twain's book has, like all works which compress into one compass a man's total imaginative powers, a way of eluding everyone's formulation. Certainly, readers like Thompson missed its essence through a fastidious concern for literary form. The common readers of 1885, on the contrary, were too beguiled by *Huckleberry Finn's* happy success as lowbrow "escape" fiction. Each of these approaches has

20. Ibid., p. 59.

demonstrable shortcomings, as has any single approach to the novel, one of the most enigmatic books in our literature.

For all his social astigmatism, Charles Miner Thompson recognized this elusive quality at the core of Twain's book. Huck Finn himself, as Thompson perceived, was an American version of a Homeric figure and "in that wild, youthful, impossible Odyssey, the record of his voyage on a frail raft down the strong Mississippi . . . assumes in a manner epic proportions." The puzzling nature of Huck's tale of adventures stemmed from the character of Huck Finn himself. *Adventures of Huckleberry Finn* is not, after all, Tom Sawyer's story. In his second return to the lost world of his own childhood Twain had chosen a different boy as the innocent eye through which to examine what the subtitles promised: "Scene: The Mississippi Valley" "Time: Forty to Fifty Years Ago." And in the complex pattern of threads connecting one boy to that world may be seen what a great writer could do with the strictly juvenile traditions of Little Men, Ike Partington, and Deadwood Dick, Jr.

At first glance, the special, defining qualities of *Adventures of Huckleberry Finn* are neither a carefully structured plot nor a nicely maintained unity of tone. Compared with both *Tom Sawyer* and *The Prince and the Pauper,* the story lacks coherence. The opening section takes its cue from the boyish pranks of *Tom Sawyer,* but once Huck is afloat, or, more precisely, once he has killed himself in Pap's cabin, the plot enters a different dimension, only to revert to farce again at the end. Beneath the surface of this rambling picaresque tale there may lie, as one modern critic has urged, the Proustian principle of repetition and variation,[21] but the visible structure seems little more than the Mississippi itself, whose current transports a pair of passive protagonists from one episode to another.

21. See Frank Baldanza, "The Structure of *Huckleberry Finn,*" *American Literature,* 27 (1955), 347–55.

Huckleberry Finn's tone is equally uncontrolled. Farce, sentiment, burlesque, melodrama, starkest tragedy, pastoral idyll —one mood or mode succeeds another in apparently aimless fashion. Compared to the sustained note of despair in *The Mysterious Stranger,* this novel is a hodgepodge of jarring tones.

In spite of these flaws (more obvious surely to adult readers than to boys and girls) the book has an imaginative intensity that transcends structural imperfections. The source of the vitality is Huck himself, whose presence and personality are felt in every sentence of his story. Any thoughtful reader must agree with Leo Marx that "the book's excellence in large measure follows from the inspired idea of having the western boy tell his own story in his own idiom." [22]

Adventures of Huckleberry Finn was not, as we know, the first boy's story Twain wrote in the first person singular. The "Boy's Manuscript" indicates that he was very early aware of the possibilities of the device Aldrich had brought to his at-

22. Leo Marx, "The Passenger and the Pilot: Landscape Conventions and the Style of *Huckleberry Finn," American Literature,* 28 (1956), 129. The critical literature on *Huckleberry Finn,* of which this perceptive essay is an outstanding instance, is now so voluminous that few writers today can hope to be wholly original. The most useful essays for this study have been Richard P. Adams, "The Unity and Coherence of *Huckleberry Finn," Tulane Studies in English,* 6 (1956), 87–103; Baldanza, "The Structure of *Huckleberry Finn"* (above, n. 21); James M. Cox, "Remarks on the Sad Initiation of *Huckleberry Finn," Sewanee Review,* 62 (1954), 387–405; T. S. Eliot, introduction to Cresset Library edition, London, 1950; Leslie Fiedler, "Come Back to the Raft Ag'in, Huck, Honey!," in *An End to Innocence* (Boston, Beacon Press, 1955), pp. 142–55; Lewis Leary, "Tom and Huck: Innocence on Trial," *Virginia Quarterly Review,* 30 (1954), 417–30; Kenneth S. Lynn, *Mark Twain and Southwestern Humor* (Boston, 1960), chap. 9; Leo Marx, "Mr. Eliot, Mr. Trilling, and Huckleberry Finn," *American Scholar,* 22 (1953), 423–40; Lionel Trilling, introduction to Rinehart Edition (New York, 1948), reprinted in *The Liberal Imagination* (New York, Doubleday Anchor Books, 1954), pp. 107–19; Philip Young, *Ernest Hemingway* (New York, Rinehart, 1952), pp. 181–212.

tention; the earlier story is, however, proof that the assumption of a narrator-hero viewpoint was of itself no guarantee of success. Yet in spite of the clumsiness of the "Boy's Manuscript" Twain knew instinctively what an effective vantage point a child's eye and mind and voice could be for the kind of realistic fiction he was prepared to write. "I perhaps made a mistake in not writing it in the first person," he admitted to Howells after finishing *Tom Sawyer*.[23] The shift to this perspective was consequently the chief innovation in the "boy's book" Twain commenced writing at Quarry Farm in the summer of 1876.

Several qualities that distinguish *Huckleberry Finn* from the "Boy's Manuscript" and *Tom Sawyer* may be attributed to Twain's happy return to this narrative technique. Using Huck to relate his own adventures gives his story stylistic unity. There are no more abrupt shifts in perspective from adult to boy, as had been the case with Aldrich and *Tom Sawyer*, no more self-conscious quotation marks to set off a boyish expression from the author's more grammatical and polished language. Vernacular realism, too, imparts immediacy, creating and sustaining the reader's sense of hearing the authentic speech of one particular boy at the exact moment of action, reflection, or illumination. Imitating faithfully Huck's idiosyncratic accents seems, moreover, to liberate Twain from some of the self-imposed or culturally derived inhibitions evident in both of his earlier novels about boys. Sticking close to the words a boy would use to recount his adventures inspires or allows Twain to treat the experiences themselves in a similarly forthright manner. The result at many points is a return to the barbed satiric spirit of the California newspaper pieces. The interior perspective also affords Twain access to certain boyish emotions evoked by nature, by society, by his own developing mind—feelings unexpressed in earlier fiction or expressed more clumsily. Thus what is essentially a commonplace literary

23. Smith and Gibson, *Mark Twain–Howells Letters*, *1*, 91.

device becomes in Twain's hands the basis for a style that opens up whole areas of life untouched before in American stories in this genre.

The most immediate sphere so illuminated is this boy's realization of the natural world around him. The conventional picture of nature in other nineteenth-century juvenile novels is much simpler than that of *Huckleberry Finn;* it may be characterized in two different ways. There is, first, the outlook displayed in Shillaber's *Ike Partington and His Friends.* In this book of adolescent pranks and neighborhood adventures, nature is a backdrop and little more. Thus when Ike and his pal embark on a river packet to return home from a summer vacation, the scene is described in these words:

> The way was long to Rivertown, and promised little of interest to the young voyagers. The river was very beautiful, bordered by deep woods and majestic rocks, whose dark shadows lay upon the waters; but they did not care about such things. They would talk for a moment to people in boats, make signals to anyone they might see on the shore, shout to hear their voices echo among the rocks; but boys are impatient, and so they were bored on board the packet.[24]

Unlike Huck, Ike considers nature unimportant, hence it is treated casually and conventionally by his author.

Another and somewhat different approach is seen in Aldrich's *Story of a Bad Boy,* in the passage already cited. Here Aldrich reconstructs a Piscataqua River sunrise with the pictorial imagination of an adult pretending to be a boy rather than through the boy himself. Though as conventional as Shillaber's, Aldrich's image is more self-consciously aesthetic. The adjectives

24. B. P. Shillaber, *Ike Partington: or, The Adventures of a Human Boy and His Friends* (Boston and New York, Lee and Shepard, C. T. Dillingham, 1879), p. 115.

—"calm," "lovely," "drowsy," "enchanted"—are those of an unsophisticated art critic. The effect of such words—and perhaps one Aldrich wanted—is to generalize the scene, rendering it indistinguishable from other mornings on other rivers.

Without the controlling presence of a narrator character, Twain often wrote in this conventional pictorial mode. Frequently it occurs in the travel books, though his uneasiness with its artificiality often leads him to undercut the sweet mood with a sharp deprecatory dig, as in this passage from *A Tramp Abroad:*

> Sometimes we drifted in the shadow of forests, and sometimes along the margin of long stretches of velvety grass, fresh and green and bright, a tireless charm to the eye. And the birds!—they were everywhere; they swept back and forth across the river constantly and their jubilant music was never stilled . . .
>
> How different is this marvel observed from a raft, from what it is when one observes it through the dingy windows of a railway-station in some wretched village while he munches a petrified sandwich and waits for the train.
>
> [9, 108]

Here the professional humorist inserts the "petrified sandwich" in order to deflate his own picture of the Neckar which he recognizes as a romantic stereotype.

When Twain wrote of his own Mississippi, however, he knew too much to be satisfied with romantic stereotypes. The author who had been a pilot in his younger days recognized that nature was something more than velvety grass and jubilant birds. For one thing, he knew that a landscape, if really looked at, was in every respect unique, that the vocabulary of Aldrich was too imprecise a tool to do justice to the endless particularity of the American scene.

138

One can observe in a work of fiction like *Tom Sawyer* Twain's initial attempts to escape the trite landscape idiom of his time and move toward a more faithful and imaginative representation of the world which boys inhabit. Consider, as an obvious example, the description of Tom's waking up on Jackson's Island:

> It was the cool gray dawn, and there was a delicious sense of repose and peace in the deep pervading calm and silence of the woods. Not a leaf stirred; not a sound obtruded upon great Nature's meditation . . . The marvel of Nature shaking off sleep and going to work unfolded itself to the musing boy. A little green worm came crawling over a dewy leaf, lifting two-thirds of his body into the air from time to time and "sniffing around," then proceeding again—for he was measuring, Tom said; and when the worm approached him, of its own accord, he sat as still as a stone, with his hopes rising and falling, by turns, as the creature still came toward him or seemed inclined to go elsewhere; and when at last it considered a painful moment with its curved body in the air and then came decisively down upon Tom's leg and began a journey over him, his whole heart was glad—for that meant that he was going to have a new suit of clothes—without the shadow of a doubt a gaudy piratical uniform. [8, 121–22]

As this passage unfolds, pictorial and realistic modes of depicting nature are displayed side by side. But it is an uneasy alliance. The various crawling creatures are everyday, specific objects, too commonplace for an Aldrich to have noticed. Yet they "obtrude" upon "great Nature's meditation," language just as self-conscious as that used to invoke Tom Bailey's world. The worm's "sniffing around" is Tom's own vocabulary; why, then, did Twain enclose it in quotation marks? Even more cloaked is the scene's underlying significance. We sense that

139

Twain is trying to express Tom's unity with nature, the source of his charm and integrity, by means of the worm who is "measuring" the boy by nature's moral yardstick. But the meaning is obscured rather than revealed by the conventional vocabulary. Twain tries to demonstrate the moment's uniqueness, but without someone inside the story to do the talking he all but fails.

Huck, of course, provides the vocabulary and the vision *Tom Sawyer* did not have. Through his eyes the river world assumes an actuality unknown to Ike Partington, Tom Bailey, or even to Tom Sawyer. For this innocently experienced lad knows the river as intimately as does the pilot in *Life on the Mississippi*. A passenger looking across the water sees "all manner of pretty pictures in it, painted by the sun and shaded by the clouds," but Huck and the pilot, as Leo Marx has demonstrated, know better. They recognize that, beautiful as nature admittedly is, each ripple has a meaning precisely the opposite of that ascribed to it by the rapturously picturesque imagination of the inexperienced traveler: that a "pretty" ripple on the water may be the surface manifestation of a hidden danger.

This insight is exemplified in Huck's famous incantation to the Mississippi River sunrise. Familiar as it is to all readers of the book, it is worth reproducing here, if only to dramatize how distinct Huck's vision is from Shillaber's and Aldrich's boy, and from the similar morning hymn in *Tom Sawyer:*

Next we slid into the river and had a swim, so as to freshen up and cool off; then we set down on the sandy bottom where the water was about knee-deep, and watched the daylight come. Not a sound anywheres—perfectly still— just like the whole world was asleep, only sometimes the bullfrogs a-cluttering, maybe. The first thing you see, looking away over the water, was a kind of dull line—that was the woods on t'other side; you couldn't make nothing else out; then a pale place in the sky; then more paleness spreading around; then the river softened up away off, and waren't black any more, but gray; you could see little dark spots drifting along ever so far away—trading scows, and such things . . . and by and by you could see a streak on the water which you know by the look of the streak that there's a snag there in a swift current which breaks on it and makes that streak look that way; and you see the mist curl up off of the water, and the east reddens up, and the river, and you make out a log cabin in the edge of the woods, away on the bank on t'other side of the river, being a woodyard, likely, and piled by them cheats so you can throw a dog through it anywheres; then the nice breeze springs up, and comes fanning you from over there, so cool and fresh and sweet to smell on account of the woods and the flowers; but sometimes not that way, because they've left dead fish laying around, gars and such, and they do get pretty rank; and next you've got the full day, and everything smiling in the sun, and the song-birds just going it!   [*13*, 163–64]

Huck's account incorporates many of the most familiar words and metaphors that a half-baked aesthete would use. The world is "perfectly still," the "nice breeze" blows "cool and fresh and sweet," everything is "smiling in the sun." Moreover, the boy does not always make the precise observation that distinguishes the realistic from the sentimental onlooker. His description is full of approximations: "sometimes," "maybe," "ever so far away," a "kind of dull line." In spite of this, there is the ring of authenticity to this image of nature that is simply not there to such a degree in other boys' books.

Primarily, this is achieved through the vernacular language which here, as everywhere in *Huckleberry Finn*, strikes the ear with the freshness of a real boy talking out loud. Twain has written not an interior monologue but an exterior one. Rhetoric (though of a special sort, not stream-of-conscious feeling) secretly organizes Huck's story from beginning to end. Using his own unliterary words (all part of what present-day pedagogues would call Huck's "active vocabulary"), the boy makes the whole scene actual to the reader. It is as if we were there watching day break with Huck as the initiated commentator at our side interpreting the vague sights and sounds. His eye, like the pilot's, picks out the snag in the current; his nose does not ignore the rotting fish. Knowledge of the ways of woodyard operators provides a humorous touch, serving the same function as the "petrified sandwich" in the description of the Neckar, but doing so with no jarring sense of incongruity. The boy is obviously well aware of evil and danger in the river world, but he is equally, and perhaps more, alive to beauty and serenity. Both qualities are part of life which the boy accepts because he is part of the natural setting.

Huck participates in his world; the other heroes of nineteenth-century juvenile fiction merely inhabit theirs. His descriptions therefore reflect intimate personal knowledge of nature in all its aspects. "We had the sky up there, all speckled with stars," he tells us at one point, "and we used to lay on our backs and look up at them, and discuss about whether they was made or just happened. Jim he allowed they was made, but I allowed they happened; I judged it would have took too long to *make* so many. Jim said the moon could a laid them; well, that looked kind of reasonable, so I didn't say nothing against it, because I've seen a frog lay most as many, so of course it could be done. We used to watch the stars that fell, too, and see them streak down. Jim allowed they'd got spoiled and was hove out of the nest" (*13*, 165–66).

Jim is a direct descendant of Uncle Dan'l of the opening scene of *The Gilded Age,* and he and Huck make ideal instruments for Twain in passages such as this one. The childlike Negro and the acute, unlettered boy communicate love of their physical world without recourse to the romantic vocabulary Twain had felt constrained to use when writing in his own voice. Their natural sense of irony, too, undercuts emotion. Thus just as the reader is touched by Huck's appreciation of life's limitless fecundity, the possibility of sentimentality is quickly destroyed by Jim's barnyard explanation. The combination of innocence and experience which the boy and the runaway slave invariably exhibit in *Huckleberry Finn* is the appropriate embodiment of the unity of thought and emotion Twain himself was vainly trying to capture in *Tom Sawyer* and *Life on the Mississippi*. Huck's particular kind of innocent eye combines the experience of the pilot with the emotion of the passenger. The happy result is an image of the river and of the entire natural world that is for once true to Twain's artistic vision.

There is, of course, another dimension to Huck's river world. This is an aspect which the boy, sensitive as he is to physical beauty, does not understand—or, if he does, cannot voice. Nature is the appropriate though treacherous home of "a community of saints" on a raft. But it is also geography and the environment that guarantees defeat for Huck and Jim. Not simply a producer of floods and fogs, which play their part in making escape impossible, the river is the moving representation of a universe so constructed that Huck's quest for freedom cannot succeed. The Mississippi runs south; this geographical detail lurks in the reader's mind throughout the later chapters of *Huckleberry Finn*, though Huck himself appears unaware of the way geography and society conspire to thwart him and Jim.

Twain's discovery of the function the great river plays as fate in *Huckleberry Finn* may have been largely subconscious. Certainly, the story's ending draws attention away from, rather than to, this dimension of Huck's odyssey. But in stories written partly for children an author's threshold of awareness of symbolism is often difficult to determine, and if the Mississippi is a shadowy symbol, nonetheless it is always there. In the huge brown stream Twain has found an appropriate representation for his growing sense—already hinted at in *Tom Sawyer* and brought out explicitly in *The Prince and the Pauper*—of an environment that surrounds, threatens, and ultimately stifles the freedom of boyhood. His sense of irony must surely have recognized how neatly the Mississippi served a triple purpose in his story: not only as vehicle for a boy's escape from "sivilization" and a thread uniting a string of picaresque adventures but as the symbol of environmental determinism, the river is "a strong brown god" in Huck's world.

Huckleberry Finn derives much of its unique power as pastoral poem from "the immediacy of the heard voice" of a boy.[25] The same is true of the novel's achievement as social history. As Twain makes Huck the alembic through which is filtered a series of impressions of the natural world, so in similar fashion Huck's innocent eye and his unspoken audible voice are made delicate instruments for registering social truth.

Twain's intentions in this direction do not clearly emerge until Huck is well along on his journey with Jim. The opening section—that is, the first sixteen chapters, evidently completed in 1876—has scarcely more social commentary than the early parts of *Tom Sawyer*, of which it is an extension in spirit. It is only after the quitting of Jackson's Island and, more specifically, after the ramming of the raft that Huck's adventures differ radically from Tom's. From that point almost to the end Huck is thrown into one new social milieu after another, always with adults, and his story thereby enters a realm entirely unlike that of any other nineteenth-century boy's story.

25. In Lionel Trilling's phrase: *The Liberal Imagination*, p. 119.

Until recently, most knowledgeable readers of Mark Twain had accounted for this shift in emphasis of *Huckleberry Finn* in terms of an imaginative response to the trip back to the Mississippi haunts of his youth which Twain made in the spring of 1882. Undoubtedly, this return to the River, which resulted in the later chapters of *Life on the Mississippi,* made a deep and melancholy impression on his mind. But it did not basically alter the structure of the novel. Walter Blair's painstaking reconstruction of the writing of *Huckleberry Finn* now makes clear that before he traveled south Twain already had in mind using Huck as social reporter. Though the trip did refill his "tank," he had already decided where this adventure story was to go. Huck's voyage, like his creator's, was to carry him down the river into a world complex enough in its social strata to delight a modern sociologist. As it turns out, Huck is a pretty fair amateur sociologist himself.

The copious notes Twain made for *Huckleberry Finn* show him drawing upon his own memories and upon his reading in the Western humorists and local colorists in the effort to chronicle definitively the folkways of his childhood. These jottings itemize many incidents in the final narrative, many more which never saw print. A random selection suggests the range of Twain's recall:

> Negro campmeeting & sermon—"see dat sinner how he run" . . .
> The country cotillion. The horse trade. Country quilting. Candy pulling . . .
> Country funeral . . .
> Duel with rifles. A village graveyard . . .
> A lynching scene. A wake. . . .
> HOUSE-RAISING. *Beef-shooting.* Debating society.
> Quilting. The world of gossip /of/ 75 yrs ago, that lies silent, stitched into quilt by hands that long ago lost their

145

taper & silkiness & eyes & face their beauty, & all gone
down to dust & silence; & to indifference to all gossip . . .
Look through notebook & turn everything in.[26]

In Huck, Twain has the ideal reporter of that bygone social
order. Simply as an unsentimental describer of the villages
themselves, Huck outstrips Twain himself. As proof, take these
two impressions of an Arkansas hamlet. The first, seen by
Twain's unaided eye, is Helena, Arkansas.

> There were several rows and clusters of shabby frame
> houses, and a supply of mud sufficient to insure the town
> against a famine in that article for a hundred years; for the
> overflow had but lately subsided. There were stagnant
> ponds in the streets, here and there, and a dozen rude
> scows were scattered about, lying aground wherever they
> happened to have been when the waters drained off and
> people could do their visiting and shopping on foot once
> more . . . Plank sidewalks on stilts four feet high were
> still standing; the broad sidewalks on the ground level
> were loose and ruinous—a couple of men trotting along
> them could make a blind man think a cavalry charge was
> coming . . .   [12, 259–61]

Here is Huck's impression of a town that might also have been
Helena:

> The stores and houses were most all old, shackly, dried-up
> frame concerns that hadn't even been painted; they were
> set up three or four feet above ground on stilts, so as to be
> out of reach of the water when the river was overflowed.
> The houses had little gardens around them, but they didn't
> seem to raise hardly anything in them but jimpson-weeds,
> and sunflowers, and ash piles, and old curled-up boots and

26. *Mark Twain at Work,* pp. 64–67, 75–76.

shoes, and pieces of bottles, and rags, and played-out tin-
ware . . .

All the streets and lanes was just mud, they warn't
nothing else *but* mud—mud as black as tar and nigh about
a foot deep in some places, and two or three inches deep in
all the places. The hogs loafed and grunted around every-
wheres. You'd see a muddy sow and a litter of pigs come
lazying along the street and whollop herself right down in
the way, where folks had to walk around her, and she'd
stretch out and shut her eyes and wave her ears whilst the
pigs was milking her, and look as happy as if she was on
salary.   [*13*, 192–94]

One of these descriptions is dead, the other is alive. In his
own person as famous traveler and writer of humorous memoirs, Twain used words and phrases that are tired. The one bit
of originality—the blind man's impression of the noisy side-
walk—is the lame hyperbole of a professional funny man.
Huck's scene, on the contrary, is impregnated with his own
vigor and humor. The words themselves are instinct with boyish imagination: "shackly," the sow that "whollops herself
right down in the way." Twain looks at Helena through the
blasé eyes of a traveler who must "do" the scene for his book.
Huck speaks to our ear, so that we are transported directly into
the village on the strength of his boyish language.

But Huck Finn is much more than an acute observer of the
seedy side of the antebellum South. His journey with a runaway
slave involves him deeply with an order that is aristocratic,
slave-holding, and "cultured," as well as shackly and shiftless.
This introduction to the whole range of Southern life—which a
vagabond boy in a small town north of St. Louis would not
normally know—constitutes Huck's social initiation. If by "initiation" one means a maturing experience which teaches a

147

young person what it means to be adult, this social introduction of Huck's is the most profound and, as it turns out, the most permanent change he undergoes. Long before he first steps on the stage in *Tom Sawyer,* "dressed in the cast-off clothes of full-grown men," Huck's life with Pap in the tanyard has made him wise to the vagaries of human nature and conduct. Similarly, Huck seems always to have understood and appreciated the natural world about him in a fashion unknown to other boys; his invocation of dawn on the river simply illustrates intimate knowledge already acquired. But a growing awareness of social fact is something we witness Huck in the act of experiencing for the first time. This widening and deepening of his social imagination prepares the way for the later awakening of Huck's moral imagination. Both dimensions of Huck's initiation are more violent and disheartening than the similar experiences of Tom Sawyer and Prince Edward. A principal reason for this is that the boy himself reports step by step his "downward path to wisdom."

Even before Huck learns for himself the moral implications of slavery he discovers that his life is controlled by an aristocracy. Its first representative is Judge Thatcher. When Huck goes to relinquish his share of the treasure—the first step in Huck's separation from society—the good Judge cannot at first understand. "He studied a while, and then he says: 'Oho-o! I think I see. You want to *sell* all your property to me—not give it. That's the correct idea.' Then he wrote something on a paper and read it over, and says: 'There; you see it says "for a consideration". That means I have bought it of you and paid you for it. Here's a dollar for you. Now you sign it.' So I signed it, and left" (*13,* 23). At this point the reader cannot be positive of the Judge's greedy selfishness, even though Miss Watson's flirtation with the slave-trader's offer makes us suspicious of even the nicest folks in St. Petersburg. But if the Judge is not cheating Huck, at least the scene alerts us to the possibility of greed

148

as social motive—a possibility abundantly realized later in the two pseudo-noblemen and others during the Wilks episode.

The Grangerfords are Southern aristocrats on a far larger scale than Judge Thatcher. In many ways they exhibit the classic virtues of gentry. The Colonel and his handsome family are kind to strangers, proud, church-going (though hardly pious), and their home is a revelation of luxury and culture to the boy from the tannery. Huck's account of the Grangerford living room is, of course, an ironic masterpiece, for the credulous boy cannot perceive, though he faithfully reports, their provincial taste.

But he can see the consequences of their pride. At the height of the feud Huck crouches in a tree and hears Southern gentlemen running along the bank, shouting "Kill them, kill them!" as they murder a thirteen-year-old boy in the water. Huck is revolted. "It made me so sick I most fell out of the tree. I ain't a-going to tell *all* that happened—it would make me sick again if I was to do that" (*13*, 160). Even more poignantly than the shooting of old Boggs, Buck's death teaches Huck the callous inhumanity underlying the Southern aristocratic code. It is significant, moreover, that although Twain makes a young boy the victim of thoughtless butchery, he avoids oversentimentalizing Buck by reporting the event through the eye of another boy who has already seen much of death—and is to see more.

Nearly all the pride, greed, and inhumanity of the well-born folk Huck meets along the river come to focus in one institution. Slavery pervades Huck's world, reaching even to the raft. For it is on that haven of liberty and fraternity that Huck must decide for himself whether to accept the moral implications of Jim's flight for freedom.

There are two events which make Huck realize that Jim is more valuable to him as a person than all the laws and standards of society. The first is the practical joke Huck plays on Jim in the fog. But it is the second proof of Jim's humanity that finally impels the white boy to make his renunciation, "All right, then, I'll *go* to hell." That is the night when Jim, having taken his friend's turn at the steering oar, sits moaning to himself. "I knowed what it was about," Huck observes. "He was thinking about his wife and his children, away up yonder, and he was low and homesick . . . and I do believe he cared just as much for his people as white folks does for their'n. It don't seem natural, but I reckon it's so. He was often moaning and mourning that way nights, when he judged I was asleep, and saying, 'Po' little 'Lizabeth! po' little Johnny! it's mighty hard; I spec' I ain't ever gwine see you no mo', no mo'! He was a mighty good nigger, Jim was" (13, 215). Then follows Jim's touching account (which Twain took from his notebook) of his slapping of his deaf child. It is only after this display of the Negro's remorse (the most poignant of all human feelings for Mark Twain) that Huck decides to defy even his own conscience and steal Jim out of slavery.

One reason why children—Buck Grangerford in one case, Jim's little deaf daughter in another—play important supporting roles to Huck Finn is that Twain believed they would help Huck dramatize social and moral issues in a novel intended to be read by boys and girls as well as by adults. The writer employs much the same strategy in delineating another facet of Southern society as Huck experiences it. That is the sentimental veneer of "culture" which overlies and attempts to justify the lives of the slave-holding gentility. Specimens of this cultural veneer are everywhere. The wrecked steamboat on which the thieves are trapped is named the *Walter Scott*, which inevitably calls to mind the semifacetious passage in *Life on the Mississippi* attributing the Civil War to the author of *Ivanhoe*. The literary and artistic remains of Emmaline Grangerford are further relics of Southern culture. They mightily impress young Huck, but even he gets the "fan-tods" after reading too much of their lugubrious sorrow.

150

The most important purveyor of literary culture in *Huckleberry Finn* is Tom Sawyer. The game of robbers Tom organizes in the spirit of *Don Quixote* seems in the opening chapters of no more significance than the Robin Hood fantasies of the earlier novel: Tom's imagination is demonstrated, as are the bookish sources of the games he leads, and Huck's mixed awe and disgust at the complicated sport. When, for instance, Tom's gang ambushes the "crowd of Spaniards and Arabs" that turns out to be a primer class, Huck reacts characteristically. Distrustful of the whole affair, he wants nevertheless to see camels and elephants, so he participates in the raid and is disenchanted. "I didn't see no di'monds, and I told Tom Sawyer so" (*13*, 18). On a small scale, this is the pattern of Huck's life.

Such harmless pranks accumulate, in retrospect, wider moral significance by the time Huck has encountered some real robbers and some fake aristocrats. The experience of pillage, murder, and traduction which the men on the *Walter Scott* initiate and the Grangerfords, the Duke and Dauphin, and Colonel Sherburn continue is thus tied to the innocent games of Tom Sawyer. All these activities, Twain suggests, *seem* to be romantic and glorious, for history and literature have thrown a mantle of appeal over them. Essentially, however, they are nothing less than cruel invasions of human dignity. Stealing little children's doughnuts and hymn books is no more defensible because it imitates a boy's version of Cervantes than is the skullduggery of the Duke and Dauphin because they are acting like real kings and noblemen of the past. "I don't say that ourn is lambs because they ain't, when you come right down to the cold facts . . . All I say is, kings is kings, and you got to make allowances. Take them all around, they're a mighty ornery lot" (*13*, 214). The "Moralist of the Main" is still at work in *Huckleberry Finn*, though he has picked up some fresh targets since writing *The Prince and the Pauper* and uses juvenile characters more subtly than he had in "Those Blasted Children."

151

The place where Tom's apparently innocent bookishness is most conspicuously connected to the other, more adult, manifestations of Southern "culture" is at Uncle Silas' farm. The elaborate, drawn-out tomfoolery there, which has so distressed modern critics, surrounds the "escape" of Jim with the aura of Baron Trenck, Casanova, "Benvenuto Chelleeny," and Henri IV. It is still cruel sport. Tom, knowing all the while Miss Watson has freed her slave, insists on doing things the "moral" way, according to the "best authorities." Huck has too much common sense to understand what Tom is about. "Picks is the thing, moral or no moral" is his reply to historical precedent. "I don't care shucks for the morality of it, nohow. When I start in to steal a nigger, or a watermelon, or a Sunday-school book, I ain't no ways particular how it's done so it's done" (13, 341).

Reversing the meaning of "morality" here is ironic, exposing the whole structure of romantic literature of the aristocratic European past as false, evil, and inhumane. Furthermore, it illuminates the meaning and extent of Huck Finn's initiation into the society of the South and its values. The boy has seen gentlemen and would-be noblemen behave with callous disregard of human feeling. He has experienced slavery itself as the incarnation of human greed and cruelty. And he has been exposed to a superficial literary tradition which attempts to justify the first two crimes. Emmaline Grangerford and Tom Sawyer are simply two innocent adolescents, yet their demonstration of the pitiful moral inadequacies of romanticism as a guide to genteel living is part of the moral daguerreotype Mark Twain has made of his South. In that picture Twain places childish characters prominently in the foreground. Primarily Huck himself as the innocently experienced narrator, but also Buck and Emmaline Grangerford, Jim's little deaf 'Lizabeth, Tom Sawyer, the innocently evil boy mastermind— all of these children play a part in a novel which soon ceases to be primarily an adventure story for boys but never ceases trying to reach both boys and grown-ups.

Not only is *Adventures of Huckleberry Finn* a richer "boy's book" than those written by Twain's contemporaries, highbrow or low, it is also the climax and summation of Mark Twain's own career to 1885. Within the loose and accommodating framework of the picaresque tale he was able to incorporate the astringent social satire of his newspaper pieces, to extend his critique of a money-centered society back in time from the post-Civil War milieu of *The Gilded Age* to the prewar world of his own boyhood, and to carry a third boy through the maturing process of violent immersion in adult affairs. In his young hero Twain created a figure reminiscent of Thomas Jefferson Snodgrass, Jim Wolf, and, strangely enough, of Prince Edward of England. For Jim, Twain drew upon his earlier sketch of the kindly, superstitious Negro, Uncle Dan'l. From *Tom Sawyer* he drafted characters, the first and final movements of the plot of *Huckleberry Finn,* and the inspiration to look again at boyhood as one version of the American success story. Around the whole he wrapped a narrative technique he first discovered in the "Boy's Manuscript."

Adventures of Huckleberry Finn is not, however, simply an abstract of Twain's career as a novelist. A good deal of its perennial and puzzling appeal may be explained by the author's personal life during the seven years of the book's gestation, by the various traditions of juvenile fiction available to him, and by comparison with earlier works of Twain. Nevertheless, an essential, elusive quality remains. Any honest assessment of "Huck Finn's Autobiography" must confront this mysterious element.

One way to formulate an answer to the enigma of the novel's hold upon the imagination is to accept and explore Lionel

Trilling's statement of its genius. "One can read it at ten," Trilling writes, "and then annually ever after, and each year find that it is as fresh as the year before, that it has changed only in becoming somewhat larger." [27] The prime reason for this cumulative growth in appreciation is that Huck Finn's Autobiography seeks to satisfy, at the same moment that it incarnates, a deep-seated urge for freedom. In a comprehensive manner, it is consummately an "escape" story. "Huck is forever lighting out," one critic has observed, and in this respect Huck repeats the pattern of most universal books about childhood. Like *Treasure Island, Alice in Wonderland,* and *The Jungle Book,* it answers a perennial human wish to get away, to be totally free of restrictions. Huck Finn's prototype was Mark Twain's model for the free individual. "In *Huckleberry Finn* I have drawn Tom Blankenship exactly as he was," Twain remarks in his *Autobiography.* "He was ignorant, unwashed, insufficiently fed; but he had as good a heart as ever any boy had. His liberties were totally unrestricted. He was the only really independent person—boy or man—in the community . . ." [28] For many youthful readers this dimension of escape—Huck's freedom to run away from it all, from parents, starched collars, regular hours, and spelling books—is the source of their delight in the novel. Clearly, Twain intended this reaction.

But the adventure story for boys which he started writing burgeoned soon into escape literature of a different sort. What commences as flight from a Sunday School "sivilization" turns into a desperate retreat from society itself. The grim events of Huck's journey down the river of experience (Philip Young reminds us that he sees thirteen corpses) reinforce as they broaden this boy's grounds for secession. Each of Huck's sym-

27. Trilling, p. 108.
28. *Mark Twain's Autobiography* (New York and London, Harper and Brothers, 1924), 2, 174.

bolic deaths and rebirths—the fake murder in Pap's cabin, the endless aliases, including the ultimate one "Tom Sawyer"—separates him from a world which he and Jim try desperately and in vain not to accept. Lighting out for the "Territory" is Huck's despairing response to loss of freedom in this area, just as "sliding out and sleeping in the woods" answers his anarchic needs at a simpler level.

Still another reading of *Huckleberry Finn* as an escape story will occur to many adult readers, as it has to Philip Young. Right from the early moment where Huck looks down on the sleeping village of St. Petersburg, his imagination seeking out forms of sadness, suffering, and death in the few blinking lights still burning below, Twain's novel records the history of a boy morbidly fascinated by death. "I heard an owl, away off, who-whooing about somebody that was dead, and a whippowill and a dog crying about somebody that was going to die," Huck reports; "and the wind was trying to whisper something to me, and I couldn't make out what it was, and so it made the cold shivers run over me" (*13*, 4). This theme echoes again and again through Huck's story, sounding with unmistakable insistence at the moment Huck climbs over the stile at Uncle Silas' farm.

> When I got there it was all still and Sunday-like, and hot and sunshiny—the hands was gone to the fields; and there was them kind of faint dronings of bugs and flies in the air that makes it seem so lonesome and like everybody's dead and gone; and if a breeze fans along and quivers the leaves, it makes you feel mournful, because you feel like its spirits whispering—spirits that's been dead ever so many years—and you always think they're talking about *you*. As a general thing it makes a body wish *he* was dead, too, and done with it all . . .

I went around and clumb over the back stile by the ash-hopper, and started for the kitchen. When I got a little ways, I heard the dim hum of a spinning-wheel wailing along up and sinking along down again; and then I knowed for certain I wished I was dead—for that *is* the lonesomest sound in the whole world. [*13*, 303–4]

In *Tom Sawyer* this melancholy note of eerie mystery was introduced, as in the graveyard scene, simply for authentic superstitious atmosphere. So, too, earlier, in *The Gilded Age*. Here, however, Huck's sensitivity to death and the possibility of dying is of a different order of intensity. One may hesitate to accept Young's explanation of Huck's raft-borne journey down the smooth, silent river as the metaphor of a death-wish. Still, one source of the novel's imaginative vitality is the tension that develops between a vital, discerning, humorous boy and the progressive fixation of that boy's healthy mind upon ghosts, death, and the pleasures of dying. Conceivably, if not the river then the "Territory" is Mark Twain's unconscious synonym for death.

If so, this is further proof that the moment of Huck's arrival at Uncle Silas' stile is the climax and turning point of the novel. Not only does it depict the moment of greatest tension between the living boy and his preoccupation with symbols of death, but it is also the point of Huck's maximum moral awareness. His "yaller dog" conscience has been conquered only a page or two earlier; he is prepared to "go to hell" for Jim. Instead, he is ignominiously reborn as "Tom Sawyer" and submits to the Evasion, thereby surrendering the moral maturity so painfully picked up on the river. Having tried to escape from Miss Watson and from an avaricious, slave-holding society, Huck now tries to escape from his own moral imagination. This reversion to moral naiveté is another of the levels on which *Huckleberry Finn* explores ambiguously the linked themes of freedom and escape.

156

The key to Huck Finn's relapse into immaturity is Tom Sawyer, for it is to oblige Tom that Huck goes along with the elaborate and degrading stunt of "freeing" Jim. But, as Leo Marx has pointed out, the ethic under which Huck and Jim have lived on the raft makes inevitable this capitulation. When the Duke and Dauphin settle their first quarrel on board the raft, Huck is delighted, "because it would 'a' been a miserable business to have any unfriendliness on the raft; for what you want, above all things, on a raft, is for everybody to be satisfied, and feel right and kind towards the others" (*13*, 174). This is Huck's creed of social harmony, the fruit of his initiation, and the most sweeping generalization about life he ever comes to. "I hadn't no objections," he says of the con-men masquerading as nobility, " 'long as it would keep peace in the family . . . If I never learnt nothing else out of pap, I learnt that the best way to get along with his kind of people is to let them have their own way." Huck Finn lives by this ethic. It governs his friendships, his lies, his aliases, indeed, all his personal relationships. It is, in fact, at the heart of his appeal as a character.

Where Huck fails is in adapting his creed to the changing conditions of his environment. He applies the ethics of tolerance and appeasement not only to strangers, frauds, and deadbeats but to his friend Tom Sawyer, with whom he cannot be for a moment without assuming the subordinate position. Assenting good-humoredly to the Evasion, with all that it implies about Jim as a human being, seems little different to Huck than letting the two rascals on the raft call themselves Duke and Dauphin. Evidently he does not recognize this involves accepting responsibility for Tom's romantic game of casual cruelty. Though, shortly before, Huck was willing "to go to hell" for Jim's sake, now he cannot see that his moral duty is telling Tom to go to the same place. Hence the appropriateness of Huck's final alias. He has achieved the ultimate ironic escape—out of his own social and moral identity into the pro-

6.

On the Trail of Success

"DEAR CHARLEY," TWAIN WROTE his business manager in the summer of 1884, "Send to me, right away, a book by *Lieut. Col. Dodge U.S.A.*, called '25 Years on the Frontier'—or some such title—I don't remember just what. Maybe it is '25 Years Among the Indians', or maybe '25 Years in the Rocky Mountains' . . . I want several other *personal narratives* of life & adventure out yonder on the Plains & in the Mountains, if you can run across them—especially life *among the Indians*. See what you can find. I mean to take Huck Finn out there." [1]

This enthusiastic note came in July from Quarry Farm, where the Clemenses, as usual, were spending the summer high on a hill overlooking Elmira. At this point *Adventures of Huckleberry Finn* was finished; publication (which would come in February) awaited the successful efforts of Webster's subscription salesmen. Meanwhile, Twain was anxious to begin another book. As had been the case in 1876, exhilaration at concluding one novel gave him the itch to start a sequel, and just as he had launched *Huckleberry Finn* in the wake of *Tom Sawyer* so now he hoped to capitalize on his own and his audience's interest with a quick successor to "Huck Finn's Autobiography."

History, however, did not repeat itself. A package of "Injun books" duly arrived at Elmira, and Twain began to work up

1. Webster, *Mark Twain, Business Man*, pp. 264–65.

the Western background for his story which, as he planned it, was to take his boys to a different part of the West than that recalled in *Roughing It*. But evidently he had deceived himself; his "tank" was empty. On September 1 he confessed to Webster, "This is the first summer which I have lost. I haven't a paragraph to show for my 3-months' working-season." [2] It was five years before Twain actually got down to writing "Huck Finn and Tom Sawyer among the Indians," and he never completed the story. Only nine chapters of the boys' adventures in the wild West had been put to paper by 1889, when his interest flagged or was diverted. Ironically, he had the chapters set up on the Paige typesetter, "that baby with the Gargantuan appetite" for swallowing his dollars. These galleys exist today in the Mark Twain Papers in California, mute evidence both of a truncated literary career and of one cause of that failure. [3]

Though it was not then apparent, the major phase of Twain's life as a writer was already past when he mailed the letter to Webster. In the field of fiction, nothing he wrote after *Huckleberry Finn* came up to its imaginative level. Moreover, simply as prose stylist Twain had by 1885 done his finest work—in the opening sections of *Roughing It* and *Life on the Mississippi*. As a pioneer explorer of boyhood, too, his best writing was completed. The fiction of the middle years—that is, of the period 1886–98—grows out of the earlier work and repeats many of its themes, but in none of the novels of this period, except *Joan of Arc*, does he place a child in center stage. The heroes of *A Connecticut Yankee in King Arthur's Court* and *Pudd'nhead Wilson* are both grown men, and if they remind us of Tom Sawyer, they are nonetheless not children.

Boys figure, to be sure, in many of the shorter pieces. Twain

2. MT to C. L. Webster (Sept. 1, 1884), in MTP. © Mark Twain Company.

3. The manuscript of "Huck Finn and Tom Sawyer among the Indians," except for three pages I discovered in the Collection of the Mark Twain Library and Memorial Commission in Hartford, has been lost.

did not forget Tom, Huck, and Nigger Jim, the favorite trio who had earned him fame and fortune. *Tom Sawyer, Abroad* (1893) and "Tom Sawyer, Detective" (1896) are two tales he actually published, and there were others that were begun though never completed. "Huck Finn and Tom Sawyer among the Indians" and a later, longer fragment entitled "Tom Sawyer's Conspiracy" are the most interesting as well as the most ambitious of several abortive attempts to repeat the successful pattern of the past.

In his Notebooks, for instance, Twain left a string of suggestions for other narratives (all of them undeveloped) that would involve his boys. As early as 1881 he wrote James Osgood to send him several of Harper's dime-novel sea stories, including "Green Hand," "Sailor's Sweetheart," "Tom Cringle's Log," and "The Cruise of the Midge." Possibly these were for Susy and Clara; more likely, however, they were for their father, for soon afterward Twain started a Tom-and-Huck story concerning an elaborate boys' naval battle on rafts in the river. Tom Sawyer, of course, played the part of Lord Nelson, while Huck narrated and a small boy named Dick Fisher commented sarcastically on the nautical proceedings.[4] In the spring of 1885, as *Huckleberry Finn* began selling well, Twain was full of ideas for other boys' stories. "Put Huck & Tom & Jim through my Mo. campaign," he advised himself at one point. "Make a kind of Huck Finn narrative on a boat—let him ship as Cabin boy & another boy as cub pilot—& so put the great river & its bygone ways into history in form of a story" was another promising germ for a story. Later, possibly under the stimulus of starting *A Connecticut Yankee in King Arthur's Court*, he outlined still another project—"A story wherein the pantaletted little children talked the stilted big-word sentimental hifalutin of Walter Scott's heroes & the other & older novels (Pamela

4. MT to J. R. Osgood, May 23, 1881, in MTP. Photostat of fragment also in MTP; original in private collection.

&c).".[5] None of these jottings came to anything. In fact, even *Tom Sawyer, Abroad,* which DeVoto properly terms the best of the shorter works of this period, breaks off suddenly in the middle of the boys' journey, as if Twain had grown tired or bored. The evidence is overwhelming that after his fiftieth birthday, Twain was a writer who had increasing difficulty doing sustained work.

The personal reasons for this situation are not hard to reconstruct. For one thing, he ceased being a writer by vocation during these years. Affairs of the Charles L. Webster Company appropriated more and more of his time and attention. Subscription publishing in the 1880's was a big-time operation, requiring a steady stream of best sellers, mass publicity techniques, and great expenditures of money. *The Personal Memoirs of U. S. Grant* alone netted the Company $150,000 and Twain himself—not the safest judge, to be sure—estimated his publishing house's assets in 1886 at half a million dollars.[6] "Money Pours In—and Out" is the title of the chapter on this period in the life of *Mark Twain, Business Man.* The Paige typesetter was only one of a number of expensive sidelines to book publishing which Twain maintained. Early in the nineties he even toyed with the notion of starting a magazine of his own, though at the same time he was complaining, "I am terribly tired of business. I think I am by nature and disposition unfit for it."[7] It was amid hectic conditions that *A Connecticut Yankee; Tom Sawyer, Abroad; Pudd'nhead Wilson;* and most of the other stories of the period were composed. If these novels and stories have neither the imaginative intensity of *Huckleberry Finn* nor the neat structure of *Tom Sawyer* or *The Prince and the Pauper,* a search for causes must begin in

5. Notebook 18, pp. 21, 31, and Notebook 21, typescript, p. 30, in MTP. © Mark Twain Company.
6. Webster, *Mark Twain, Business Man,* pp. 340–54.
7. Ibid., p. 353.

the writer's daily affairs. Twain had virtually relegated art to the corners of his life.

Another and more pervasive reason for his literary troubles, particularly in relation to writing about children, lay in the spreading pessimism of his thought. After finishing *A Connecticut Yankee* in 1889, he wrote Howells that if he could do the book over again, "there wouldn't be so many things left out. They burn in me; & keep multiplying & multiplying; but now they can't ever be said. And besides, they would require a library—& a pen warmed-up in hell." [8] This sense of outrage at human folly and evil erupts again and again in his fiction during these years. Hank Morgan's uncharacteristic diatribes against the knights and the Church, Pudd'nhead Wilson's Calendar (equally out of keeping with the character of this small-town lawyer who hopes finally to be accepted as one of the boys), "The Man That Corrupted Hadleyburg," "Captain Stormfield's Visit to Heaven" (endlessly rewritten, forever suppressed)—all reflect the increasing misanthropy. Bankruptcy and Susy's tragic death in 1896 were signal events in the most somber period of Twain's life, but they merely intensified an outlook that had already turned bleak.

Corrosive opinions about life in general and human nature in particular were nothing new to him. But as a writer of fiction he had usually been able to keep them in proximate artistic equilibrium in the earlier novels. One way this had been accomplished was by tempering with the wholesome, candid eye of childhood the private fulminations Twain felt about "the damned human race." Boyhood's perspective, consummately in *Huckleberry Finn* and successfully in *Tom Sawyer* and *The Prince and the Pauper,* had mediated between Twain's twin impulses toward savagery and sentimentality.

Now, however, he turned to writing books in which children

8. MT to W.D.H., Sept. 22, 1889, *Mark Twain–Howells Letters,* 2, 613.

either played subordinate roles to adults, as in *A Connecticut Yankee* or *Pudd'nhead Wilson,* or re-enacted boyish adventures somewhat removed from the real world of adult society, as in *Tom Sawyer, Abroad* or "Tom Sawyer, Detective." In either case, the writer's control weakened as his misanthropy often burst out of the dramatic context. Unity of effect was destroyed in the heat of such personal explosions; inevitably, fiction came to resemble tracts or parables. Twain was working in the direction of *What Is Man?,* his pessimistic "Gospel" of complete determinism, in which all pretense at fictional form is abandoned.

The combination of these social and personal perplexities had, naturally, a great deal to do with the content of Twain's writing; they affected also its form. Snatching time from an ever-accelerating round of business affairs, he took to writing quick, careless books that would bring in the money. Exploiting his reputation as America's most popular writer, then making up for this by alternately venting and suppressing his animus against the public, he was an artist at odds with himself. The pattern of his literary work was similarly chaotic. First he planned to take Huck Finn out West; then, hoping to capitalize upon the popularity of the historical romance, he turned to *A Connecticut Yankee in King Arthur's Court.* Completing this, he returned to Huck and the West, only to be diverted by the importunities of Mary Mapes Dodge (who had for years been after him to do something for the *St. Nicholas*) to write *Tom Sawyer, Abroad,* a boy's version of Jules Verne. Then, as a fad for Sherlock Holmes swept America in the early Nineties, Twain hurriedly turned out *Pudd'nhead Wilson* and, later, "Tom Sawyer, Detective." As far as one can tell from the fragmentary manuscript, "Tom Sawyer's Conspiracy" was to be yet another detective story. Sandwiched among these various bids for popularity was *Joan of Arc,* a labor of love, part history, part fiction.

Perennially careless about formal structure anyway, he indiscriminately used these conventional genres—the historical romance, the boys' adventure tale, the detective story—because they had established formulas, could be easily and rapidly (as he thought) composed, and were readily marketable. After all, he had secured the approval of the classes with *The Prince and the Pauper* and of the masses with *Huckleberry Finn*, so he could now afford to appropriate the techniques of popular fiction. Never contemptuous of the dime-novel audience, Twain genuinely preferred writing for the "Belly and the Members," as he expressed it, instead of for highbrows. It both earned more money and suited his temperament.

To say that Twain employed the forms of trashy literature does not mean that he wrote trash. In spite of manifest defects, the mark of his imagination and the cast of his vigorous thought are evident in each of the works written during these years. Furthermore, his interest in children and in their relationships with adults was still strong. The boy figures in *A Connecticut Yankee* and *Pudd'nhead Wilson* are subordinated to older characters, but they play significant roles in the action and satire. The lesser pieces, involving Tom, Huck, and Jim, re-examine old problems—for instance, environmental constraint and moral freedom, ways boys learn of the world, the importance of training in the formation of personality—which had been broached before. Some fresh answers to these questions are put forward. Moreover, in this period of general (though by no means universal) decline in Twain's control over his art we may see in the serene good humor of such a work as *Tom Sawyer, Abroad* that childhood still served him as the safest perspective from which to view the world as literary experience.

Twain's original intentions for *A Connecticut Yankee in King Arthur's Court* were, as he outlined them to "Mother" Fairbanks in 1886, for a conventional historical romance, gentle enough in tone and treatment to appeal to the same readers who had welcomed *The Prince and the Pauper*. "Of course in my story I shall leave unsmirched & unbelittled the great & beautiful *characters* drawn by the master hand of old Malory . . ." he assured her. "I am only after the *life* of that day, that is all: to picture it; to try to get into it; to see how it feels & seems. I shall hope that under my hand Sir Galahad will still remain the divinest spectre that one glimpses among the mists & twilights of Dreamland across the wastes of the centuries; and Arthur keep his sweetness & his purity." [9] Precious little remains in the finished novel of this promise of reverent and sympathetic treatment of Camelot's residents. Once Twain entered his sixth-century Dreamland and saw "how it feels & seems" to live in feudalism, his satiric impulse got the better of his desire to please readers like Mrs. Fairbanks. Consequently, Hank Morgan's visit to Arthur's kingdom turns up nearly every social shortcoming that a commonsensical and provincial Yankee of the nineteenth century could find to criticize in feudal Britain. As Hank, nicknamed the Boss, travels incognito with King Arthur through the realm (in imitation of Miles Hendon and Prince Edward), he systematically attacks the whole framework of medieval life. From the absurdly uncomfortable armor of knighthood to *droit du seigneur* to the superstitious piety of medieval Catholicism, everything out of the past is represented as either ridiculous or pernicious by the mechanic from East Hartford.

Since the Boss voices so many of the truculently nineteenth-century notions of Twain himself, the reader's temptation is to identify Hank Morgan strictly as the mouthpiece of his creator. When, for instance, Hank and King Arthur encounter a poor serf who has been out helping track down a fellow slave accused of burning a manor house, Hank is horrified at this lack of class solidarity. "It reminded me of a time thirteen

9. MT to Mrs. Fairbanks (Nov. 16, 1886), in Wecter, *Mark Twain to Mrs. Fairbanks*, p. 258.

centuries away, when the 'poor whites' of our South who were always despised and frequently insulted by the slave-lords around them . . . were yet pusillanimously ready to side with the slave-lords in all political moves for the upholding and perpetuating of slavery" (*14*, 298), he observes, and both the sentiment and phraseology are straight out of *Life on the Mississippi*. Similar confusion between Yankee speaker and Missouri accent appears at other points in the narrative, as, for example, when Hank quotes from the historian Lecky, who was (next to Robert Ingersoll) Mark Twain's favorite agnostic and iconoclast.

Hank Morgan was not meant to be Twain's mouthpiece pure and simple. Sometimes (as above) he is that; more often, however, the Boss is a fictional personage in his own right, an actor in the story and himself an object of the double-edged satire. Though Twain's chief target is sixth-century superstition, the Boss, too, is held up to laugh at; his blatantly nineteenth-century prejudices—naive scientific optimism, skepticism, and materialism—are as exaggerated as the presuppositions of the medieval mind in the Knights and in Merlin. Moreover, at the climactic Battle of the Sand Belt, in which Hank, Clarence, and the fifty-two boy cadets annihilate twenty-five thousand knights, their victory is short-lived and Pyrrhic. Trapped within the circle of rotting corpses, the Boss and his practical gadgeteers fall prey to Merlin's sabotage, signifying Twain's reluctance to settle his feud with feudalism entirely on the terms of the nineteenth century.

An even more obvious way in which Twain registers his humorous awareness of Hank's limitations, both as hero and as mouthpiece, is through one of the dominant metaphorical patterns of *A Connecticut Yankee*. This central metaphor, by which Twain seeks to give coherence to his satire, involves the child. Adult characters, as well as the eras and institutions they typify, are related to one another chiefly in the way they resemble children or adolescents. Hank Morgan himself, for instance, though a man of forty, is depicted essentially as an adolescent. He has a fifteen-year-old switchboard sweetheart back in Hartford (telephones were a great novelty in 1889). As soon as he arrives in Camelot he takes as his closest friend Clarence, a teen-ager to whom Hank teaches all the handy ways of a modern mechanical gadgeteer. In the final showdown with the massed knights and the Church, Hank gathers about himself and Clarence a little force of loyal boys and with them defeats feudalism in a debacle that reminds an adult reader of nothing so much as a small boy's dream of revenge upon a grown-up system that has frustrated him.

In the Boss' eyes, however, neither the young cadets nor himself behave like petulant kids, but the Knights of the Round Table do. After listening to their interminable bragging tales of jousts and quests, Hank is disgusted. "Many a time I had seen a couple of boys, strangers, meet by chance, and say simultaneously, 'I can lick you,' and go at it on the spot," he remarks, "but I had always imagined until now that that sort of thing belonged to children only, and was a sign and mark of childhood; but here were these big boobies sticking to it and taking pride in it clear up into full age and beyond." Then the sympathetic coda: "Yet there was something very engaging about these great simple-hearted creatures, something attractive and lovable. There did not seem to be brains enough in the entire nursery, so to speak, to bait a fish-hook with . . . There was a fine manliness observable in almost every face; and in some a certain loftiness and sweetness that rebuked your belittling criticisms and stilled them" (*14*, 21–22). This contradictory attitude of the Boss, calling the Knights immature boys and admirable men in successive breaths, typifies Twain's own ambivalent feelings about human nature as well as his muted impulse to ridicule heroes of the past.

168

Another form of his satiric metaphor is to ridicule the Knights through the eyes of other, younger characters. Hank's imagination—like his creator's—naturally thinks of young people and his eye is always aware of their presence. Hence, when he himself rides out of Arthur's castle, clad in the ridiculously uncomfortable armor of a knight, he reports quite seriously the reactions of a jeering crowd of small boys who stood at the gate. "They said 'Oh, what a guy!' And hove clods at us. In my experience boys are the same in all ages. They don't respect anything, they don't care for anything or anybody. They say 'Go up, baldhead' to the prophet going his unoffending way in the gray of antiquity; they sass me in the holy gloom of the Middle Ages; and I had seen them act in the same way in Buchanan's administration . . ." (*14*, 92). As boyish irreverence toward the past is Hank's own stance, naturally he welcomes it even though he himself is inside the armor being laughed at.

Pomposity is not the only failing childish characters help to uncover. They also dramatize the presence of organized cruelty in medieval Britain, as when the Boss and the King during their educational tour are seized and sold as slaves. On the London road the gang of slaves meet a pitiful procession. A young girl of eighteen, with a baby at her breast, is being carried by on a cart. In the wagon also is her coffin, for the young mother has stolen a piece of linen and must hang for it. Morgan and King Arthur then witness the execution.

> After his [the priest's] prayer they put the noose around the young girl's neck, and they had great trouble to adjust the knot under her ear, because she was devouring the baby all the time, wildly kissing it, and snatching it to her face and her breast, and drenching it with tears, and half moaning, half shrieking all the while, and the baby crow-

ing, and laughing, and kicking its feet with delight over what it took for romp and play. Even the hangman couldn't stand it, but turned away. [*14*, 361]

Twain has manifestly modeled this melodramatic episode upon the burning of the women heretics in *The Prince and the Pauper*. Details are as graphic as in the earlier scene, but the use of the baby here to extract every ounce of pathos from the child-mother's death is surely less convincing than was the grief of the daughters of the two Anabaptists. The shift is characteristic of Twain's dissolving sense of fictional fitness; in such details may be seen his split personality—the sardonic satirist and the soft-hearted man of feeling—in the very process of separating. Ahead in one direction lie *What Is Man?* and *The Mysterious Stranger*, in the other, "The Death Disk" and "A Horse's Tale."

Hank Morgan's mockery of knight errantry in comparing the members of the Round Table to boisterous boys is little more than a recurrent metaphor in *A Connecticut Yankee*. It is one humorous sidelight to the satire but less dramatic a use of childhood than either the urchins who derisively clod the Boss in his armor, or the baby ignorantly prattling in her mother's arms on the scaffold. Such touches prove that a childish society is not only laughable but evil. But the chief role children play in this novel is a more dramatic one than any of these. That is at the climax of the action, when the Boss, having aroused the Church's ire and brought the Interdict down on Britain, retreats to Merlin's Cave with Clarence and the fifty-two "fresh, bright, well-educated, clean-minded young British boys—none younger than fourteen, and none above seventeen years old"— to prepare for Armageddon.

"Why did you select boys?" Hank asks Clarence, who has arranged all the electrical wiring and the bombs, and has provisioned the fortress. "Because all the others were born in an atmosphere of superstition and reared in it," Clarence replies. "It is in their blood and bones. We imagined we had educated it out of them; they thought so, too; the Interdict woke them up like a thunderclap! It revealed them to themselves, and it revealed them to me, too. With boys it was different. Such as have been under our training from seven to ten years have had no acquaintance with the Church's terrors, and it was among these that I found my fifty-two" (*14*, 422).

Clarence, of course, is acting upon the enlightened notions which the Boss has drilled into him. His reactions have been learned at the "civilization-factory" where Hank turns slaves into *men*. "Training—training in everything; training is all there is *to* a person" is Hank Morgan's motto. "We speak of nature; it is folly; there is no such thing as nature; what we call by that misleading name is merely heredity and training. We have no thoughts of our own, no opinions of our own; they are transmitted to us, trained into us." Here, pretty clearly, the Boss is speaking for Twain particularly in the words that follow:

All that is original in us, [Hank continues] and therefore fairly creditable or discreditable to us, can be covered up and hidden by the point of a cambric needle, all the rest being atoms contributed by, and inherited from, a procession of ancestors that stretches back a billion years to the Adam-clam or grasshopper or monkey from whom our race has been so tediously and ostentatiously and unprofitably developed. And as for me, all that I think about in this plodding sad pilgrimage, this pathetic drift between the eternities, is to look out and humbly live a pure and high and blameless life, and save that one microscopic atom in me that is truly *me*: the rest may land in Sheol and welcome for all I care. [*14*, 150]

Such bitter words as these ring false in the mouth of the practical and optimistic young mechanic from East Hartford. But they express precisely the post-Darwinian pessimism of Twain himself. As happens increasingly in the fiction of these years, the boyish actor's mask has slipped, revealing the features of a tired and world-weary man.

Exactly how hopeless Twain's outlook becomes is revealed in the aftermath of the Battle of the Sand Belt. Ostensibly of course, Hank, Clarence, and the cadets have won a smashing victory over the forces of superstition. The adolescents have, symbolically speaking, destroyed their fathers, the old order, the authority principle; America has murdered its ancestor. But like the escape of Huck Finn the rebels' moment of victory is brief. Clarence reports the defeat that swiftly follows. "We were in a trap, you see—a trap of our own making. If we stayed where we were, our dead would kill us; if we moved out of our defenses, we should no longer be invincible. We had conquered; in turn we were conquered" (*14*, 446).

Surrounded by the stinking corpses of a dead social order, the Boss and his boys are sickened by the poisonous air. Then, as if to drive home even more ironically the novel's paradigmatic ending, Merlin the magician "disguised as a woman . . . a simple old peasant goodwife" slips into the Cave and casts a spell over the Boss. He sleeps for thirteen hundred years, awakening only to tell his story and die. If the knights are symbolic fathers, then Merlin, the incarnation of antireason, becomes the mother-figure who completes by subterfuge the defeat of boyhood's dream of revenge, reform, and escape. Lost along with boyhood are the values of the nineteenth century which Hank and his friends represent—"hard unsentimental common sense and reason" with all the social, political, and economic consequences thereof.

Lost, too, in the battle is the very principle of human freedom and self-determination. For in a world wholly determined

172

by heredity and training, even "civilization-factories" do not work. The factories themselves are blown up. Their products— "*men*" not slaves and yet not actually grown men but fresh-faced boys—are defeated by their own successful use of scientific efficiency. This ironic holocaust, like the river in *Huckleberry Finn*, is the dramatic symbol of Twain's deterministic universe. Boyhood—humanity's last, best hope for starting fresh, for living according to Enlightenment notions of reason— cannot, in spite of every mechanical invention, either rescue society or escape from it.

A Connecticut Yankee in King Arthur's Court, though not ostensibly a novel of boyhood, touches upon several of the themes already aired in *Huckleberry Finn*, and, more particularly, *The Prince and the Pauper*. Twain may originally have intended only an amusing parody of Malory's *Morte D'Arthur*, something popular and good-natured enough to prove acceptable on both sides of the Atlantic. But as the novel turned out, criticism of the English feudal tradition was far from gentle; furthermore, *A Connecticut Yankee* cut deeper into more fundamental problems of human experience than perhaps its author had planned. In the process of discovering the dimensions of his narrative, he fell back upon a familiar cast of characters to dramatize the issues that appeared. As a consquence, children, in particular teen-aged boys, provide in this novel not simply a metaphor for ridicule, but also a moral norm, an angle of vision, and, at the last, a paradigm of Twain's hardening determinism. Though essentially adult satire, *A Connecticut Yankee in King Arthur's Court* drives home its pessimistic message by means of the childish figures who embody and enact the ambiguous values in the light of which Mark Twain judges the past and its institutions.

During the summer of 1889, before *A Connecticut Yankee* was yet published, Twain finally got back to his project of taking Huck Finn and his friends out into the wild West. His timing was hardly accidental, for at this period a craze for the American West swept the country, manifesting itself in many aspects of popular life and culture. Younger readers participated in the dime-novel cult of hero-worship for Deadwood Dick—or, by now, Deadwood Dick, Jr.—that still flourished sturdily in spite of opposition from parents and pedagogues. Grown-ups who disdained Beadle and Adams nevertheless enjoyed the poems and stories of western writers like Bret Harte, Joaquin Miller, and Helen Hunt Jackson, whose *Ramona* in 1884 had been a best-seller. Twain himself, of course, had already a solid reputation as a western story-teller with *Roughing It*. In many middle-class homes there was a Rogers plaster group which illustrated western life. On the national scene, too, the West figured prominently in the news of the day. Washington, Montana, and North and South Dakota entered the Union in 1889, and Idaho and Wyoming the following year. The Battle of Wounded Knee, late in 1890, finally concluded a long series of bloody Indian uprisings that had fired the American imagination and made a culture hero of George A. Custer. Few fields in 1889 held out more promise for a writer sensitive to fashion's prevailing winds than did life on the high plains of the American West. "Huck Finn and Tom Sawyer among the Indians" was planned to cash in on this rich bonanza.

Because the story is fragmentary—Twain completed only enough of the narrative to make twenty-three galleys when set up by the Paige machine, possibly eighty or ninety book pages—"Huck Finn and Tom Sawyer among the Indians" does not reveal much that is fresh about Twain's boys. Tom is still the clever bookish organizer, whose grandiose and flattering notions about Indians are derived from Cooper's novels. Huck remains as he was at the end of his *Adventures*, quizzical and acquiescent. Jim, unfortunately, plays but a shadowy part. The author preferred, in these opening chapters, to emphasize local color and the novel appeal of western character types. Thus in the course of a truncated narrative the boys learn from a Mexican how to pack a mule, fall in with a family emigrating to Oregon, and meet a typical plainsman-trapper. There is a buffalo hunt, a raid from unfriendly Indians, a brush with some rascally white horse-thieves, a prairie cloud-burst, and, as the fragment ends, the promise of a general Indian uprising. "Note also the characteristic plan," DeVoto points out, "to get in all typical plains experiences and sights." [10]

The most striking figure in the story is Brace Johnson, the handsome plainsman under whose guidance the Mills family is venturing into the country of the "Dakotah Sioux." Beloved of Peggy Mills and idolized by everyone, this stalwart figure, a Miles Hendon in buckskins, is described by Huck in terms much like those Edward L. Wheeler once used to create Deadwood Dick. "According to my notions," Huck tells us, "Brace Johnson was a beautiful man. He was more than six foot tall, I reckon, and had broad shoulders, and he was as straight as a jackstaff, and built as thin as a race-horse. He had the steadiest eye you ever see, and a handsome face, and his hair hung all down his back, and how he ever could keep his outfit so clean and nice, I never could tell, but he did. . . . And as for strength, I never see a man that was any more than half as strong as what he was, and a most lightning marksman with a gun or a bow or a pistol. He had two long-barreled ones in his holsters, and could shoot a pipe out of your mouth, most any distance, every time, if you wanted him to." [11] Were it not for the little personal touch about Huck's pipe, this description would be pure dime-novel stereotype.

10. DeVoto, summary of plot of "Huck Finn and Tom Sawyer among the Indians," in MTP.

11. "Huck Finn and Tom Sawyer among the Indians," galley 15, in MTP. © Mark Twain Company.

More interesting than Brace's resemblance to a Beadle and Adams hero is his theology; at least, it is more interesting to Huck, who reports at some length Brace's "Injun religion" notions about God. To the young plainsman, there are actually two Gods—a Good one and a Bad one. Since the Good God is anxious to help man anyway, there is no use, Brace believes, spending time placating him. But the Bad God is someone to watch out for; "so the sensible thing was to keep promising and fussing around him all the time, and get him to let up," as Huck explains. Brace tries as devoutly as possible not to offend his Bad God, but inadvertently eats some meat on Friday, which is strictly taboo. "We had been pretty cheerful, before that," Huck relates, "galloping over them beautiful Plains, and popping at Jack rabbits and prairie dogs and all sorts of things, and snuffing the fresh air of the early mornings, and all that, and having a general good time; but it was all busted up, now, and we quit talking and got terrible blue and uneasy and scared . . ."[12]

In these passages Twain seems simply to be poking fun at both Huck's theological naiveté and Brace's aboriginal superstitions. But these latter were not an ironist's fabrications; they were bona fide details of Indian religion Twain discovered in Colonel Richard Dodge's *The Plains of the Great West* (1877) and *Our Wild Indians* (1883), the two books Twain asked Charles Webster to send him in 1884. As a matter of fact, he read widely in Western lore and tried sincerely to make "Huck Finn and Tom Sawyer among the Indians" an accurate as well as a melodramatic portrayal of the region.[13] The tone

12. Ibid., galley 16.
13. Other books Twain probably consulted include Irving's *Astoria* ("Send me Washington Irving's" is a notation Twain crossed out in the letter to Webster); Fearon's *Sketches of America: Narrative of a Journey of Five Thousand Miles through the Eastern and Western States of America*, London, 1819; Hall's *Travels in North America in the Years 1827 and 1828*, Edinburgh, 1829; Richardson's *Beyond the Mississippi: Life*

of Huck's comments suggest, moreover, that Twain himself took seriously certain aspects of Brace's "Injun religion." In his own copy of *Our Wild Indians,* for example, Twain noted with evident approval one Indian belief which he put into his young plainsman's theology. In the margin next to Dodge's discussion contrasting the red man's Great Spirit with the white man's Deity, he penciled this reaction: "Our illogical God is all-powerful in name, but impotent in fact; the Great Spirit is not all-powerful, but he does the very best he can for his injun and does it free of charge." At another point, Twain was even more emphatic. "We have to keep our God placated with prayers," he wrote in the margin, "and even then we are never sure of him—how much higher and finer is the Indian's God." [14]

In the semifinished state of Huck's story this kind of private skepticism is submerged beneath the surface of a fast-paced narrative meant mostly for boys. But Huck's artless admiration for Brace Johnson, extending to that hero's heterodoxies, hints at some revealing directions the story might have followed if it had been finished. "Huck Finn and Tom Sawyer among the Indians" is an unusually clear instance of the way Twain attempted to import into juvenile popular fiction his private philosophical problems. As before, the persona of the vagabond boy from the tanyard serves very neatly as the medium through whom to project both facets of his fiction.

In another respect, too, Huck's narrative of life among the Indians is, in spite of incompleteness, symptomatic of its author's state of mind. For these comments on Indian religious beliefs and practices reveal how influential were books on the

and Adventure on the Prairies, Mountains, and the Pacific Coast, Hartford, n.d.; and Captain Marryat's Second Series of a Diary in America, Philadelphia, 1840. These four last were owned by Twain; two of them (Fearon and Hall) bore marginalia in his hand; all were sold at auction April 10, 1951. See Mark Twain Library Auction Catalogue, in MTP.

14. Quoted in Mark Twain Library Auction Catalogue, April 10, 1951, Item 132, in MTP. © Mark Twain Company.

American West, like those of Washington Irving and Colonel Dodge, in opening up for Twain and for his readers the wholly new fields of anthropology and comparative religion. After all, Indian tribes such as Huck and Tom encounter were the nearest primitive societies Americans could read about in the 1880's and 1890's. The fact that they were fast disappearing added to their romantic appeal and made them proper topics for a commercial writer to exploit. Twain, however, saw something more in Dodge's accounts of Indian life. To one far gone in religious skepticism, as he certainly was by 1889, the primitive notions Brace Johnson has embraced provide excuse for voicing the marked relativism he himself felt. This reaction to the romance of the Plains Indian may have been idiosyncratic and conceivably unpopular; Twain may have ceased writing "Huck Finn and Tom Sawyer among the Indians" because he was not sure his audience would take to serious talk about Good Gods and Bad Gods.

If it proved somewhat risky for Twain to present realistically and sympathetically details of Indian belief, it was doubly dangerous to get involved, as Twain soon did in Huck Finn's story, in an honest portrayal of Indian behavior. Here, far more than with Brace Johnson's heresies, the requirements of plot and audience collided head on. With an eye to an exciting and characteristic action, Twain instigated a violent and, as it turned out, bloody series of adventures for Huck, Tom, and Jim. In company with the Mills family, they move far out into dangerous Indian territory. Brace, the only member of the expedition familiar with the ways of the red men, is delayed; he comes up too late to prevent a band of bloodthirsty Sioux from butchering all the male Millses and carrying off little Flaxy, Jim, and seventeen-year-old Peggy Mills. Tom and Huck escape, but when they tell Brace what has happened, the young plainsman is nearly beside himself with fear for his sweetheart, for he knows what Indians do to their female captives. In fact, the Sioux mutilated the bodies of the Mills men so horribly that, as Huck puts it, "it would not do to put it in a book." [15] Brace had given Peggy a small dirk with which to kill herself if captured. But just as the fragment breaks off, Huck finds the dirk. When he shows it to Tom, the latter cannot at first see why they must not show the knife to Brace, but must pretend that Peggy is dead. Huck hesitates to speak frankly of rape; but "at last I came out with it and then Tom was satisfied," he relates cryptically.

What "it" involved in actuality Twain knew very well from Colonel Dodge. As that veteran Indian fighter explained in *Our Wild Indians,* "Cooper, and some other novelists, knew nothing of Indian character and customs when they placed their heroines prisoners in their hands. I believe I am perfectly safe in the assertion that there is not a single wild tribe of Indians in all the wide territory of the United States which does not regard the person of the female captive as the inherent right of the captor; and I venture to assert further that, with the single exception of the lady captured by the Nez Percés, under Joseph, in Yellowstone Park, no woman has, in the last thirty years, been taken prisoner by any wild Indians who did not, as soon after as practicable, become a victim to the brutality of every one of the party of her captors." [16] At other points in his memoirs, Dodge goes into even greater detail on this score.

Given Twain's juvenile and family audience and, even more significantly, his personal reticence about sexual matters, one can sense how much more embarrassing these facts about Indian life were than mere matters of theology. Since the plot of "Huck Finn and Tom Sawyer among the Indians" is built

15. "Huck Finn and Tom Sawyer among the Indians," galley 9, MTP. © Mark Twain Company.

16. Richard I. Dodge, *Our Wild Indians* (Hartford, American Publishing Company, 1882), p. 529.

around Peggy Mills' abduction and rescue (as the narrative breaks off Brace and the two boys are still in pursuit) it seems safe to surmise that the story foundered on this rock. As far as the narrative is carried, it is an honest portrayal of life on the plains. But there were limits to Twain's forthrightness. He could perhaps reconcile tensions between his private and public views on religion, but when it came to rape and white slavery, he stopped writing. It may well have been with relief that he turned, as he soon did, to *Tom Sawyer, Abroad,* where Mary Mapes Dodge and not Colonel Dodge could be his guide on the trail of successful fiction.

Twain had better luck with his next attempt to further the adventurous careers of his three youthful villagers from St. Petersburg. *Tom Sawyer, Abroad* is scarcely longer than "Huck Finn and Tom Sawyer among the Indians," but it hangs together well enough to be called a finished piece. At any rate, Mrs. Dodge thought so, for she paid $5,000 for it and ran it in *St. Nicholas* from November 1893 to April 1894. The Clemens family had spent the summer of 1890 at Onteora in the Catskills in company with Mrs. Dodge. It was at her suggestion and for her youthful readers that *Tom Sawyer, Abroad* was written.

Most informed readers of this *nouvelle,* in some respects the most charming and poised of all Mark Twain's works about childhood, have suspected the influence of Jules Verne, in particular of *Five Weeks in a Balloon.*[17] But a nearer and more important source is to be found in the biography of her famous father which Susy, aged thirteen, wrote during 1885 and 1886. At one point in this artlessly acute sketch of Mark Twain, Susy recounts a bedtime story which her father once told his daughters. It concerned a group of children in a country schoolhouse in wintertime. The only source of heat was from a single regis-

17. See D. M. McKeithan, *Court Trials in Mark Twain and Other Essays* (The Hague, M. Nijhoff, 1958), pp. 156–68.

ter in the floor, and the big boys were mistreating the smaller children, pushing them away from the warmth. One of the bullies got his finger caught in the register. Suddenly, several of the children went out into the cold. At this point, Susy's account takes on a marked dreamlike quality.

> Then they went and borrowed quite a few baloons & went up in the air & then went up higher & higher & higher & higher & they let out a bird. The children were frozen when they put out a bird. The bird didn't know where he was & he went among the clouds, & pretty soon he came back sailing back again & they sailed & sailed & sailed & went over oceans & seas & pretty soon they landed in Africa. Quite a few plain people & a few Indians came & some lions & tigers, & the lions nibbled at the frozen children & couldn't bite them. Then a man came & said they were missionarys on the half shell & they must be thawed out so they thawed them out & pretty soon they got growed up to be women & men & were very good missionarys & converted many, & a[t] last were eaten at a barbeque—[18]

This amusing anecdote may, of course, owe something to Verne, but it conforms closely to the plot of *Tom Sawyer, Abroad* and must at least be accounted an intermediate source. Since this story was Twain's first actual appearance in *St. Nicholas,* he might reasonably be excepted to employ a plot which had demonstrated appeal for his own daughters. After all, the Clemens children had been accepted perfectly seriously as literary arbiters since the writing of *The Prince and the Pauper.*

Twain's decision to send the three "errornorts," Tom, Huck, and Jim, traveling over Africa, Egypt, and part of the Holy

18. Unpublished manuscript of Susy Clemens' biography of Mark Twain, pp. 81–82, in the Collection of C. Waller Barrett, New York City. © Mark Twain Company.

Land was prompted also by memory of his own hugely successful *Innocents Abroad*. From the *Quaker City* excursion,
Twain knew something of the Near Eastern terrain at first
hand. For a writer now harried by other distractions, this
memory was doubtless a comfort; it seemed necessary only to
convert the satiric adult travelogue into a gentler story for
children. Other writers familiar to Twain—including Jacob
Abbott, whose *Rollo Abroad* series was in the Clemens family
library—might show him how to catch this tone. Though
Twain did not share Abbott's strenuously didactic purpose,
he may have paid some attention, reading aloud from Rollo's
travels to Susy, Clara, and Jean, to one style of juvenile travel
fiction.

Whatever the inspiration, the final text of *Tom Sawyer,
Abroad* demonstrates that he was careful to fit his tale to Mrs.
Dodge's model. After it was written, the manuscript was pains-
takingly edited. Every conceivable crudity of expression was
removed. Even so apparently innocuous a word as "fool" was
replaced by softer substitutes, "chucklehead," "blatherskite,"
"shad," "animal." Similarly, "God" (never, of course, a word
used in vain) likewise was eliminated and "heaven" put in its
place. Other modifications in the same vein were made, all
reinforcing Twain's original intent, which was to write at last
an unequivocally juvenile story.[19] Very likely, Mrs. Dodge
found nothing whatever to complain of in the story of Tom,
Huck, and Jim aloft in a balloon over Africa.

Though *Tom Sawyer, Abroad* is an adventure story exploiting the novelty of exotic locale and unusual event, everything
else about the story comes directly out of Twain's earlier Mississippi River stories. After the mad Professor has dropped to
his death in the Atlantic, Tom and Huck and Jim remain as

19. The manuscript of *Tom Sawyer, Abroad*, with these corrections in
Twain's hand, is in the Berg Collection, New York Public Library. ©
Mark Twain Company.

the only characters, except for an occasional African. The three are in personality, speech, and outlook unchanged from their last appearance at Uncle Silas' farm. Tom is still out to make a name for himself by organizing outlandish adventures, which, this time, are suggested by his reading of Scott. Huck is the same skeptical, sympathetic narrator, glad for a chance to get away in the balloon from the hateful people nagging at him to behave. "Land, I warn't in no hurry to git out and buck at civilization again," he remarks. Jim, too, is the same warm-hearted, superstitious companion he was on the raft. It is he, and not the other two, who returns the little child to the Arab woman after Tom and Huck have rescued it from the brigands.

The balloon itself, of course, is a new kind of raft. The three "errornorts" drift comfortably along, elevated safely above the dangers of the desert. Whenever it becomes necessary to avoid lions, brigands, sandstorms, or fleas, they have only to touch the controls. This mode of escape is often invoked. When attacked by fleas, for instance, Huck reports, "we went up to the cold weather to freeze 'em out, and stayed a little spell, and then come back to the comfortable weather and went lazying along twenty to twenty-five miles an hour, the way we'd been doing for the last few hours. The reason was, that the longer we was in that solemn, peaceful desert, the more the hurry and fuss got kind of soothed down in us, and the more happier and contented and satisfied we got to feeling, and the more we got to liking the desert, and then loving it" (19, 57). Quite clearly, Huck and his friends aloft are enacting Mark Twain's own dream of escape.

Even from the elevated perspective of the balloon, however, life is not always peaceful. As they cruise along, the boys observe one caravan attacked by bandits, another wiped out completely by a sudden sandstorm. But their eeriest brush with death in the desert is when they glide over a group of men and camels lying lifeless in the sand. "We dropped down slow and stopped," Huck recounts, "and me and Tom clumb down and went among them. There was men, and women, and children. They was dried by the sun, and dark and shriveled and leathery, like the pictures of mummies you see in books. And yet they looked just as human, you wouldn't 'a' believed it; just like they was asleep . . . Most of the clothes had rotted away; and when you took hold of a rag, it tore with a touch, like spider-web. Tom reckoned they had been laying there for years" (19, 62–63). The dreamlike quality of this episode is typical of the whole story; it is as if the silent gliding of the balloon across the desert softens without blurring the cruel outlines of the adult world below. Death is there, but it resembles sleep. In other places and in other moods the threat of death is treated otherwise—usually Twain makes of it a joke, as when Huck dangles just above the snapping jaws of a lion or Jim huddles atop the Sphinx dodging the bullets of the Egyptian soldiers.

These modulations in the tone of Twain's handling of his boys' relations to adult experience (conceived of quite simply as the danger of death) constitutes both narrative technique and meaning in *Tom Sawyer, Abroad*. Projecting the dangers from below by turns as a joke, a spine-tingling adventure, or a melancholy instance of human cruelty is the exciting pattern of events that juvenile adventure stories ought to exhibit. In addition, however, the rising and falling of the balloon in response to the adult activities down on the ground represents the way children can (and must) adjust to grown-ups. The balloon's perspective constantly shifts, and the boys themselves make the adjustments; but it is the threatening presence of adults—the mad Professor, brigands, soldiers—which make Tom, Huck, and Jim hop.

This matter of childhood's proper perspective on the real world is introduced obliquely and humorously when Jim is landed on the head of the Sphinx. Tom and Huck remain in the balloon to see how Jim looks. "Then we sailed off to this and that and t'other distance," Huck reports, "to git what Tom calls effects and perspectives and proportions, and Jim he done the best he could, striking all the different kinds of attitudes and positions he could study up, but standing on his head and working his legs the way a frog does was the best. The further we got away, the littler Jim got, and the grander the Sphinx got, till at last it was only a clothes-pin on a dome, as you might say. That's the way perspective brings out the correct proportions, Tom said; he said Julus Cesar's niggers didn't know how big he was, they was too close to him" (*19*, 108). The ironies of this speech—that it is a Negro who cavorts like a frog for the edification of the two white boys, that "clothes-pin on a dome" aptly suggests both Twain's and Huck's jaundiced view of humanity at this time, that Huck's artless reference to "Julus Cesar's niggers" neatly underscores Tom's outlook—are embedded but not hidden in the humorous narrative.

Such a mixture of good-natured story-telling and philosophizing marks the whole fabric of *Tom Sawyer, Abroad*. Out of the action emerges a series of existential questions which the boys in the balloon debate: why Indiana is pink on a map but not that color when traversed in a balloon; whether a "*my*ridge" (Huck's term for a mirage) is real or not; what a metaphor is; the difference between "knowledge and instink." The result is a children's adventure tale that raises so many epistemological queries that the very term "errornorts" begins finally to take on Joycian significance, as if Twain were exploring modes of adolescent experience that could avoid the errors of adulthood. Twain's treatment of these matters, as DeVoto has pointed out, is in the form of a dialogue, with Tom Sawyer representing both the literary imagination and Yankee common sense, while Huck and Jim exemplify the intuitive provincial mind with all its "prejudices, ignorances, assumptions, wisdoms, cunning." [20]

In the extended debate between "knowledge and instink"

20. Bernard DeVoto, ed., *The Portable Mark Twain* (New York, Viking, 1946), 32.

Tom, of course, is the rationalist. It is he who scouts Jim's superstitious explanation of the "*my*ridge"—"Mars Tom, hit's a *ghos'*, dat's what it is"—and directs the balloon to a real oasis by following a flock of desert birds in search of water. When Huck sides with Jim in these discussions, Tom is disgusted. "I'm lost in the sky with no company but a passel of low-down animals," he groans, "that don't know no more than the head boss of a university did three or four hundred years ago" (*19*, 67).

The two simple souls are, however, fully capable of pricking the balloon of Tom Sawyer's conceit, especially as that trait is expressed through Tom's literary imagination. When Tom suggests they organize a crusade, in the manner of "Richard Cur de Loon and the Pope," Jim cannot at first understand what a crusade is. When it is explained, he and Huck cannot accept history's justification for killing strangers. Tom again waxes sarcastic; "here's a couple of sapheaded country yahoos out in the backwoods of Missouri setting themselves up to know more about the rights and wrongs of [crusaders] than they did!" But the yahoos have the last word. "Well, Mars Tom," Jim replies, "my idea is like dis. It ain't no use, we *can't* kill dem po' strangers dat ain't doin' us no harm, till we've had practice . . . But ef we takes a' ax or two, jist you en me en Huck, en slips acrost the river to-night arter de moon's gone down, en kills dat sick fam'ly dat's over on the Sny, en burns dey house down, en—" (*19*, 11).

Huck's position in these arguments is intellectually neutral but emotionally identified with Jim: "the trouble about arguments is, they ain't nothing but *theories*, after all, and theories don't prove nothing, they only give you a place to rest on, a spell, when you are tuckered out butting around and around trying to find out something there ain't no way *to* find out" (*19*, 78). When Tom and Huck wander about the streets of Cairo looking for Joseph's granary, Huck is amazed that Tom is able to choose precisely the right one from as many as forty old tumbled-down sheds. "Well, I says to myself, how *does* he do it? Is it knowledge or is it instink?" Tom puts a brick from "Joseph's granary" in his pocket to give to a museum back home. When Huck substitutes another brick for the original one, in order to test Tom's acumen, the youthful archeologist is completely fooled. "I think that settles it—" Huck decides, "it's mostly instink, not knowledge. Instink tells him where the exact *place* is for the brick to be in, and so he reconnizes it by the place it's in, not by the look of the brick. If it was knowledge, not instink, he would know the brick again by the look of it the next time he seen it—which he didn't. So it shows that for all the brag you hear about knowledge being such a wonderful thing, instink is worth forty of it for real unerringness. Jim says the same" (*19*, 118–19).

In passages like this *Tom Sawyer, Abroad* verbalizes for the first time themes which remained submerged or implicit in the action of the earlier stories about boyhood. Tom's imagination, fed on fiction and history but often blind to personal feelings, is shown up by Huck's and Jim's humane credulity in a manner even more explicit than in *Tom Sawyer* or *Huckleberry Finn*. The superiority of instinctual perception over trained intelligence is here vigorously proclaimed; it had merely been suggested before. Unlike Hank Morgan, Tom is never permitted in his balloon debates to win a clear-cut victory for common sense. Huck's admiration for his sophisticated friend's historical and literary tastes is more tempered than in any of the earlier stories.

In every respect, *Tom Sawyer, Abroad* is essential to an understanding of Twain's lifelong exploration of childhood. For not only does this story bring into the open many of the writer's characteristic intellectual concerns, it shows their shape in Twain's mind in the early nineties, a time when the writer was desperately casting about for ways of holding in balance opposing forces that threatened to destroy his artistic powers. *Tom Sawyer, Abroad* represents one of the last times Twain was able to juggle into significant literary form his antithetical notions of human nature and behavior, of man's place in a universe possibly devoid of meaning. Perhaps it was the cheery influence of *St. Nicholas* that enabled (or forced) him to mute his destructive pessimism. More likely, it was the happy thought of taking Tom, Huck, and Jim aloft in a balloon. Placing the innocent eye of boyhood in the aerial perspective of the high-soaring airship gave Twain a double filter, as it were, against the barbarities of adult life below. As a consequence death became a form of sandy sleep, and epistemological problems grew less perplexing as the three "errornorts" demonstrated how much more bearable life could be in a balloon even than on a raft. To be sure, *Tom Sawyer, Abroad* offers no real solution to the questions it raises. All problems dissolve into nothing as Aunt Polly sends word to the three airmen atop Mount Sinai to return home at once. There the story ends abruptly. Literally and figuratively, matters are left up in the air. After all, if Twain did rehearse the plot of *Tom Sawyer, Abroad* in the bedtime story Susy relates, he knew that as long as children remain in the balloon they are "frozen," that lions cannot nibble them there. Descending from the balloon means to grow up to be women and men and "at last to be eaten at a barbeque." Like the nursery anecdote from which it probably grew, *Tom Sawyer, Abroad* implies more than it states. If Mark Twain intended a full-fledged defense of childhood's instinctual mode of dealing with an evil and deadly world of adults, this purpose remained unfulfilled. That would have to wait until his imagination turned, as it did in 1893, to the story of Joan of Arc, the Maid of Orleans.

Mark Twain had mixed feelings about his brash young creature, Tom Sawyer. Generally he was contemptuous of

Tom's pretensions and took pains to deflate his adolescent egotisms. But the boy's combination of imagination, self-dramatization, and common sense was, after all, a part of Twain himself and could never be wholly derided. Indeed, he liked Tom and reproduced his essential characteristics in many guises—in Tom Canty, in Hank Morgan, in Pudd'nhead Wilson, and in several minor personages of the travel books.

Tom Sawyer fitted admirably the requirements for the hero of a detective story, and of course *The Adventures of Tom Sawyer* in a sense is the story of a successful sleuth. But it was not until 1896 that Twain made his young boy into the special, recognizable detective stereotype he is in "Tom Sawyer, Detective." That this did not take place sooner is in part due to the tastes of Twain's readers. During the early nineties there suddenly developed a market for detective fiction, stimulated by the craze for Conan Doyle. Sherlock Holmes, to whom Twain's friend Joe Twichell introduced him at this time, invaded America in the winter and spring of 1890, when *The Sign of the Four* ran in *Lippincott's Magazine.* Soon *A Study in Scarlet* and the subsequent stories became so popular here that English readers, who had originally received the goings-on in Baker Street somewhat coolly, were quite won over. By 1894 Sherlock Holmes was a best-seller on both sides of the ocean.[21]

"Tom Sawyer, Detective" and, to a lesser degree its predecessor, *Pudd'nhead Wilson,* were intended to cash in on this popular fad. Tom's adventure, which ran as a serial in *Harper's Magazine* in June 1896, bears some of the earmarks of a burlesque of Sherlock Holmes, but it is such an involved and tedious tale that the reader is scarcely aware of Twain's satiric intent. "Tom Sawyer, Detective" is perhaps Twain's poorest

21. See Howard Haycraft, *Murder for Pleasure: The Life and Times of the Detective Story* (New York, D. Appleton, Century, 1941), pp. 49–50, 100.

short story. The intricate murder plot is carefully worked out (something unusual for Twain) and Huck is again pressed into service as narrator. But the detective story convention, which demands no delineation or development of character, proved precisely the wrong form for a tired writer to adopt. The melancholy fact that Twain's narrative, descriptive, and even humorous powers had at least temporarily gone to seed is emphasized by the frenetically busy plot. Moreover the characters—Tom, Huck, the Phelpses, and their neighbors—who in the last chapters of *Huckleberry Finn* were, in spite of moral backsliding, genial and vivid figures, now appear as dull caricatures of themselves. The scene is again the Phelps farm in Arkansas, but Uncle Silas himself is now unrecognizable as a nervous, irritable murder suspect. The peaceful plantation has been transformed into a nightmarish feuding-ground. Tom and Huck move in a miasma of suspicion, fear, and confusion, which Tom magically but mechanically dispells in the final courtroom scene. This destruction of the partly idyllic close of *Huckleberry Finn* might have been a significant and moving sign of social and spiritual decay if it were forcefully handled. But the story (which as Twain explains in a footnote was copied from an actual murder case in Sweden) dominates everything; its unfolding prevents him from pausing at any one point to develop an appropriate atmosphere. Even death itself is less significant than unraveling the identity of its perpetrator. Tom triumphs in the courtroom, but his victory over slower-witted adults is virtually without meaning; it is simply a contrived demonstration of elementary logic in a stupidly evil situation. Quite clearly, Twain was not as emotionally involved in proving here the power of reason as he had been in *Tom Sawyer, Abroad* about expressing sympathetic feelings for "instink." If any story of Twain's deserves the name of potboiler, it is "Tom Sawyer, Detective." Twain himself realized this. In his Notebook he made an entry for June 1, 1896, which doubtless conveyed a judgment of the story appearing in *Harper's Magazine* that very month. "What a curious thing a 'detective' story is," he wrote. "And was there ever one that the author needn't be ashamed of, except 'The Murders in the Rue Morgue'?" [22]

Two years earlier, in 1894, the attempt to exploit the detective story had been less calculated and more successful. *Pudd'nhead Wilson*, as F. R. Leavis has pointed out, is by no means a flawless novel, and many of its imperfections stem from Twain's use of a detective-story plot,[23] but as a social study of the American village it ranks with *Tom Sawyer*, *Huckleberry Finn*, and "The Man That Corrupted Hadleyburg." In Pudd'nhead Wilson himself Twain created his most mature hero. Roxy, the handsome mulatto girl, is Twain's solitary attempt to do what Hawthorne accomplished in Zenobia of *The Blithedale Romance;* not only is Roxy a sexually mature person but one of the few credible female characters in Twain's fiction who is neither a girl nor a grandmother.

Pudd'nhead and Roxy are in no sense children. Twain's portrait of Dawson's Landing contains children of course, as all villages have them, but for once they are neither major characters nor moral norms by which the older townspeople are judged. Instead of these usual roles, children in *Pudd'nhead Wilson* play the part of victims. They are victims of slavery and of the social system erected on that institution. From their cradles, Tom Driscoll and Valet de Chambre (familiarly known as Chambers) are raised together by Roxy. One of these babies is Roxy's own illegitimate son. His father is a Virginia-born aristocrat and bequeaths to his offspring blond hair and pure blue eyes; physical appearance, however, does not save the boy

22. Notebook 30[II] (June 1, 1896), typescript, p. 32, in MTP. © Mark Twain Company.

23. See introduction by Leavis to Grove Press Edition of *Pudd'nhead Wilson* (New York, 1955), pp. 9–31.

from the slave's status. Indistinguishable from this mulatto baby is Roxy's other charge, a blond and blue-eyed scion of Percy Northumberland Driscoll, another FFV and leading citizen of Dawson's Landing. Mrs. Driscoll has died in childbirth and Roxy is given her baby to raise. His social identity is determined in quite another direction from Roxy's own son, for he is white. But the only sure test of the identities of the two tow-heads, so nearly twins in appearance, is the fingerprint taken by the town's amateur sleuth, Pudd'nhead Wilson.

A whole chain of social and psychological dislocations ensues when Roxy, in a fit of despairing rage at the system that might some day sell her son down the river, switches the two babies in their cradles. The black baby who is white in appearance becomes white in point of social fact. The white child with the fair skin becomes the Negro slave. Both are sons of Virginia aristocrats, yet this exchange completely reverses their lives. The dramatic situation of *The Prince and the Pauper* has, in effect, been transferred to a slave-holding American village.

Tom Driscoll, the white-black-white child, grows into the most thoroughly unpleasant person in all of Twain's writings.[24] Chambers, the white-white-black boy, becomes a humble, courageous servant and companion to his obnoxious fellow. This personality development is not gradual, it happens overnight. " 'Tom' was a bad baby from the very beginning of his usurpation," Twain observes. "He would cry for nothing; he would burst into storms of devilish temper without notice, and let go scream after scream and squall after squall . . . The baby Tom

24. In "Villagers—1840–43" Twain identified as the prototype for Tom Driscoll a Hannibal youth by the name of Neil Moss. "The envied rich boy of the Meth. S. S. Spoiled & of small account. Dawson's. Was sent to Yale—a mighty journey & an incomparable distinction. Came back in swell eastern clothes, & the young men dressed up the warped negro bell ringer in a travesty of him—which made him descend to village fashions. At 30 he was a graceless tramp in Nevada, living by mendicancy & borrowed money. Disappeared." "Villagers, 1840–43," pp. 4, 5, in MTP. © Mark Twain Company.

would claw anybody who came within reach of his nails, and pound anybody he could reach with his rattle" (*16*, 26–27). By the time the boys reach school age Tom is a thorough coward and makes Chambers fight all his battles. Eventually Chambers does such a good job of defending his white master that all the neighborhood is afraid. "Tom could have changed clothes with him, and 'ridden in peace', like Sir Kay in Launcelot's armor," Twain reports sardonically.

An even more pointed twist to the problem of identity in *Pudd'nhead Wilson* occurs one day when the boys are swimming in the river. Tom begins to drown. Since it is a common trick for boys to pretend to struggle in the water and then blandly swim away when a rescuer approaches, no one pays attention to Tom's thrashing—except Chambers, who "believed his master was in earnest, therefore he swam out, and arrived in time, unfortunately, and saved his life." From this time on, the boys of Dawson's Landing torment Tom by referring to Chambers as "Tom Driscoll's 'nigger-pappy'—to signify that he had had a second birth into this life, and that Chambers was the author of his new being" (*16*, 32). The ironic implications of this event are myriad and mysterious. Perhaps Twain means simply to call attention to their transposed identities. Possibly he is suggesting symbolically the generic obligation all white children owe to blacks who, like fathers, selflessly take care of them. Or, again, this remark may mean that Tom's despicable social character has in essence been fathered by the slavery system which also has produced Chambers, the faithful servant.

As this episode indicates, the possibilities for deciding what constitutes the child's true self are virtually endless in *Pudd'n-head Wilson*. The two boys have true physical identities, but only Pudd'nhead's fingerprints can prove what these are. The babies have racial identities, but these are determined by social convention. Roxy learns to her sorrow that she can manipulate her son's social identity only by doing irreparable ruin to his personality and character. Tom's vicious cowardice (culminating in murder and, more callous yet, in selling his own mother down the river) is represented as the inevitable consequence of his status as a white boy which molds his personality in a certain direction. Twain does not excuse Tom's evil deeds, but he sees them as induced by a slave-holding environment that condones license among its gentry. Similarly, the black boy's sterling qualities do not appear so much Chambers' achievement as the natural reaction of an inferior upon whom certain demands—in the form of humility, strength, obedience—are made. This powerlessness of the two children in the face of environment adds special irony to the fact that one of them owes his life to the other.

Amid these confused switches in identity (complicated by the disguises necessary to a detective-story plot) the sole test of the boys' true selves remains the fingerprint. It is the sign of "that one microscopic atom in me that is truly *me*" of which Hank Morgan spoke in *A Connecticut Yankee*. It is the sign, too, of the scientific method, of reasonable common sense searching beneath the confusing surface of crime and disorder in the society of Twain's childhood. Pudd'nhead Wilson employs the fingerprint to discover Tom Driscoll, the black boy masquerading as white, as the murderer of his own foster-father. The guilty secret of Dawson's Landing is slavery.

Just as Tom, though a murderer, is the victim of circumstance, so is Chambers an equally pitiable pawn of overpowering forces. When Pudd'nhead clears up the mystery, Chambers is restored to his "rightful" place as heir and white man. But it is too late. "He could neither read nor write, and his speech was the basest dialect of the negro quarter," Twain remarks. "His gait, his attitudes, his gestures, his bearing, his laugh—all were vulgar and uncouth; his manners were the manners of a slave. Money and fine clothes could not mend these defects or cover them up; they only made them the more glaring and the more pathetic. The poor fellow could not endure the terrors of the white man's parlor, and felt at home and at peace nowhere but in the kitchen. The family pew was a misery to him, yet he could nevermore enter into the solacing refuge of the 'nigger gallery'—that was closed for good and all" (*16*, 202). Twain pinpoints the tragedy, but his inability or disinclination to dramatize Chambers' dilemma, so promising in ironies, is further evidence of declining artistic vigor. He exhausted his creative impulse in this novel in uncovering the usurper and establishing the scope of the crime; tracing psychological aftereffects, conveniently enough, were not part of the Sherlock Holmes pattern.

As *Pudd'nhead Wilson* shows more clearly than "Tom Sawyer, Detective," Twain was attracted to the mystery story genre because, among other things, he could exploit thereby a lifelong penchant for mixed identities and disguises while at the same time expressing through this limited literary form the crude determinism of his "Gospel." Furthermore, when the masquerade involved, as it did in Pudd'nhead's story, a Negro passing for white, Twain could introduce a recurrent theme of his earlier fiction, slavery as the archetypal source of evil in the world of his childhood. But Twain was apparently dissatisfied with the way he had combined these elements in the two detective narratives he published. In 1898, doubtless recognizing that his most successful fiction had been built around childish figures, Twain made one final (and, as it turned out, abortive) try at writing a good detective story. Under the controlling presence once again of Huck Finn as narrator, he began in that year his last mystery story, "Tom Sawyer's Conspiracy."

This fragmentary tale, composed in Vienna in the Hotel Metropole where the Clemenses were passing the winter, was as usual the fruit of childhood memories. As early as 1884 he had jotted down the germ from which this narrative grew.

"Villains *very scarce*. Pater-rollers & slavery" was Twain's cryptic entry in his *Notebook*. It referred to the tense days in the 1850's when fear of abolitionist raids from across the river made the atmosphere of Sam Clemens' village thick with suspicion. "Pater-rollers" was a slang phrase for Missouri vigilantes who patrolled Hannibal streets after dark, enforcing the curfew on slaves and protecting their property from kidnapping. The notion of building this situation into a narrative with Tom and Huck as central figures may have occurred to Twain as he finished *Huckleberry Finn;* the date of the initial idea is suggestive. But the tale did not assume clearer shape until 1896. Some time in November of that year Twain made a fuller notation of an action: "Have Huck tell how one white brother shaved his head, put on a wool wig & was blackened & sold as a negro. Escaped that night, washed himself, & helped hunt *for himself* under pay." [25]

In "Tom Sawyer's Conspiracy" Clemens spins this absurd plot out to considerable length before dropping the project. In the process, however, a number of highly subversive comments are made about Southern society. Some of these are intended as boyish joking; others have an edge that reminds the reader of the San Francisco sketches. In this respect and in others the fragment is a hodge-podge of elements from earlier works.

As usual, Tom Sawyer initiates the action; it is *his* conspiracy. The time is late spring, when time hangs heavy on Huck's and Tom's hands. The boys meet on Jackson's Island to plan some devilment. Tom wants to start a revolution, a civil war, but finally settles on a conspiracy, one that will put even St. Bartholomew's Day in the shade. "It was to get the people in a sweat about the Ablitionists," Huck explains.[26] The

25. Notebook 31[I], typescript, p. 22, in MTP. © Mark Twain Company.

26. "Tom Sawyer's Conspiracy," p. 26, in MTP. © Mark Twain Company.

first step is to print up some handbills and post them all over town. The posters purport to come from the Sons of Freedom, and bear an eye and eyebrow, unfortunately printed upside down, which puzzles Huck at first. "And I asked him what that nut was for, at the top, & he said it wasn't a nut, it was an eye & an eyebrow, & stood for vigilance & was emblumatic. That was him—all over; if a thing hadn't a chance in it somewheres for the emblumatics it warn't in his line, & he would shake it & hunt up something else." [27]

When the handbills appear on trees and doors, all St. Petersburg is thrown into a panic by Tom's emblematic eyeball. Jake Flacker, the town's slow-witted detective, takes charge, and a vigilance committee is formed. Then the boys plan to dress Tom up in wig and blackface as an escaped Negro slave and let Huck sell him to Bat Bradish, the town slave-dealer who is, as his name suggests, conveniently near-sighted. But when the boys approach Bradish's cabin they discover that two white men have thought of the identical stratagem. One white man, blackened to resemble a runaway slave, lies in chains in the cabin. Tom and Huck flee, but later return to find that some one has apparently robbed and murdered Bat and the disguised "white nigger" has fled. The incriminating footprints, however, turn out to be Jim's, and the boys' faithful companion, who was in the vicinity as part of their conspiracy, is arrested and accused of murder. "Everybody was raging about the murder," Huck relates,

> & didn't doubt but Jim was in with the Sons of Freedom & been paid by the gang to murder the nigger-trader, & there'd be more—every man that owned niggers was in danger of his life; it was only just the beginning, the place was going to swim in blood, you'll see. That is what they said. It was foolish talk, that talk about Jim, becuz he had

27. Ibid., p. 95.

always been a good nigger & everybody knowed it; but you see he was a free nigger this last year & more, & that made everybody down on him, of course, & made them forget all about his good character. It's just the way with people.[28]

While Jim is in jail, Huck and Tom go to ask the owners of Jim's wife and children if his family could come to visit Jim, "& their marsters was very good & kind, but couldn't spare them now, but would let them come before long—maybe next week—was there any hurry?" Though Huck is surprised at this casual cruelty, Jim is not. "Jim was dreadful sorry, but knowed it couldn't be helped & he had to get along the way things was," Huck observes sadly; "but he didn't take on, becuz niggers is used to that." [29]

These characteristic comments of Huck's remind us of *Huckleberry Finn*, and there is even at one point talk of escape "to Illinois & the everlasting woods" to indicate that Twain had his earlier novel in mind. But the revolt against a slave society proves, as before, only a boyish gesture. Huck defers to Tom's histrionic imagination as he did in the Evasion. The inevitable courtroom climax is arranged to make Tom a hero, "the way he done in Arkansaw." "That Arkansaw business had just pisoned him, I could see it plain," Huck comments; "he wouldn't ever be satisfied to do things in a plain common way again." [30] As "Tom Sawyer's Conspiracy" closes, the two rascals are discovered to be none other than the Duke and the Dauphin, whom Tom cleverly proves—by means of a footprint and a pair of false teeth belonging to "the white nigger in the lean-to"—to be the murderers of Bat Bradish. Boyhood again has triumphed —at least, Tom Sawyer has.

Though morally incoherent, "Tom Sawyer's Conspiracy" is

28. Ibid., pp. 156–57.
29. Ibid., pp. 216–17.
30. Ibid., p. 161.

the most interesting boyhood story Mark Twain never finished. It tries to combine the Bad Boy manner of *Tom Sawyer,* the detective plot of *Pudd'nhead Wilson* and "Tom Sawyer, Detective," and the narrative technique and some of the moral atmosphere of *Huckleberry Finn.* As fiction, it is disjointed, incomplete, typically Twainian; nevertheless the social situation it portrays is highly promising as a source for dramatic action. Moreover, in the emblematic eyeball of Tom's Sons of Freedom, he created an ironic and appropriate symbol of boyhood. Most obviously, the eye is a moral searchlight thrown upon slavery. But the eyeball on the handbill is printed, in boyish ignorance, upside down, suggesting that boyhood's moral vision is untrustworthy. Indeed this adventure reveals that the eye of Tom Sawyer, as in previous escapades, is virtually blind to pervasive immorality in his community even though this youthful Sherlock Holmes knows how to get things done. Huck's insight, on the other hand, is far clearer, but he lacks Tom's practical knack of manipulating the adult world. Because these two cannot combine their talents, the Sons of Freedom succeed only in disturbing for a few hectic weeks the peaceful tenor of their Missouri village. The secret oath of Tom Sawyer's cabal —"To run the conspiracy the best it knowed how in the interests of Christianity & sivilization & to get up a sweat in the town"—remains largely unfulfilled.[31] What might have been a companion piece to *Huckleberry Finn* became instead something closer in tone to "Tom Sawyer, Detective."

The most conspicuous quality of the "Conspiracy" is a sense of incompleteness. Literally, it is unfinished, like "Huck Finn and Tom Sawyer among the Indians." In addition, one has the more general impression of a broken-off narrative that simply "got tired," which was Twain's experience in writing *Tom Sawyer, Abroad.* Evident, too, in the account of Tom's final escapade is a radical falling-off of inventive powers, artistic

31. Ibid., p. 33.

apathy expressing itself in trite situations all too familiar to Twain's readers (there is, for instance, a town doctor who physics Tom with the same corrosive cures first itemized nearly thirty years earlier in the "Boy's Manuscript").

To be sure, Twain had returned to his most successful group of characters, to his favorite setting, to the boyish perspective. This last was most encouraging, for wherever Huck Finn is, *there* is sure to be trenchant speech and moral vision. Moreover, in the inverted eyeball of the Sons of Freedom poster Twain created a device which, had he possessed the true symbolic imagination of, say, a Hawthorne, might have been developed into a literary structure comparable to *Huckleberry Finn* or *The Scarlet Letter*. Here, perhaps, is the most melancholy fact of all—that the man who could conceive a situation as promising as that of "Tom Sawyer's Conspiracy" and could endow it with a potentially rich symbolic meaning that remained embedded in the characters and action was no longer able to combine his ingredients into an artistic whole.

The failure of the story is typical of virtually all the novels and stories of these middle years in Twain's career. In these works he appears plainly to be the victim not only of his social and commercial environment but of his own cast of thought. The author of *A Connecticut Yankee* and *Pudd'nhead Wilson* and of the shorter pieces discussed here was falling deeper and deeper into a deterministic pessimism that defied his best efforts at artistic expression. The relative success of *Tom Sawyer, Abroad* is in large part attributable to the perspective on his problems Twain was temporarily able to establish by looking through the immature eyes of three innocents suspended above the adult world.

Before succumbing to the despairing view of human nature voiced in *What Is Man?*, Mark Twain made a desperate effort to resolve his personal and ideological dilemmas. In 1893, forsaking the trail of success and the hope of quick profits from popular potboilers, he had begun to work on an entirely different kind of novel. He turned away from the deceptive task of wooing the readers of Conan Doyle, Jules Verne, and Colonel Dodge to writing the story of a little French maiden of the fifteenth century. *The Personal Recollections of Joan of Arc* was an unhappy writer's private answer to the doubts and failures of his middle years.

7.

Joan of Arc: The Child as Goddess

FEW NATURAL EVENTS in the history of American letters seem in retrospect less accidental than the wind which, one day in 1849, supposedly blew the leaf from a book about Joan of Arc across the path of a thirteen-year-old printer's apprentice in Hannibal, Missouri. Clearly Mark Twain himself, who came later to believe in a world wholly determined from the beginning, regarded the event as the first, if not the last, turning point in his life.[1] As he subsequently recounted the story, the random page fascinated the boy. It described the Maid's persecution in prison by the rough English soldiery who had stolen her clothes. Young Sam hurried home to ask his mother and brother whether Joan of Arc was a real person. For the first time, apparently, the remote past had touched Sam Clemens.

The course of Twain's career as writer took symbolic shape from this casual event. Joan of Arc's story opened simultaneously the worlds of history and literature to the young boy, who grew into a man absorbed by the past and by the urge to represent it through fiction. Four medieval stories—*The Prince and the Pauper, A Connecticut Yankee in King Arthur's Court, Personal Recollections of Joan of Arc, The Mysterious Stranger*—

1. See Wecter, *Sam Clemens of Hannibal*, p. 211, and Paine, *Mark Twain*, 1, 81–82. Neither biographer accounts for the fact that this episode, to which Twain often referred in later life, is unmentioned in "The Turning Point of My Life," in *What Is Man?*.

were fruits of this dual devotion to history and fiction. For a writer intimately in touch, by the seventies, with a very large audience, this choice of theme often created difficulties. The public's lukewarm reception of *The Prince and the Pauper* showed that tales of medieval life were by no means as popular as other themes Twain might develop. In fact, *A Connecticut Yankee* was the only one of these stories that Twain himself considered a financial success. In one sense or another, each of the others was written out of personal, not commercial, considerations.

Certainly *Joan of Arc* was. "That is private & not for print, it's written for love & not for lucre, & to entertain the family with, around the lamp by the fire." So he described to Mrs. Fairbanks, in January of 1893, the romance he was composing amid the "serene and noiseless life" which the Clemenses were momentarily leading in Settignano, outside Florence.[2] At this time it was indeed a sacrifice for Twain to write for love. He was in the midst of recurrent financial troubles with the omnivorous Paige typesetter, and his publishing company and other business ventures were swallowing large portions of the Clemens fortune. The Panic of 1893 was about to break, and this would shortly bring him to the very brink of bankruptcy. Yet in spite of these and other private anxieties, Twain took time from more marketable work—*Tom Sawyer, Abroad,* "The £1,000,000 Bank-Note," *Pudd'nhead Wilson*—to begin his story of the Maid of Orleans.

2. MT to Mrs. Fairbanks (Jan. 18, 1893), in Wecter, *Mark Twain to Mrs. Fairbanks,* p. 269. The history of the writing of *Joan of Arc* Twain himself recorded in his Notebooks: "Every book, from Huck Finn & Prince & Pauper on, was read to the household critics chapter by chapter nightly as it was written. Joan was thus read: the first half at the Villa Viviana [*properly* "Viviani"] winter of '92–3; the third quarter at Etretat [France] Aug & Sep '94—("wait till I get a hankerchief, papa")—the final chapter in Paris Nov. Dec. 94 finished in the next month (Jan '95) I think." Notebook 31[II] (last date indicated Jan. 6, 1897), typescript, pp. 49–50, in MTP. © Mark Twain Company.

On the face of it, *Joan of Arc*—or, more properly, *Personal Recollections of Joan of Arc, By Sieur Louis de Conte (Her Page and Secretary), Freely Translated out of the Ancient French into Modern English from the Original Unpublished Manuscript in the National Archives of France by Jean François Alden*—was an unusual sequel to *Pudd'nhead Wilson*. From an American locale familiar alike to author and audience, Twain turned now to fifteenth-century France and its remote rivalry of Burgundian and Armagnac. Fresh from creating Roxy, a vibrant, fallible, and feminine figure, he undertook to depict a virginal maiden who lived and died like a saint. The cynical quips of Pudd'nhead's Calendar were followed by a story necessarily imbued with the atmosphere of Roman Catholic hagiolatry. Tom Driscoll the rascal gave place to Joan; the child as victim of circumstance became the child as victorious general of the armies of France. Nothing Twain wrote during the middle years illustrates better than *Joan of Arc* the stubborn presence of contradiction and paradox in the career of this writer.

Indeed, of all his books *Joan of Arc* appears the most incongruous product of Mark Twain's imagination. Equally distant in tone from the boisterous humor of *Huckleberry Finn* or "1601" and the hopeless pessimism of *What Is Man?* and *The Mysterious Stranger,* this romance has usually been dismissed as an aberration. Perhaps for this reason it has remained the least known and least read of Twain's major novels. Yet as an image of childhood the book is doubly significant, not simply as Twain's first and only novel about a young girl but also as his most extended exploration of the relations between children and adults in terms of religious experience. In this sense, *Joan of Arc* is a companion piece to *Tom Sawyer, Abroad.* Having dramatized the epistemological issues of "knowledge and instink" in the tale of the balloon, Twain was prompted by his own doubts to plumb theological depths in the story of "the most noble life that was ever born into this world save only One." The result is a novel unsuccessful as art but fascinating as a reflection of the mind of Mark Twain. Understanding the enigmas of *Joan of Arc* is an essential critical task. Moreover it is one enjoined upon his readers by the author himself, who in 1908 remarked, "I like the *Joan of Arc* best of all my books; & it *is* the best; I know it perfectly well." [3]

In a note made some time later, Twain remarked that fourteen years of labor went into *Joan of Arc*—twelve years of study and two of writing. Paine tells of a bibliography, compiled "not much later than 1880," of books about the young girl.[4] The interest first aroused by the stray page in Hannibal had thus been sustained, or at least renewed, during the Nook Farm years, though Twain had then been too preoccupied with business, entertaining, traveling, and writing other novels to do anything more with Joan than to study her story.

This cult Mark Twain shared with the nineteenth century. Before that time Joan of Arc had been wreathed in the mists of legend. Reviled by the Englishmen Holinshed and Shakespeare in the sixteenth century, neglected in the seventeenth, ridiculed by Voltaire in the eighteenth, and then idealized by Southey and Schiller in the early nineteenth century, Joan became, during Twain's own lifetime, a figure of new fascination to writers and to readers.

Joan's modern popularity began in 1841. In that year appeared both J. E. J. Quicherat's remarkable collection of the records of the Maid's trial at Rouen in 1431 and Michelet's fifth volume of the *Histoire de France*, separately titled *Jeanne D'Arc*. Michelet's work had already been translated into English and

3. Quote in Paine, *Mark Twain*, 2, 1034.
4. Ibid., p. 958.

published in America by 1845. It is possible, judging from the description in Paine, that the page Sam Clemens picked up in 1849 was from this very volume.[5]

Other writers—Lamartine and Dumas in France, J. R. Green, Janet Tuckey, Andrew Lang in England, John Lord and Francis Lodge in America—followed Michelet. Even Emily Dickinson, though she seemed secluded from popular currents in her father's house in Amherst, composed in 1861 a brief lyric in the Maid's honor.[6]

Such writers found a ready audience, too, among the readers of Twain's generation. In the summer of 1885, for instance, Olivia Clemens reported in her diary that thirteen-year-old Susy was reading Schiller's *Jungfrau von Orleans* aloud to her and they were both finding it "delightful." [7] The culmination of these years of interest did not come until 1920, the year of Joan of Arc's canonization. But as if to underscore the connec-

5. "The 'maid' was described in the cage at Rouen, in the fortress, and the two ruffian English soldiers had stolen her clothes. There was a brief description and a good deal of dialogue—her reproaches and their ribald replies" (Paine, *1*, 81). Michelet's version, in the American edition, tallies in part with this: "On the Sunday morning, Trinity Sunday, when it was time for her to rise, (as she told him who speaks,) and said to her English guards, 'Leave me, that I may get up.' One of them took off her woman's dress, emptied the bag in which was the man's apparel, and said to her, 'Get up.'—'Gentlemen,' she said, 'you know that dress is forbidden me; excuse me, I will not put it on.' The point was contested until noon; when, being compelled to go out for some bodily want, she put it on." M. Michelet, *History of France, from the Earliest Period to the Present Time,* trans. G. H. Smith (New York, 1845), *2*, 164. All references hereafter are to this edition.

6. For the treatment of Joan of Arc in nineteenth-century history and letters see Lord Ronald Gower, *Joan of Arc* (London, 1893), pp. 289–319; and Helen H. Salls, "Joan of Arc in English and American Literature," *South Atlantic Quarterly, 35* (1936), 167–84. For the poem "A Mien to Move a Queen" see Thomas H. Johnson, ed., *The Poems of Emily Dickinson* (Cambridge, Mass., Harvard University Press, 1955), *1*, 202–3.

7. Olivia Clemens' Journal (July 2, 1885), p. 13, in MTP.

tion between the little saint and Twain, Joan was beatified in 1909, a few months before Twain's death.

With many of these nineteenth-century writers Twain was perfectly familiar. He owned and had read carefully copies of Michelet, Janet Tuckey, J. R. Green, and Dr. John Lord; of the eleven books cited in a preface to *Joan of Arc,* Twain owned at least seven, for they are preserved in the Mark Twain Papers.[8] These all bear copious underlinings and marginal comments in Twain's hand—unmistakable evidence of close and critical reading. Few men in his generation were as widely read in the lore of Joan of Arc as Twain himself.

The chief reason for this unusual breadth of knowledge was that the story of the Maid of Orleans touched him deeply. The image he constructed of her in his novel was the result of much thought; it answered not only to his intellectual interests but also to his personal emotional needs. Intellectually, Joan of Arc attracted Twain because she epitomized an age-old struggle of common folk against the twin institutions of cruelty and oppression, the Crown and the Church. In this respect, *Joan of Arc* repeats themes of *The Prince and the Pauper* and *A Connecticut Yankee.* Emotionally, the pull was even stronger. In Twain's eyes Joan was the incarnation of youth and purity and power. She was the unique instance in history of the young girl whose innocence not merely *existed* but *acted* in the gross world of adult affairs. She was the peerless human being, and it was of the utmost importance that she remain eternally a young girl.

To young maidens, hovering on the edge of adult experience,

8. Marius Sepet, *Jeanne D'Arc,* Tours, 1887; Michelet, *Jeanne D'Arc,* Paris, 1873; Comtesse de Chabannes, *La Vierge Lorraine: Jeanne D'Arc,* Paris, 1890; Lord Ronald Gower, *Joan of Arc,* London, 1893; John O'Hagan, *Joan of Arc,* London, 1893; and Janet Tuckey, *Joan of Arc,* "The Maid," London, 1880. Copies of Green and Lord were listed in *Mark Twain Library Auction Catalogue,* April 10, 1951.

Mark Twain had a lifelong partiality. There were, first of all, his three daughters, in particular Susy Clemens. As Susy reached maidenhood she assumed a special place in her father's heart. Natural parental affection was reinforced by Susy's extraordinary gifts of sensitivity in speech and writing; the biography she wrote of her father made him intensely proud of his daughter. In the wider Nook Farm life at Hartford was the Saturday Morning Club, the group of girls who had met regularly at Twain's home during those exciting weeks in 1878 when they had listened to and criticized installments of *The Prince and the Pauper*.[9] In later years this special fondness for young girls expressed itself in several ways. Paine tells of one Bermuda holiday which Twain spent largely in the company of Margaret Blackmer, aged twelve. The lonely old man, whose infant son, favorite daughter, and beloved wife were all dead, found the child so charming that he organized the Angel Fish Club, or The Aquarium. To this select group he elected only himself and a dozen teen-aged girls whose youthful beauty reminded him of the pretty tropical fish.[10]

Even more suggestive of the psychological depth underlying this interest in girlhood is the fragmentary, posthumous "My Platonic Sweetheart," composed in 1898. This story purports to be a true account of a dream he had recurrently throughout his adult life. In it Twain, always seventeen, has for a lover a fifteen-year-old maiden "girlishly young and sweet and innocent." The pair of "ignorant and contented children" move across a phantom landscape conversing in eloquent, cryptic phrases which lose their meaning to the awakened dreamer. Twain comments on his dream:

> She was always fifteen, and looked it and acted it; and I was always seventeen, and never felt a day older. To me

9. See Ellsworth, *A Golden Age of Authors*, p. 224.

10. See Paine, *Mark Twain*, 3, 1435–41, and Twain's Notebook 38 (1905) (June 1908), typescript, p. 3, in MTP.

she is a real person not a fiction, and her sweet and innocent society has been one of the prettiest and pleasantest experiences of my life. I know that to you her talk will not seem of the first intellectual order; but you should hear her in Dreamland then you would see! [11]   [27, 303]

The timeless and sexless quality of Twain's devotion to girlhood—strikingly suggestive in emotional intensity to similar sentiments in Poe, Dickens, and Lewis Carroll—is explicit here. That he regarded Joan of Arc also specifically as a "platonic sweetheart" is clear from his treatment of the Maid in his romance. There is, for example, no hint of sexual development in his growing heroine, in spite of the interesting fact that Michelet, whom Twain followed often very closely, comments upon this very aspect of Joan's history. "She had the divine right to remain," Michelet observes at one point, "soul and body, a child. She grew up strong and beautiful; but never knew the physical sufferings entailed on women." In a footnote the French historian quotes from the testimony of several Domremy women to the effect that Joan never menstruated.[12] Twain knew this passage, for in the margin of his own copy of Michelet he wrote, next to this paragraph: "The higher life absorbed her & suppressed her physical (sexual) developement." [13] Anyone familiar with Twain's skittishness about sex in his books, not to mention the social attitudes of his day, will not be surprised at his silence on this score. Still, it is a detail that throws light upon Joan's strictly childish appeal for him. The notion that the Maid was believed to have remained a

11. The details of this story are so numerous and suggestive that they have not failed to attract the attention of psychologists, amateur and professional. For an interesting discussion of the less platonic aspects of Twain's dreams see A. E. Jones, "Mark Twain and Sexuality," PMLA, 71 (1956), 595–616.

12. Michelet, History, 2, 133.

13. Mark Twain's copy of Michelet, Jeanne D'Arc, p. 10, in MTP. © Mark Twain Company.

child in body as well as in spirit must have pleased him and added force to his iterations of her immaculate girlishness.

Similar sentiments about girlhood animate the whole of *Joan of Arc,* in which the aged narrator, Sieur Louis de Conte, in addition to being an actual historical personage, is the most transparent of personae. Twain discovered the "young man of noble birth" with the convenient initials in Michelet's history and translated a minor figure into the central intelligence around which his story is constructed. By doing so the novelist introduced himself and his private feelings into the stream of history.

Joan of Arc is the most historical of all Twain's novels and shows on every page its debt to the history books he read so carefully. "I have never done any work before that cost so much thinking and weighing and measuring and planning and cramming, or so much cautious and painstaking execution," he wrote H. H. Rogers in January 1895, as he was finishing the book in Paris. Speaking of the final scenes in Rouen, he went on:

> Although it is mere history—history pure and simple— history stripped naked of flowers, embroideries, colorings, exaggerations, inventions—the family agree I have succeeded . . . The first two-thirds of the book were easy; for I only needed to keep my historical road straight; and therefore I used for reference only one French history and one English one—and shoveled in as much fancy work and invention on both sides of the historical road as I pleased. But on this last third I have constantly used five French sources and five English ones and I think no telling historical nugget in any of them has escaped me.
>
> Possibly the book may not sell, but that is nothing—it is written for love.[14]

14. MT to H. H. Rogers (erroneously April 29, 1895), in Paine, *Letters,* 2, 623–24. Wecter corrects Paine's mistake in the month in *Mark Twain to Mrs. Fairbanks,* p. 275.

Twain's boyish sense of accomplishment is reflected also in the itemized list of "Authorities examined in verification of the truthfulness of this narrative" printed in a preface to *Joan of Arc*. Besides Quicherat's *Condamnation et réhabilitation de Jeanne D'Arc* and Fabre's *Procès de Condamnation de Jeanne D'Arc*, Twain lists six biographies by Frenchmen and three by Englishmen. Since we have his personal copies of seven of these, it is clear that he was neither boasting to his friend Rogers nor trying to hoodwink the reading public.

At one point in the novel Sieur Louis observes, "the office of history is to furnish serious and important facts that *teach*" (*18,* 63). As usual, the page speaks for his creator. Twain's careful display of his documentation is proof that *Joan of Arc* was written to teach others about the most perfect human that ever lived. Children especially (though not exclusively) seem to be the audience he had in mind, as William Dean Howells was the first to point out.[15] For an ex-newspaperman whose career opened with satiric squibs against Sunday-school books, this turn is somewhat ironic.

Now, as was the case with *The Prince and the Pauper,* Twain's commitment to historical "truthfulness" involves him in the effort to deal impartially with Joan of Arc. Certain of the writers he has leaned upon try to write realistically and rationally about the Maid; others, in their sympathy and prejudice, make scant effort to do so. Michelet and Sepet, though both staunch Armagnac sympathizers, are of the first group. Michelet, in particular, seems to have influenced Twain more than any of the eleven writers he lists. On internal and external evidence he is the "one French history" Twain told Rogers he used for the first two-thirds of his romance.[16]

---

15. W. D. Howells, *My Mark Twain* (New York, 1910), p. 151.
16. Besides furnishing Twain with the most complete treatment of Louis de Contes (as his name is spelled in *Jeanne D'Arc*), Michelet's *History* is directly cited several times in the text (*17,* 191; *18,* 18, for example). The wording of Joan's reply to the Archangel (*17,* 69), her

It is chiefly from Michelet that Twain derives the inspiration for what realism *Joan of Arc* possesses. The French historian places Joan in the context of political and religious events of her day. He sees her as the manifestation on the one hand of the medieval Virgin cult and on the other of the spirit of French nationalism. Joan's successes are related to contemporary military and political realities. When the girl-general is fearful, imprudent, or opportunistic Michelet usually says so. Although patriotic and absurdly Anglophobic, he expresses the spirit of the nineteenth century—rationalistic, anticlerical, nationalistic. Mark Twain's *Joan of Arc* partakes of this spirit.

But the letter to Rogers also mentions as a historical guide "one English one." That book, I believe, is Janet Tuckey's *Joan of Arc, "The Maid."* This little volume, which, to judge from the underlinings and comments, Twain read as carefully as any other source, is manifestly designed for a family, even a childish, audience. Miss Tuckey's Maid is a less impartial and candid creation than Michelet's. Language and the details of military life are less graphic. Unsupported legends find an uncritical welcome, and in the process Joan becomes an angel

---

leavetaking from her Domremy playmates (*17*, 89), and numerous other specific details seem closer to Michelet than to any other source. Twain's marginalia in his French copy of Michelet indicate a close and early reading; many of the opening passages are translated in the margin as if he had read Michelet first and was not sure of his French. In his copies of Gower and Chabannes, he has written Michelet's name in the margin as if testing certain passages against Michelet's version. An illustration from one edition (not Twain's one of 1873) of *Jeanne D'Arc* was tucked inside Twain's copy of Sepet. More general in its influence is Michelet's blend of candor, humor, anticlericalism, and sympathy for Joan. At one point the Frenchman remarks, "To travel at such a time with five or six men-at-arms was enough to alarm a young girl. An English woman, or a German, would never have risked such a step; the *indelicacy* of the proceeding would have horrified her" (Michelet, *History*, *2*, 135). In his French copy Twain wrote indignantly next to this passage: "How stupid! A *Joan of Arc* would do it, no matter *what* her nationality might be. That spirit has no nationality." © Mark Twain Company.

whose final end is a pathetic victimization of ideal innocence. Miss Tuckey's book is also of the nineteenth century—it is saccharine, churchly, genteel. Twain's romance likewise partakes of this spirit.

For, faced with dissimilar, almost opposing, images of Joan of Arc, Twain has not decided between them: he has accepted and used both. To do so, of course, fits with the twin tendencies toward sentimentality and realism which characterize virtually all of Twain's fiction. Furthermore, to be both blunt and gentle, pious and anticlerical, cynical and awe-struck in the face of Joan's history fits the character of Twain's alter ego, Sieur Louis de Conte. Through his eyes we see the saint's life and death unfold; he supplies, consequently, the novel's unifying structure, the means by which Twain has altered and embellished the historical narrative.

One of the characteristic features of Mark Twain's fiction is his dramatic use of a narrator. *Joan of Arc* derives much of its power from the character who tells the story. Although it is not clear from the early Domremy chapters, Louis de Conte bears a striking resemblance to the narrators Twain created many years earlier for both *Roughing It* and "Old Times on the Mississippi"—that is, he is two people at once, the fifteen-year-old boy who leaves Domremy to follow Joan and the old cynic who relates the tale many years later. This double role is made explicit in comments such as this:

> My wound gave me a great deal of trouble clear into the first part of October; then the fresher weather renewed my life and strength. All this time there were reports drifting about that the King was going to ransom Joan. I believed these, for I was young and had not yet found out the littleness and meanness of our poor human race, which brags about itself so much, and thinks it is better and higher than the other animals. [*18*, 109]

The stripling who hears and believes the rumors is carefully differentiated from him who speaks; he is brother to the greenhorn in the opening chapters of *Roughing It* and the cub of "Old Times," just as the old misanthrope is a parallel figure to the old-timers in each of the earlier works.[17] It is as if a middle-aged Mark Twain were looking back at himself, the thirteen-year-old boy, Sam Clemens, and commenting on his own naiveté. In this sense *Joan of Arc* is a double initiation. At the same time that a saint is being made of an innocent village maiden her page is becoming an embittered old man.

One reason, however, for the weakness of *Joan of Arc* as a novel is that Twain does not sufficiently dramatize these two narrators or the process by which "the boy" (as Twain identified him in early marginal notes in his reading) is transformed into the misanthrope. Louis' initiation is already over when he records Joan's career. As a result, the novel, already somewhat desiccated by historical fact and occasional footnotes, loses that freshness which Huck Finn, for example, was able to give to the far more dramatic account of his initiation.

In the opening chapters these effects of the page's disenchantment are less apparent, and this section is in many respects the most successful part of the novel. Certainly it is most completely of Twain's own manufacture. Always at home in treating childhood, he expands the village scenes far beyond the accounts of Michelet or Tuckey. His narrator becomes almost a believable boy and Joan a real girl as the history of their life in the woods and fields is told. The specifically pastoral quality of these chapters is likewise Twain's own idea. Ignoring the sources which point out that the D'Arc family were not simple farmers but prosperous villagers and that Joan was not often afield, Twain casts Joan almost exclusively in the role

17. See Henry Nash Smith, "Mark Twain as an Interpreter of the Far West: The Structure of *Roughing It,*" in *The Frontier in Perspective* (Madison, University of Wisconsin Press, 1957), pp. 205–28.

of shepherdess.[18] In so doing he draws a distinct line between her life in the open fields, where all is idyllic peace beneath the Fairy Tree, and that of the village, where violence and evil can and do occur.

Perhaps the most graphic instance of the violent realism of Louis' recollection of village life occurs when the Burgundians raid Domremy. Twain developed this episode from brief references in the histories. Both Michelet and Miss Tuckey dismiss the event in a sentence or two, but he constructs an extended scene of wartime pillage. To the bare facts supplied by the records Twain adds such details as the "wrecked and smoke-blackened homes" to which Joan and her friends return to discover "in the lanes and alleys carcasses of dumb creatures that had been slaughtered in pure wantonness . . ." The climax is reached as Joan and the others reach the village square:

> At last we came upon a dreadful object. It was the madman—hacked and stabbed to death in his iron cage in the corner of the square. It was a bloody and dreadful sight. Hardly any of us young people had ever seen a man before who had lost his life by violence; so this cadaver had an awful fascination for us; we could not take our eyes from it. I mean, it had that sort of fascination for all of us but one. That one was Joan. She turned away in horror, and could not be persuaded to go near it again. [17, 53]

The village lunatic, Joan's friend, along with every other outcast person and animal in Domremy, is wholly Twain's creation. His gory death repeats the pattern of violence which all of Twain's childish characters confront. Joan of Arc, in spite of her carefree life in the fields, is no more spared the sight of

18. See, on this point, Michelet, 2, 132; Tuckey, p. 25; Gower, p. 5; O'Hagan, p. 39. O'Hagan, for instance, writes: "She attended almost wholly to the house, but rarely going to the fields to keep her father's sheep." Twain here chooses to follow the Countess de Chabannes, whose opening chapter is entitled "La Bergère."

blood than is Tom or Huck or Prince Edward or Theodor Fischer.

De Conte's account of Joan's childhood is a mixture of pastoral idyll and a realistic, even gruesome, picture of medieval village life. But as saint and secretary leave Domremy to fulfill their fates at Orleans, Rheims, and Rouen, the balanced tone of Twain's romance changes. The credulous, boyish side of the narrator's mask is discarded and with it the depiction of outdoors life as innocence. The unhappy old man takes over the story. At the same time the pastoral idyll gives way to blatant melodrama. Whereas Joan and her companions are pictured in the village with considerable individuality (especially in their speech), in later scenes all the characters tend to be projected as stereotypes. Joan herself, of course, is the virtuous heroine. The Paladin is her comic bodyguard with the heart of gold. Cauchon and Loyseleur, the Bishop and Priest who control the trial at Rouen, are the arch-villains. The sometimes absurd excesses of melodramatic simplification are suggested by Louis' description of Bishop Cauchon:

> . . . I asked myself what chance an ignorant poor country-girl of nineteen could have in such an unequal conflict; and my heart sank down low, very low. When I looked again at that obese president, puffing and wheezing there, his great belly distending and receding with each breath, and noted his three chins, fold above fold, and his knobby and knotty face, and his purple and splotchy complexion, and his repulsive cauliflower nose, and his cold and malignant eyes—a brute, every detail of him—my heart sank lower still. [18, 123–24]

The radical degree to which Twain conceived this novel as melodrama and undercut thereby his own claim to "historical truthfulness" is aptly suggested by a note he made on the flyleaf of one of the history books he read. "Have several of her play-

216

mates," he scribbled, "come all the way, hoping somehow to save her—she glimpses them when she knows she is en route to the stake & they don't—a little later they crowd in & get a glance—it is then that the boy closes with Oh, my God!" [19] History would not allow this Tom Sawyer scheme to be carried out, but in places where the facts are hazier he gratuitously added scenes that were often lurid with passion, mystery, or sentiment.[20]

The tensions between Twain's intellectual aims and his emotional predilections, the pull of "truthfulness" against the image of Joan as his "platonic sweetheart," as it were, are everywhere evident in *Joan of Arc*. The sentimental innocence of the boy, though more palpable in the Domremy chapters, runs all through the narrative; we see it particularly in the melodramatic touches. Side by side with this maudlin sentiment, however, exists the mocking laughter of the old secretary, whose cynicism is directed not at Joan but at himself and at all men. Sieur Louis de Conte, being so thoroughly of two minds about Joan's life, is indeed an ambiguous interpreter of its meaning.

"What can we say to it in the last year of this incredulous old century, nodding to its close?" asked William Dean Howells

19. Penciled notation, flyleaf, Comtesse de Chabannes, *La Vierge Lorraine, Jeanne D'Arc*, in MTP. © Mark Twain Company.

20. One such interpolation is the whole of Bk. II, chap. 19, a ghost story complete with candles at midnight, a haunted room, and groans behind a wall, climaxing in the discovery of "a rusty sword and a rotten fan" (*17*, 245). This episode was evidently added to the narrative after an evening at the Villa Viviani. Olivia Clemens noted in her journal: "Yesterday Mme. Villari and Mrs. Charles Leland called and we sat around the fire telling ghost stories. Mme. Villari told of friends of hers taking to pieces an old house to rebuild, in tearing down the walls they came upon a room that they did not know existed, it was entirely walled up, all that was found in this room was a fan and a sword." Olivia Clemens' Journal, entry "Florence, Italy, 1892–3," in MTP. © Mark Twain Company.

of the "preposterous," "impossible" facts of the Maid's life as his friend had presented them.

> We cannot deny it. What was it all? Was Joan's power the force dormant in the people which her claim of inspiration awoke to mighty deeds? If it was merely that, how came this poor, ignorant girl by the skill to lead armies, to take towns, to advise councils, and to change the fate of a whole nation? . . . Could a dream, an illusion, a superstition, do this? [21]

Such was the fundamental question *Joan of Arc* raised for Howells; nor could he go on to give Twain's answer to the matter of Joan's power, because there was no such clear-cut answer in the novel. Howells could see that Joan was more to Twain than the expression of French nationalism, but he could not tell, judging from the novel alone, whether her power came from a divine source or from the girl's own soul.

At this level of meaning, *Joan of Arc* is indeed a perplexing mixture. A devotional exercise for a Roman Catholic girl couched in profoundly Protestant terms, it is also a celebration of the world's most perfect human by an oldish man who has lost his faith in mankind. The novel is, moreover, a case history of a religious mystic whose puissance seems to emanate from her own intuition rather than from the temporary indwelling of Holy Voices. These ambiguities are implicit in the structure of the book not simply because the historical Joan was, and is, an enigma but also because Sieur Louis de Conte cannot resolve his own doubts.

Actually, in the course of the story Louis offers three explanations of Joan's life and accomplishments. First, she may be considered purely as the amanuensis of supernatural powers which, because of her heritage, her reliance upon saints and sacraments, and her allegiance to the Pope are to be regarded

21. *My Mark Twain*, p. 155.

as specifically Christian and Catholic. This, the grave church-men of Poitiers are glad to confess, is the answer to "that elusive and unwordable fascination, which was the supremest endow-ment of Joan of Arc." Though the priests appropriate Joan's power and declare "This child is sent of God," Sieur Louis himself will not admit that Joan's superhuman abilities are a Catholic Christian's special gift from Heaven, for in his world-weary eyes the Church is a very fallible institution. Even before the dreadful disenchantment of the trial at Rouen, Louis' name for the doctors of the Church is the "holy hair-splitters." Fre-quently the secretary (whose boyish faith as he hid in the woods and watched the Archangel approach Joan was un-questioned) has the chance to make Christian explanations for the events he witnesses. He seldom does so, for to the old man the Church is not the exclusive channel through which the Maid is empowered to do her mighty miracles. "She could have reminded these people," Louis observes on one occasion, "that Our Lord, who is no respecter of persons, had chosen the lowly for his high purposes even oftener than he had chosen bishops and cardinals" (18, 205). In the jaundiced eyes of her servant, at any rate, Joan cannot be adequately explained as Catholic Christian. Her faith does not explain her power, but rather the reverse.

A second and stronger possibility is that the child's mysterious mastery over the adult world derives, as Howells and Michelet believed, from the people. "To the Dwarf, Joan was France, the spirit of France made flesh" de Conte remarks, and then adds, "and God knows it was the true one" (17, 225). On an-other occasion Louis calls Joan "a mirror in which the lowly hosts of France were clearly reflected" (18, 29). And yet, as the romance moves toward its tragic conclusion, this theory is more and more eroded by the facts of life as Louis comes to know them. This same dwarf, who both believed Joan to rep-resent the people and was one of them himself, turns out to be

219

a cruel and bloodthirsty soldier. Colonel Sherburn's shooting of old Boggs in *Huckleberry Finn* is no more disgusting a demonstration of human brutality than the scene in which the Dwarf strangles a Burgundian soldier.

The venom of Twain's own cynicism imbues Louis' account of this episode with jarring intensity. "One heard the muffled cracking of bones," he reports grimly:

> The Burgundian's eyes began to protrude from their sockets and stare with a leaden dullness at vacancy. The color deepened in his face and became an opaque purple. His hands hung down limp, his body collapsed with a shiver, every muscle relaxed its tension and ceased from its function. The Dwarf took away his hand and the column of inert mortality sank mushily to the ground.
>
> We struck the bonds from the prisoner and told him he was free. His crawling humbleness changed to frantic joy in a moment, and his ghastly fear to a childish rage. He flew at that dead corpse and kicked it, spat in its face, danced upon it, crammed mud into its mouth, laughing, jeering, cursing, and volleying forth indecencies and bestialities like a drunken fiend. It was a thing to be expected: soldiering makes few saints. Many of the onlookers laughed, others were indifferent, none was surprised. But presently in his mad caperings the freed man capered within reach of the waiting file, and another Burgundian promptly slipped a knife through his neck, and down he went with a death-shriek, his brilliant artery-blood spurting ten feet as straight and bright as a ray of light. There was a great burst of jolly laughter all around from friend and foe alike; and thus closed one of the pleasantest incidents of my checkered military life.   [*18*, 37]

Yet these bloodthirsty soldiers are little better than the King himself, who is "a sceptered ass" to Louis. From the top to the bottom of French society the page finds nothing but venality, cruelty, weakness. At the end we are prepared to discount the page's assertions of Joan as the spirit of France as the credulous hopes of the young boy. What the old man later learns undercuts, and all but denies, this explanation of Joan of Arc.

A third possibility suggests itself finally as the truest key to Joan of Arc's life. Her power is not intellectual—it defies rational explanation by the best university minds; nor is it social —the people are a great beast, the Church simply a group of people. Her supernatural deeds must, then, emanate from some mysterious source anterior to reason and to human institutions. That this source is mysterious is everywhere insisted upon by Twain's commentator:

> Who taught the shepherd-girl to do these marvels—she who could not read, and had had no opportunity to study the complex arts of war? . . . It is a riddle which will never be guessed. *I* think these vast powers and capacities were born in her, and that she applied them by an intuition which could not err. [*17*, 304]

The translator of Louis' history, Samuel L. Clemens, can no more elucidate the matter clearly than the old page. "Joan of Arc, a mere child in years, ignorant, unlettered, a poor village girl unknown and without influence . . . laid her hand upon this nation, this corpse, and it rose and followed her." So runs the "Translator's Preface." Twain himself, in his own voice, falls back on wonder (as, curiously enough, does Michelet, for all his rationalistic nationalism). Nowhere in the records Twain has combed can he isolate a sufficient First Cause for the career of this "noble child, the most innocent, the most lovely, the most adorable the ages have produced."

But has the novel not already suggested one source? If the church or the people cannot, may not the Fairy Tree "explain" Joan of Arc? This Tree is the central symbolic vehicle for Mark

Twain's pastorale. Mentioned in passing by all his historical sources, the Fairy Tree in Twain is the haunt of the fairies who befriend Joan and the other children until banished by the superstitious village priest. Beneath the Fairy Tree, too, Joan is first visited by the Archangel Michael. The boys and girls of Domremy sing a hymn to the Tree whose words, entirely Twain's creation, evoke the mood of Joan's life. Since it plays so central a role in establishing the theme of *Joan of Arc* it is worth quoting in its entirety.

L'Arbre Fée de Bourlemont
Song of the Children

Now what has kept your leaves so green,
  Arbre Fée de Bourlemont?
The children's tears! They brought each grief,
  And you did comfort them and cheer
  Their bruisèd hearts, and steal a tear
    That, healèd, rose a leaf.

And what has built you up so strong,
  Arbre Fée de Bourlemont?
The children's love! They've loved you long:
  Ten hundred years, in sooth,
They've nourished you with praise and song,
And warmed your heart and kept it young—
    A thousand years of youth!

Bide always green in our young hearts,
  Arbre Fée de Bourlemont!
And we shall always youthful be,
  Not heeding Time his flight;
And when, in exile wand'ring, we
Shall fainting yearn for glimpse of thee,
    Oh, rise upon our sight!   [*17*, 13–14]

This sacred song is referred to at key points in the narrative so often that it resembles an operatic motif. The Tree and song together constitute Twain's most notable addition to the Joan of Arc legend.

It is not easy to say whether the Fairy Tree means more to Joan of Arc, dead at nineteen, or to Sieur Louis, who lives unhappily on into old age. For both, the Tree signalizes childhood, happiness, unity with nature, the past. The most touching demonstration of its appeal to both comes at an unlikely point in the story, at the banquet following King Charles' coronation at Rheims. After the speech-making, it is the weak-willed King's happy thought to surprise Joan with the singing of the children's song.

> Then out of some remote corner of that vast place there rose a plaintive voice, and in tones most tender and sweet and rich came floating through that enchanted hush our poor old simple song "L'Arbre Fée de Bourlemont!" and then Joan broke down and put her face in her hands and cried. Yes, you see, all in a moment the pomps and grandeurs dissolved away and she was a little child again herding her sheep with the tranquil pastures stretched about her, and war and wounds and blood and death and the mad frenzy and turmoil of battle a dream.   [18, 55]

The Tree is the talisman of Joan's oneness with nature; it asserts that she is "born child of the sun, natural comrade of the birds and of all happy free creatures" (18, 124–25). It gives her the "seeing eye," "the creating mouth," those innate, mysterious qualities which neither the doctors, nor the soldiers, nor Joan's own page can otherwise account for. A vision of the Tree appears to Joan in prison and aids her as much as the Holy Voices to meet death. For the Fairy Tree is the sign of Paradise. It is a pagan sign, not specifically Christian, being associated with children, fairies, open fields, and animals of the forest rather than with Saint Catherine and Saint Margaret. Furthermore, it signifies a Paradise existing eternally in the past, not a future Christian heaven.

Twain would not have us think that Joan and her companions are less devout Catholics for their allegiance to the Fairy Tree, so clearly a pagan nature symbol. Their childish faith and love encompass both modes of grace. Just as the Archangel appears to Joan under the branches of the Tree, so do the two visions of paradise coexist at her death in Joan's innocent soul. The Fairy Tree that rises upon her sight in prison shares its power with the Cross, in the sight of which she dies.

The Fairy Tree is the comprehensive symbol through which Joan's life approximates for Twain the pattern of myth. Her sacrificial death (so like Christ's) [22] completes the cycle of the nature goddess begun by a pastoral childhood, continued through an heroic, miraculous career, and climaxed by the Passion at Rouen. Through her death—and clearly this is the significance of her life to Louis de Conte—Joan of Arc escapes from time, from old age, from loss of faith. The vision of the Fairy Tree redeems life.

This interpretation of his heroine clearly fitted Mark Twain's own spiritual condition which was in many respects identical in its perilously balanced pessimism and nostalgia with that of his spokesman. That he could represent Joan simultaneously as Christian, democrat, and nature goddess, and yet not exclusively as any of these, argues a spiritual ambivalence, a tension among skepticism, determinism, and faith which was, by 1896, far from being resolved.

Joan of Arc both exemplifies this dilemma and offers a way

22. A flyleaf notation in Twain's copy of *La Vierge Lorraine, Jeanne D'Arc* reads: "Several great Historical trials:
    Christ before Pilate
    Joan's two trials
    That man in the time of Mary [.]"
MTP. © Mark Twain Company.

out. Sieur Louis, with his mixture of irony, resignation, and rage at the human race, is the literary spokesman for the philosophical contradictions (if one may so grace the simplicities of Twain's thought) of *What Is Man?* More significant, however, is Joan of Arc herself. The Maid embodies and transcends all contradictions. Depicted as girlishly human in speech and manner, she escapes the stain of depraved humanity by her indestructible innocence. A devout Catholic, her loyalty to her Voices places her in righteous opposition to that fallible institution the Church. Her bond with the Fairy Tree, on the other hand, establishes a link with nature, with a prerational source of knowledge, with a pre-institutional source of piety, with an eternal world of values not subject to the pains, disappointments, doubts, and contradictions of adult life. For it is *adult* life which creates ambiguities for Sieur Louis de Conte. *Joan of Arc,* though it culminates in the victimization of childhood, affirms that state as the only form of life worth living— and dying—for.

Twain was not alone in his spiritual confusions, nor was he the only artist in the 1890's who found in childhood, in a romantic return to nature, in a coupling of Christian and pagan imagery, resolution of the loss of faith and the crippling effects of scientific determinism. At the same time that he was composing *Joan of Arc* Henry Adams was working his way toward a private cult of the Virgin. William Dean Howells, in *A Boy's Town* (1890) had just celebrated childhood in terms even more nostalgic than *Joan of Arc.* Stephen Crane, in the imagery of *The Red Badge of Courage* and "The Monster," was mixing pagan and Christian symbols in an attempt to replace by art the lost Methodism of his unworldly father. Further afield, the artists and architects of the White City at Chicago were carefully blending Christian and pagan motifs and ornaments and Frederick L. Olmsted was introducing nature into that plan with his "wooded isle" landscape arrangement. In France, where Twain completed *Joan of Arc*, a similar mixing of themes was taking place in certain symbolist poems and on the canvases of Paul Gauguin.

Joan of Arc has, to be sure, no direct tie with *Mont-Saint-Michel and Chartres*, *The Red Badge of Courage*, the Columbian Exposition, or the paintings of Gauguin. Yet a common pattern may perhaps be discerned in these manifestations of *fin de siècle* art. Certain artists, of whom Twain was one, were simultaneously struggling to assert spiritual values in the face of massive forces making for religious decay. Some of these forces may be identified as scientific determinism, the ugly spread of industrialism, imperialism, the worship of wealth. What concerns readers of *Joan of Arc* is not the nature of these forces but rather the form of the response. In this historical romance Twain utilizes some of the ideas abroad in the air of his time. Like Adams, he worships a Virgin whom he has, along with his friend Howells and, to a lesser degree, Stephen Crane, made into a child. He merges the image of a Roman Catholic saint with that of a primitive nature goddess much as Saint-Gaudens would mix pagan and Christian elements in the decoration of a frieze or Gauguin would place a halo about the head of a half-naked Tahitian maiden. Thus, though *Joan of Arc* was Twain's private act of devotion, it partook of certain of the spiritual and artistic currents in the Western world of 1896.

What strikes the casual reader as an incongruity in Mark Twain's career shows, upon inspection, to have an appropriate inevitability. Far from being an unlikely topic for him to hit upon, Joan of Arc had all the earmarks of a predetermined subject for his pen. At a particular moment in his life Twain found that the Maid of Orleans gave him a means of dramatizing his own and his age's spiritual dilemma without the embarrassing obligation to resolve the dilemma. For, after all,

Joan was "the *Riddle* of the Ages . . . All the rules fail in this girl's case." To the aging man who was both a realist and romantic in his writing, a determinist and a moralist in his thinking, an agnostic and yet a deist in his worship, Joan of Arc permitted a temporary haven. That haven lay in the timeless past of childhood, symbolized by the Fairy Tree of Bourlemont, a kind of Jackson's Island in the fifteenth century, where even death at the stake was but a necessary stage in the cycle of a girl goddess.

8.

Nightmares and Dreams

THE FINAL, UNHAPPY CHAPTER of Mark Twain's life is well
known. Equally familiar is his desperate response to fate, for
he was a man who reacted extravagantly to misfortune. "You
have seen our whole voyage," he wrote Joe Twichell after
the death of Susy. "You have seen us go to sea, a cloud of
sail, and the flag at the peak; and you see us now, chartless,
adrift—derelicts; battered, water-logged, our sails a ruck of
rags, our pride gone. For it is gone. And there is nothing in
its place." [1]

Twain had cause to despair. For a man whose emotional
life was built around his family, the blows dealt him were
devastating. His favorite daughter died suddenly, painfully,
alone; this was in 1896, shortly before the family was to be
reunited after the wearisome lecture tour around the world
which recouped the Clemens fortunes. Olivia Clemens, never
a strong person, went rapidly into decline after Susy's death
and for the next eight years was a total invalid. Her death in
1904 at Florence was a release. The final body-blow was the
death of Jean, Twain's youngest, who suffered from epilepsy
and succumbed suddenly to a heart attack on Christmas eve
1909.

This succession of private calamities made it doubly difficult for Twain to accept the fact of growing old. His letters

1. MT to Rev. J. H. Twichell (Jan. 19, 1897), in Paine, *Letters*, 2,
640.

to Howells and Twichell during the last dozen years of his life are filled with railings against old age and death. The fame an admiring world heaped on him, culminating in the scarlet robe from Oxford, did little to relieve the deepening disillusionment of his final years. "Life was a fairy-tale, then, it is a tragedy now," he wrote some old friends upon receiving an invitation to their golden wedding anniversary.[2]

Twain had lost his wife, his son, two of his daughters, and a host of friends. Stick by stick, the emotional furniture of his house of intellect was stripped away. What remained, however, was his writing desk. In the face of what he regarded as disaster, the aging artist took refuge in work. He plunged into writing with a ferocity born of the urge to make sense of catastrophe. The first-fruits of sublimation were two elegies, "In Memoriam," a poem composed after Susy's death, and its prose sequel, "The Death of Jean." The latter is the more personal and poignant document of grief; indeed, it hangs continually on the edge of mawkishness. What redeems "The Death of Jean" is not simply terrible sincerity of emotion but also the identification of Twain's private loss with the general sense of lost innocence and youth that for thirty years had informed his fiction. "And last night I saw again what I had seen then," he wrote of Jean's body lying in its coffin on Christmas eve, "—that strange and lovely miracle—the sweet, soft contours of early maidenhood restored by the gracious hand of death! When Jean's mother lay dead, all trace of care, and trouble, and suffering, and the corroding years had vanished out of the face, and I was looking again upon it as I had known and worshipped it in its young bloom and beauty a whole generation before." (*26*, 122). This was written barely four months before Twain's own death, and one cannot fail to sense here the writer's own yearning for the "gracious hand." But the phrases themselves—"the sweet, soft

2. MT to Mrs. Gordon (Jan. 24, 1906), ibid., p. 787.

contours of early maidenhood," "the corroding years," "young bloom and beauty"—reverberate with meanings derived not only from the present tragedy but also from *Joan of Arc,* "A Horse's Tale," "Marjorie Fleming, The Wonder Child," "Eve's Diary," stories about young girls written by Twain during the last unhappy years of his life.

The writing of these stories had been another way to assuage grief. "I work all the days, and trouble vanishes away when I use that magic," he confided to Joe Twichell; "I have many unfinished books to fly to for my preservation." [3] To Howells he made a more specific comment. "For several years I have been intending to stop writing for print as soon as I could afford it. At last I can afford it, & have put the pot-boiler pen away." Then he added, "What I have been wanting is a chance to write a book without reserves—a book which should take account of no one's feelings, and no one's prejudices, opinions, beliefs, hopes, illusions, delusions; a book which should say my say, right out of my heart, in the plainest language & without a limitation of any sort. . . . I believe I can make it tell what I think of Man, & how he is constructed, & what a shabby poor ridiculous thing he is, & how mistaken he is in his estimate of his character & powers & qualities & his place among the animals." [4]

The book "without reserves" turned out to be *The Mysterious Stranger.* Much revised and published only after his death, this *nouvelle* of an angelic boy's visit to a medieval Austrian village was Twain's last major work. Quite apart from the grief-ridden atmosphere in which it was composed, the conditions surrounding the genesis of *The Mysterious Stranger* were for Twain unusual. Released simultaneously from pressures of audience, family, friends, neighbors—all

3. MT to Rev. J. H. Twichell (Jan. 19, 1897), ibid., pp. 641–42.
4. MT to W. D. Howells (May 12, 1899), *Mark Twain–Howells Letters, 2,* 698–99.

those forces that operated at Nook Farm and helped so much to shape his earlier work—he was freer than ever before to make this novel exactly what he intended: "the right vessel to contain all the ordure I am planning to dump into it." [5] Together with some slighter pieces like "Letters from the Earth" and "Little Bessie Would Assist Providence" (both unpublished fragments), *The Mysterious Stranger* presents us with the "symbols of despair" (to use DeVoto's appropriate phrase) of a village agnostic grown old and bitter. The novel exhibits Twain's mind at one extreme of its violent oscillation, at that pole where a meaningful universe is now rejected and one in which human freedom (hence human responsibility) is seen as illusion.

We know there always existed an opposite pole to Mark Twain's misanthropy. At the other end of his mind Twain was a man with strong emotional attachments not only to specific human beings but to the potential dignity of the human condition itself. Strongest of all his intuitive sympathies, of course, was his feeling for children. This predilection persisted right alongside his burgeoning pessimism. Thus only a few years before *What Is Man?* he wrote *Tom Sawyer, Abroad;* a few years later he was busy with "Eve's Diary" and "A Horse's Tale." Such vacillations characterize the writer's whole career. From the "Snodgrass Papers" right up to *Joan of Arc* we have noted this curious compulsion for contradictions, expressing itself between different works and also within a single novel or story. Hence the persistence of a sentimental impulse throughout his period of blackest despair should not be wondered at. Like the Angel Fish Club which he established about this time, his attachment to childhood and his special fondness for young maidens survived even the onslaught of his rage against the cosmos.

Since virtually all of Twain's last works which exhibit this

5. Ibid., p. 699.

sentimental side deal with girls, one is tempted to wonder whether the aged writer did not unconsciously divide his allegiance along sexual lines. "The Death Disk," "A Horse's Tale," "Eve's Diary," and "Marjorie Fleming, the Wonder Child" are, on the surface at least, happy pieces in which the power and beauty of girlhood are celebrated. *The Mysterious Stranger,* on the other hand, attempts to demonstrate "what a shabby poor ridiculous thing" man is, and does so principally in terms of boyish characters. Closer scrutiny shows, however, that in spite of attractive plausibility this notion does not do justice to the inner coherence which Twain's bifocal vision actually had. Though *The Mysterious Stranger* manifests superficially a nihilism that totally contradicts the mood of idyllic, innocent happiness of the other stories—notably, "A Horse's Tale"—a closer look at the fabric of both sorts of fiction uncovers a sympathetic thread running through the story of young Satan's visit to Eseldorf and, conversely, a melancholy, elegiac tone underlying the saccharine narratives of Cathy Alison and her cousins. In other words, Twain allowed both spirits to enter and form a necessary element of both stories. Despair *and* sentimentality are inseparable here, as in the novels and stories of earlier years, because they formed consistent and complimentary aspects of his view of reality. In this fundamental respect his imagination was entirely static.

More than any other factor, I believe, the unchanging dualism of his mental temper explains why he continued, long after the nostalgic appeal of Hannibal had evaporated, to select boys and girls as favorite fictional characters. To the last, he saw the world of childhood as the appropriate battle ground upon which his violently contradictory views of human nature and destiny could deploy themselves without ever reaching a definitive outcome. As had been the case with *Joan of Arc,* he could not bring himself, either in *The Mysteri-*

ous Stranger or in the genial little tales of these last years, to deny the hopeless determinism of the one or the fond idealizing of maidenhood so typical of the other. All his life Mark Twain found it difficult to settle down.

The germs from which *The Mysterious Stranger* eventually grew were implanted many years before Twain finally began writing it in 1898. One of the earliest inspirations apparently occurred in the summer of 1867. At that time he had just come East as roving correspondent for the *Alta California*. Behind him lay the satiric newspaper sketches, the trip to the Sandwich Islands, and the first lectures of the "Moralist of the Main." Ahead lay the *Quaker City* excursion, *Innocents Abroad*, Elmira, and Nook Farm. Young and poised on the brink of a brilliant career, Twain was in a receptive frame of mind.

During his rambles about New York City the red-haired, drawling Westerner saw and recorded a great variety of Eastern sights for his California readers. In one of the city's libraries he happened upon an old copy of the Apochryphal New Testament in an edition of 1621. Twain was plainly fascinated by the old tome. He commented at length upon this unusual but somewhat unnewsworthy item, as if the Apochrypha were so entirely novel to him that it would naturally seem so to his fellow Westerners. "It is rather a curious book," he remarked. "This book has many chapters devoted to the infancy of the Savior and the miracles he wrought. For instance: Chapter 15: Jesus and other boys play together and make clay figures of animals. Jesus causes them to walk; also makes clay birds which he causes to fly, and eat and drink. The children's parents are alarmed and take Jesus for a sorcerer, and order them to seek better company . . . Chapter 19: Jesus charged with throwing a boy from the roof of a house, miraculously causes the dead boy to speak and acquit him . . . makes fish-pools on the Sabbath, and causes a boy to die who broke them down; another boy runs against him, whom he also causes to die . . . His society was pleasant, but attended by serious drawbacks." [6]

Though he called these legendary anecdotes of the boy Christ "frivolous and trifling," there is good reason to believe they made a lasting impression. The notion of depicting the Son of God as a sort of boy magician doubtless appealed then to the youthful skeptic who had already privately rejected the Presbyterian orthodoxy of his mother; later the mature novelist would find the same idea aptly suited to the inner requirements of his final novel.

By a process made familiar by John Livingston Lowes the memory of the divine boy went down into Twain's unconscious. In 1898, over thirty years after that first peek into the Apochrypha, the dormant seed began to germinate. On September 21, 1898, Twain's Notebook received this entry: "Story of little Satan, Jr. who came to Hannibal, went to school, was popular and greatly liked by those who knew his secret. The others were jealous and the girls didn't like him because he smelled of brimstone. He was always doing miracles—his pals knew they were miracles, the others thought they were mysteries." [7] Characteristically, he had sidestepped the problem of blasphemy by transforming young Jesus into "little Satan, Jr.," but in essentials—a divine boy introduced into the life of an actual village—we have the eventual outline of *The Mysterious Stranger.* God is about to become a Bad Boy.

During the following weeks Twain played with the idea. He could not at first decide whether to make his story of the superhuman youth extravagantly funny (as the name "little

6. Franklin Walker and G. Ezra Dane, eds., *Mark Twain's Travels with Mr. Brown* (New York, A. A. Knopf, 1940), pp. 251, 252–53.

7. Albert B. Paine, ed., *Mark Twain's Notebook* (New York, Harper and Brothers, 1935), entry of Sept. 21, 1898, p. 369.

Satan, Jr." suggested) or to strike a more serious satiric note. In November, for instance, he jotted down this embryonic episode: "In the early days he takes Tom & Huck down to stay over Sunday in hell—gatekeeper doesn't recognize him in disguise & asks for tickets . . . They wipe the tears of the unbaptised babies roasting on the red hot floors—one is Tom's little niece that he so grieved to lose—still, as she deserves this punishment he is able to bear it." [8] The edged satire of the concluding phrase here is some distance from the tone of the opening remark, and very different indeed from this idea for the same kind of Satanic boys' story he wrote down about November 8: "Write Xmas story, Title The Good Little Boy who went to Hell. Treats the little devils to fans & ice cream. Gives papa-Satan an asbestos prayerbook, partly converts him, & secures certain palliations [ameliorations], privileges & advantages for Christian babies, St Bartholomew Catholics who got snatched out of life without the saving last sacraments, & They are allowed to go outside and cool off, Sundays. Goes to heaven and gets privileges there for good little children—they are allowed to spend their Sundays in hell." [9] Here even the projected title recalls Twain's California sketches, and his old inerradicable penchant for extravagant burlesque has operated to lead him away from the original dramatic situation. Unchanged, however, is the fierce moral indignation that forty years before had earned him the nickname of the "Moralist of the Main."

Eventually, Twain chose serious rather than burlesque ridicule as the basic tone for *The Mysterious Stranger*. Furthermore, instead of moving his story of young Satan about from earth to heaven to hell, Twain, who commenced

8. Notebook 32[II] (last date Nov. 11, 1898), typescript, p. 51, in MTP. © Mark Twain Company.
9. Notebook 32[II] (last date Nov. 8, 1898), typescript, pp. 49–50, in MTP. © Mark Twain Company.

writing the novel in Vienna, selected the sleepy, symbolic hamlet of Eseldorf (Assville) as a medieval Austrian setting for the miraculous appearances of Satan's nephew. This final choice of locale came, however, only after several abortive versions of the story had been abandoned. One of the most interesting of these rehearsals was one with Hannibal as the setting and Twain's childhood friends and neighbors (thinly disguised) as actors.

The opening scene of this version of little Satan's story discloses Hannibal in wintertime, with Sid, Tom, and Huck sliding down the hill to school. A new boy appears, "apparently about fifteen," neatly dressed and very handsome. He goes by the name of Forty-four and at first speaks only French.[10] Within a few minutes, however, he memorized the entire English grammar, as well as whole books of mathematics, Latin, and Greek—all to the immense astonishment of the kids and of Archibald Ferguson, the old schoolmaster. After nonchalantly breaking the arm of the school bully, Forty-four settles down in the home of the Hotchkisses (a ménage modeled on that of Orion Clemens, Twain's scatterbrained brother). Everything "the miraculous boy" does mystifies and delights the townspeople. He converses with animals, has an inexhaustible supply of gold coins in his trousers, causes a table laden with rich viands to appear, providing a banquet served by tiny devils who considerately stand on metal plates so as to keep from scorching the furniture. When a terrible blizzard strikes, Forty-four rescues thirteen villagers from the snowdrifts. Gradually, the angelic

10. A plausible explanation of the significance of Satan's odd alias is offered by Kenneth Lynn. Developing a suggestion by Henry Nash Smith, Lynn reminds us of two Jewish boys Twain knew as a boy in Hannibal. Their name was Levin; so their collective nickname was Twenty-two ("Twice Levin—twenty-two"). Lynn analogizes "Twice Twenty-two—forty-four." See *Mark Twain and Southwestern Humor*, pp. 280–81.

adolescent comes to prefer human life to his own condition. He stops his sudden visits back to Hell, ceases performing miracles, gets religion, and finally falls in love with Annie Fleming, a Missouri maiden of eighteen.[11] Consequently, as the fragment ends—for in characteristic style Twain completed only six chapters of the Hannibal *Mysterious Stranger* together with some notes for subsequent sections—young Satan has all but renounced angelic status in favor of human life. The recoverable idyll of village boyhood seems to have temporarily bemused Twain's imagination and we are once again back in the atmosphere of *Tom Sawyer,* except that this time boyhood demonstrates its superiority by virtue of superhuman cleverness.

The Hannibal version of *The Mysterious Stranger* is a comedy. Though it contains premonitions of its successor (particularly in Forty-four's acerb comments upon man's Moral Sense), in tone the unfinished tale alternates between the fabulous and the genial. As the century waned, however, and Twain's cast of mind steadily darkened, this boisterous mode of depicting possible relations between humans and superhumans became less and less suitable. His growing rigidity of thought manifested itself in many ways. Two of the most revealing forms it took were *What Is Man?*, the "gospel" of pessimism he began writing also in 1898, and in Twain's private reading, particularly in books about psychology and popular science. One of the more revealing of these latter expressions of his cosmic philosophy is his own copy of James Mark Baldwin's popular introduction to psychology, *The Story of the Mind,* which appeared in 1899. Twain's marginal comments in this little volume reinforce the doctrine of man as a machine—the doleful answer to the query of *What Is Man?*.

Cast in the form of a dialogue, *What Is Man?* repeats in

11. See MS of Hannibal version of *The Mysterious Stranger* in MTP.

skeletal form the double perspective of many of Twain's novels. That is, a Young Man, as naive as the greenhorn in *Life on the Mississippi,* asks questions of an Old Man who is as cynically wise as Sieur Louis de Conte after his career as page to a saint is over. Inevitably not much dramatic interest is generated. Over and over again the refrain is repeated: "Man the machine—man the impersonal engine. Whatsoever a man is, is due to his *make,* and to the *influences* brought to bear on it by his heredities, his habitat, his associations. He is moved, directed, COMMANDED, by *exterior* influences—*solely.* He *originates* nothing, not even a thought." The Old Man will not even allow Adam the least bit of freedom to think originally. "Adam probably had a good head," he admits, "but it was of no sort of use to him until it was filled up *from the outside.* He was not able to invent the triflingest little thing with it . . . A man's brain is so constructed that *it can originate nothing whatever.* It can only use material obtained *outside.* It is merely a machine; and it works automatically, not by will-power" (*26,* 5, 7).

The impotence of the human mind to act independently—that is the melancholy message the Old Man asserts and which the Mysterious Stranger echoes with sardonic insistence. They are, of course, voicing the convictions of Twain himself. By the mid-nineties, he had come to rest in a philosophy which, rejecting the Christian explanation of human freedom of the will, accepted uncritically those aspects of popular evolutionary thought that regarded man as caught in a cul-de-sac of environmental forces from which there is no escape. In *Mark Twain at Work* Bernard DeVoto has explained Twain's private reasons for adopting such a form of environmentalism, one far starker in its human prospects than formulations of Herbert Spencer or William Graham Sumner. DeVoto argues that Twain's whole purpose as a writer during his last years was to absolve himself from imagined guilt for the dire family calamities that engulfed him. "Art is the terms of an armistice made with fate," DeVoto asserts, and goes on to analyze Twain's determinism in these terms: "He had tried to say: it was not my fault, I was betrayed. But the accusation could not be stayed so easily. He had tried to say: it was not my fault, for the fixed universe of inescapable law intended from the beginning that this should happen." [12]

To see Twain's determinism as psychologically rather than intellectually necessary is doubtless a sound insight; it helps, for one thing, to bridge the apparent gap between the two sides of his mind. But to such an explanation must be added evidence for the writer's honest wrestling with the intellectual problems of his generation. Though uneducated in a formal sense and hence like all self-taught men full of surprising depths and shallows, Twain nevertheless was generally familiar with the fields of popular science, philosophy, and, as it emerged, psychology. From what we know of his conversation and letters and from the contents of his library he followed the Darwinian dialogue of his age. He owned and read with attention some, at least, of the works of John Fiske, Andrew D. White, and William James, as well as more popular formulations like C. W. Saleeby's *Evolution, the Master-Key*.[13]

One of these books which Twain read carefully was James Mark Baldwin's *The Story of the Mind*, a copy of which its author sent with the affectionate inscription "From one Mark to Another." [14] Twain's underlinings and marginal comments indicate that his imagination responded vigorously to Baldwin's explanations. Moreover the form these responses took

12. DeVoto, *Mark Twain at Work*, pp. 129, 130.
13. See *Mark Twain Library Auction Catalogue*, April 10, 1951, in MTP, especially Items 15a, 28a, 61a, 7c, 69c, 74c, D3, D47.
14. MT's copy of James Mark Baldwin, *The Story of the Mind* (New York, D. Appleton and Company, 1899), is in the Mark Twain Library, West Redding, Connecticut.

is strikingly similar to the language of *The Mysterious Stranger*. In the introduction, for instance, Baldwin remarks upon the genesis of human mentality, "we must think of it [the Mind] as a growing, developing thing, showing its stages of evolution in the ascending animal scale, and also in the unfolding of the child . . . and as revealing its possibilities finally in the brutal acts of the mob, the crimes of the lynching party, and the deeds of collective righteousness performed by our humane and religious societies." Twain marked this whole passage, for the author of *Huckleberry Finn* knew at first hand man's capacities in the direction of mobs and lynching parties. He twice underscored the word "brutal" and underlined (very likely with grave reservations) "humane" and "deeds of collective righteousness." *The Mysterious Stranger*, on which Twain may well have been working as he read Baldwin, contains (like the earlier novels) a number of graphic depictions of mobs and lynching parties.[15]

To be sure, Twain did not need a Princeton professor to inform him of man's inhumanity to his fellows. The question raised by *The Story of the Mind* is not literary influence, but rather evidence of intellectual awareness on Twain's part of scientific opinion concerning man's freedom as a thinking animal. On this score, Baldwin both reassured and upset him. The psychologist presented the latest theories linking all forms of life into one organic chain; at one place he wrote, "there is the rise of the evolutionary theory, which teaches that there is no absolute break between man and the higher animals in the matter of mental endowment; and that what difference there is must itself be the result of the laws of mental growth." [16] Twain more or less accepted this; "no frontier" he wrote carefully in the margin. Then Baldwin continued, "the more adequate the science of the human mind has be-

15. *The Story of the Mind*, pp. 6–7.
16. Ibid., p. 24.

come the more evident has it also become that man himself is more of a machine than has been supposed." Twain emphatically agreed. In fact, he went further; "He is wholly a machine" he asserted at the edge of the page. "Man grows by certain laws," Baldwin continued; "his progress is conditioned by the environment, both physical and social, in which he lives; his mind is a part of the natural system of things." Here Twain differed completely. Twice underscoring "growth," he wrote indignantly in the margin, "There is no mental *growth*. There is extension of mental *action*, but not of capacity." [17]

"Man is wholly a machine. There is no growth or change, only more of the same automatic, inevitable response to external stimuli." This, in essence, is the intellectual position Twain held during the period in which *The Mysterious Stranger* was written. Since there are clear indications in earlier works of his tendency to think in these terms, one must be careful about ascribing all of the writer's rigid determinism, as DeVoto is inclined to do, to an attempt to rationalize guilt feelings arising from the death of loved ones. Like all works of the fictional imagination, *The Mysterious Stranger* is the product of Twain's total experience. Its final form depends no less upon a young man's casual reading of the Apochrypha than upon other books read or personal tragedies endured.

Some of the literary effects of these influences may be seen in the final version of *The Mysterious Stranger*, a vastly different story from its Hannibal predecessor. Gone is Forty-four, the obliging young angel whose miraculous deeds demonstrate his good will. Instead appears Philip Traum, a charming but cynical nephew of Satan whose miracles are both more God-like and more inhuman than Forty-four's. In place of Tom, Huck, and Sid, there are three quite different boys—Theodor Fischer, son of the local organist, and his two pals, Seppi and Nikolaus. Eseldorf itself is projected far less graphically than

17. © Mark Twain Company.

was Hannibal. The village is viewed from a curious perspective, through the haze of time and distance; it is a dream town.

We learn Eseldorf's true status only gradually, and do so through the innocent eye of Theodor, the last boyish narrator in Twain's fiction. In a manner not unlike *Moby-Dick* Twain's novel has a divided focus. Philip Traum (like Ahab) is ostensibly the chief figure. However, it speedily becomes clear that all of Traum's actions are not only perceived through Theodor's mind but are directed toward illuminating that Ishmael-like mind with a sense of the true nature of things. What is happening is a cosmic initiation, with Theodor as the neophyte and Philip Traum the master of ceremonies.

The relation between the divine boy and the human is a complex one. Theodor's reaction to young Satan's instructive miracles—as, for instance, when he creates a crowd of tiny human figures, sets them to work, but casually crushes the life out of them when they begin quarreling—is a mixture of wonder and revulsion. To Theodor's young and naive mind, Satan's nonchalant murder of the tiny creatures is literally a brutal act. But Philip shows him that brutes never behave as badly as humans. Like Satan himself, animals lack a moral sense, and hence they cannot wrongfully inflict pain. "When a brute inflicts pain," he explains to the three boys,

> he does it innocently; it is not wrong; for him there is no such thing as wrong. And he does not inflict pain for the pleasure of inflicting it—only man does that. Inspired by that mongrel Moral Sense of his! A sense whose function is to distinguish between right and wrong, with liberty to choose which of them he will do. Now what advantage can he get out of that? He is always choosing, and in nine cases out of ten he prefers the wrong. There shouldn't be any wrong; and without the Moral Sense there couldn't be any. [27, 50-51]

242

These are indeed confusing words and deeds for Theodor to comprehend. On the one hand Philip Traum has the attributes of God—he creates effortlessly all forms of good things, and elicits the most ecstatic adoration from the boys. But just as effortlessly he commits the most inhumane deeds and does them in the same spirit of innocent ruthlessness a leisurely cat would display in devouring a mouse. He appears genuinely to like Theodor, Seppi, and Nikolaus, and yet his scorn for humanity is comprehensive. He blames men for misusing their miserable moral sense, but in the next scene will prove that man has absolutely no freedom of choice to exercise that sense. Satan by turns laughs and rages at human behavior; he will at one moment consider man's frailties so contemptible as to be beneath notice and then launch into a detailed diatribe against the evils of colonialism. Philip Traum is a thinly masked mouthpiece for the contradictions of Twain's own tortured mind. Philip Traum is one part Bad Boy, one part God, and one part Mark Twain.

As he had done many times before, Twain uses children as the chief vehicle for his cosmic allegory. Thus when he is anxious to demonstrate the inevitability that Man's moral sense will produce pain and suffering, he shows the villagers of Eseldorf dealing with a suspected witch. "They chased her more than half an hour, we following to see it," Theodor tells us,

> and at last she was exhausted and fell, and they caught her. They dragged her to a tree and threw a rope over a limb, and began to make a noose in it, some holding her, meantime, and she crying and begging, and her young daughter looking on and weeping, but afraid to do or say anything.
> They hanged the lady, and I threw a stone at her, although in my heart I was sorry for her; but all were

243

throwing stones and each was watching his neighbor, and if I had not done as the others did it would have been noticed and spoken of. Satan burst out laughing.

[27, 114–15]

This scene, which echoes earlier episodes in *The Prince and the Pauper, Huckleberry Finn,* and *A Connecticut Yankee,* marks a fictional high-water mark in Twain's misanthropy. Never before had the writer taken such explicit pains to show that boys are no different in their moral cowardice from other people. Theodor's confession (so different in its implications from Huck's unconscious lapses) pinpoints with dismaying clarity the end of Twain's belief in children's moral superiority.

Boys are as craven as grown-ups for several reasons. For one thing, they have the moral sense, that well-nigh infallible human instinct to do wrong and inflict pain. Moreover, boys cannot fail to throw stones at witches because, like everyone else, they are slaves to public opinion. "Monarchies, aristocracies, and religions are all based upon that large defect in your race," Traum tells Theodor, his words ringing with the same scorn Colonel Sherburn's had for Huck Finn, "the individual's distrust of his neighbor, and his desire, for safety's or comfort's sake, to stand well in his neighbor's eye" (27, 118).

But Theodor throws a rock at the unfortunate woman for a more comprehensive reason than either of these. This boy lives in a world in which this act, like all others, is absolutely predetermined and inevitable. "Among you boys you have a game," Satan explains, "you stand a row of bricks on end a few inches apart; you push a brick, it knocks its neighbor over, the neighbor knocks over the next brick—and so on till all the row is prostrate. That is human life. A child's first act knocks over the initial brick, and the rest will follow inexorably. If you could see into the future, as I can, you would see everything that was going to happen to that creature; for nothing can change the order of its life after the first event has determined it" (27, 81). Such determinism, Satan tells the three boys is neither ordered nor foreordained by God. "No. The man's circumstances and environment order it." Even were a person to try to assert his own will in opposition to the predetermined condition of things, such an act would itself be part of the pattern, "a thought bound to occur to him at that precise moment, and made certain by the first act of his babyhood" (27, 82–83).

Satan does not bother to notice how this assertion flatly contradicts his earlier remark about man's liberty to choose whether he will do right or wrong. *The Mysterious Stranger* contains so many such ambiguities that as a coherent *Weltanschauung* it can be regarded only as the end-product of a tired mind grappling with ideas foreign or inaccessible to it. Twain was no philosopher. But he *was* a literary artist; and while no reader can fail to notice the metaphysical fuzziness, neither can one miss the imaginative intensity generated at several points in the narrative. The emotional impact thus produced —and it occurs, as might be expected, most frequently in connection with Theodor and his friends, not with Satan— signals both the book's success as fiction and its inadequacy as philosophy. As the reader's sympathies are aroused, the world of Eseldorf is seen through Theodor's eyes. Gradually it is perceived that the various intellectual confusions spring from Twain's dramatic structure as well as from metaphysical imprecision. As Edwin Fussell has convincingly demonstrated, *The Mysterious Stranger* is the fictional representation of the mental process of a boy thinking his way from the mistaken belief that the material world is real to final awareness that the only reality lies in dreams.[18] That is Satan's objective in

18. See E. W. Fussell, "The Structural Problem of *The Mysterious Stranger*," *Studies in Philology*, 49 (1952), 95–104.

Theodor's initiation. "It is true, that which I have revealed to you," Satan says at the last; "there is no God, no universe, no human race, no earthly life, no heaven, no hell. It is all a dream—a grotesque and foolish dream. Nothing exists but you. And you are but a *thought*—a vagrant thought, a useless thought, a homeless thought, wandering forlorn among the empty eternities!" To which Theodor adds, "He vanished, and left me appalled; for I knew, and realized, that all he had said was true" (27, 140).

Philosophically speaking, of course, solipsism can be a coherent system only in a deaf-mute; even to assert it is to deny it. But Twain creates the illusion of order by constructing his story so that, at each stage of Theodor's enlightenment, both character and author accept as "real" that segment of experience being tested. This is the reason, among others, for Twain's reiterated use of his tried-and-true device, the division of his chief character into two distinct personalities. Satan and Theodor Fischer are two boys, one of whom represents the intellectual, amoral, and nihilistic side of Twain's mind and the other embodies the emotional and moral values that are in process of dissolution. In rough fashion, therefore, the two fit the classic pattern of earlier novels first established by Tom and Huck and repeated, with minor variation, by the pauper and the prince, Tom Driscoll and Chambers, Sieur Louis and Joan.

Within this dramatic and ideological framework, changes taking place in Theodor's innocent imagination are both accepted as valid and shown to be simply the illusion of change. Thus though we come to recognize that nothing *actually* exists, that literally everything is a dream, yet we cannot help sympathizing with the boy's dismayed reactions to Satan's revelations. For instance, one of Traum's favorite lessons is to demonstrate how an apparent tragedy like the death of a loved one is, in the omniscient mind, often known to be a happier fate than others that might have occurred. He proves this by telling Theodor that Nikolaus will die by drowning two weeks hence, that this death is far preferable to, say, forty-six years of painridden paralysis. Poor Theodor and Seppi (who learns the grisly secret) go through torments of pity and remorse during that fortnight. Twain's evocation of that grief (so close to his own experiences) is genuinely moving. "No, my mind was filled with Nikolaus," Theodor relates,

> my thoughts ran upon him only, and the good days we had seen together at romps and frolics in the woods and the fields and the river in the long summer days, and skating and sliding in the winter when our parents thought we were in school. And now he was going out of this young life, and the summers and winters would come and go, and we others would rove and play as before, but his place would be vacant; we should see him no more. Tomorrow he would not suspect, but would be as he had always been, and it would shock me to hear him laugh, and see him do lightsome and frivolous things, for to me he would be a corpse, with waxen hands and dull eyes, and I should see the shroud around his face . . .   [27, 89]

In imagery Huck Finn might have used, Twain here voices his private grief and says a requiem on a writing career spent as the champion of childhood. Theodor's elegy indirectly mourns the lost world of Cardiff Hill and Jackson's Island. "It was an awful eleven days," he goes on to remark, "and yet, with a lifetime stretching back between today and then, they are still a grateful memory to me, and beautiful. In effect they were days of companionship with one's sacred dead, and I have known no comradeship that was so close and precious" (27, 94). The dream of innocence is dead, as we realize when Theodor confesses that he is an old man recalling the past and not the young boy actually living through Nikolaus' last days.

The emotional charge infused into this and other scenes argues eloquently, though surreptitiously, that cynicism and solipsism are not *really* Twain's most deeply felt convictions. His more genuine sentiments are expressed by various characters in *The Mysterious Stranger,* one of whom is the mother of the dead Nikolaus, Frau Brandt. Accused of blasphemy and witchcraft (the medieval equivalents, in a sense, of Twain's own sin in writing this book), the grief-stricken woman is led to the stake. Turning to the people of Assville, she delivers a farewell. "Pronounce your sentence and let me go; I am tired of your society," she says.

> So they found her guilty, and she was excommunicated and cut off from the joys of heaven and doomed to the fires of hell; then she was clothed in a coarse robe and delivered to the secular arm, and conducted to the market-place, the bell solemnly tolling the while. We saw her chained to the stake, and saw the first thin film of blue smoke rise on the still air. Then her hard face softened, and she looked upon the packed crowd in front of her and said with gentleness:
>
> "We played together once, in the long-agone days when we were innocent little creatures. For the sake of that, I forgive you."   [27, 107]

This pardon in the name of childhood for society's inhumanity evokes at once the whole of Mark Twain's past. Hannibal and its various fictional images, similar scenes of sacrifice in *The Prince and the Pauper* and *Joan of Arc,* Twain's lifelong interest in history and in the roles innocence and integrity had played therein—all of these are implied or recalled in the tired martyr's speech. Symbolically, at least, Prospero is laying down his wand.

248

When, therefore, Twain reaches the solipsistic climax of *The Mysterious Stranger* and asks his reader to accept in all seriousness that none of these experiences is actual but only the merest figment of dreamy illusion, the demand is too great. The story of Theodor Fischer's initiation is too convincing as fiction to persuade as philosophy. Its maker has dramatized the divided camps of his own imagination so effectively that Satan's revelation of the cosmic joke of existence cannot erase or diminish the memory of certain boys and their friends—a mother, a kindly old priest, a good-hearted lawyer, all figures out of Twain's earlier fiction. These characters, though not without their flaws as literary creatures, are more "real" than Philip Traum, whose name suggests not merely his symbolic significance but also the limits of his dramatic potentiality.

Though they disliked each other's work, Mark Twain and Henry James would surely have agreed on this one point: to function at all, the artist must celebrate life. James expressed it once in the preface to *The Wings of the Dove* (a novel also begun in the last years of the waning century): "The poet essentially *can't* be concerned with dying ; . . . The process of life gives way fighting, and often may so shine out on the lost ground as in no other connexion." [19] By virtue of a similar commitment, Twain's achievement—of sustaining until the final page a desperately delicate balance between despising mankind and loving certain individuals, between intellectual assertion of a meaningless universe and intuitive awareness of love's reality—makes *The Mysterious Stranger* a work of very modern dimensions. Characteristically, Twain was able to bring off this feat by viewing once again the bitter truths of human life from the double perspective of boyhood and old age. Looking through the innocent eye as well as through the

19. Henry James, *The Art of the Novel, Critical Prefaces,* ed. R. P. Blackmer (New York, Scribner's, 1946), pp. 289–90.

tired mind enabled him, in a nostalgic sense at least, to keep writing worth-while fiction right to the end of his unhappy life.

During the years that *The Mysterious Stranger* was simmering in various forms in Twain's imagination—from the summer of 1898 until about 1906—his pen, now released from potboiler duty, was also busy with a quite different sort of fiction. Nothing indicates so eloquently his split vision as the fact that "The Death Disk" and "A Horse's Tale" were composed simultaneously with drafts of *The Mysterious Stranger*. Both Abby Mayfair and Cathy Alison, the saintly little heroines of these two tales of military life, are figures closer in spirit to Little Lord Fauntleroy than to Theodor Fischer and his friends. If the pendulum of despair swung Twain in *The Mysterious Stranger* close to Melville's mood of *The Confidence Man*, the opposite swing brought him back into the neighborhood of Frances Hodgson Burnett.

As I have tried to demonstrate, Twain never considered himself wholly apart from the juvenile tradition in American letters. *Tom Sawyer*, *The Prince and the Pauper*, and *Tom Sawyer*, *Abroad* were consciously aimed at boys and girls (among other readers), nor had the restrictions of such an audience (in spite of Van Wyck Brooks) much hindered Twain from writing what he wanted. That he still thought of his fictional career in these capacious terms is suggested by an entry made in the Notebooks as late as July 1898. "Creatures of Fiction" is the heading for a possible story Twain suggested to himself. There followed a list of juvenile figures: "Hans Brinker, [Lau]rence Hutton, Tom Bailey, [Bob Sawyer] Uncle Remus's Little Boy, George Washington, (with hat check) Sanford & Merton, Rollo & Jonas, Mary & little lamb, Tom & Huck, Prince & Pauper, Casabianca." Then Twain added the germ for a narrative: "Last comes Mogli on ele-

250

phant with his menagerie & they all rode away with him. It is a hot day. The place is a grassy meadow with scattering shade trees, a [small] prairie hid away in the forest—very still & sad, buzzing insects. They appear one or two at a time, & get acquainted, & talk. Climb trees when the menagerie appears." This idea evidently held Twain's fancy, for a few pages later he made a further notation: "Add: burial of Babes in Wood & of Cock Robin. The Midshipmate. Make Casabianca sing 'All in the Downs the Ship lay moored' & dance hornpipe. Introduce Mother Goose & her people." [20] Modern readers, intent upon constructing a mythopoeia for Mark Twain and proving *Huckleberry Finn* the Great American Novel, may be appalled at his casual listing of Huck Finn and Mother Goose side by side. To the last Twain ignored nice distinctions in literary form, grouping the serious and trivial together in cavalier fashion.

"The Death Disk" is not so blatantly juvenile a tale as the projected "Children of Fiction," but its sentimental appeal to children first and adults after is unmistakable. Twain toyed with this historical anecdote off and on for years. There is a Notebook entry as early as 1883 which records his reaction to an incident he read in Carlyle's *Cromwell* about a little girl who is called upon to determine the death of some soldiers in the Roundhead army. At first, under the stimulus of writing a stage version of "The American Claimant," he was all for turning this episode into a grand, dramatic tragedy. This proved but a temporary enthusiasm, however, and the story hung fire in his imagination for years. Finally, in 1902 he actually wrote a brief play which was produced, with some success, at the Carnegie Lyceum in New York. Some time later he redid the play as a short short story—"the shortest thing

20. Notebook 32[I] (July 16, 1898), typescript, pp. 26–27, in MTP. © Mark Twain Company.

I ever wrote, I think"—and it appeared in *Harper's Maga-zine*.[21] "The Death Disk" is of literary interest only because it explores anew one of his favorite fictional situations—the meeting of an innocent child with death in a grisly form. Abby Mayfair is asked by Oliver Cromwell to be God's instrument of justice in the trial for disobedience of three of his officers. In order to decide which of the three shall die (as a warning to the army) the Lord General gives three disks of sealing wax to the little child. Whichever officer receives the red disk from the girl's hand must die. As she walks behind the three blindfolded men she recognizes her own father, and places "the prettiest one" in his hand. The bathos of this situation is carried through to the very end; at the last moment, however, the child remembers that Cromwell had promised her any-thing she wished. She demands her father's pardon and the tragedy is averted. "God be thanked for the saving accident of that unthinking promise," concludes Cromwell, "and you, inspired by Him, for reminding me of my forgotten pledge, O imcomparable child!" (*23, 282*).

Cathy Alison is another "incomparable child" whose power and purity shine forth in a military setting. But in her case death is not averted, and "A Horse's Tale," which opens in the same Elsie Dinsmore spirit as "The Death Disk," descends with chilling abruptness to a bloody conclusion. The differ-ence between the two in large measure follows from the un-usual circumstances surrounding the genesis of the later story. One summer day in 1905, the actress Minnie Maddern Fiske approached Twain and asked him to help her in a campaign to abolish, of all unlikely things, bull-fighting in Spain. Twain's antivivisectionist sympathies were at that time common knowl-edge, for he had already written "A Dog's Tale." Mrs. Fiske suggested that a parallel story, exposing the cruelties of the

21. See Notebook 17 (May 1883 – August 1884), typescript, p. 6, in MTP; also Paine, *Mark Twain*, 2, 763, 3, 1194, 1246.

peculiar Latin institution, might be done in the form of a short story "of an old horse that is finally given over to the bull-ring." [22] Twain wrote her at once. "I shall certainly write the story. But I may not get it to suit me, in which case it will go in the fire." [23] As it turned out, this caveat by the aged writer jealous of his hard-won freedom proved unnecessary. Within a month "A Horse's Tale" was finished and appeared the next year.

As fiction this is, in Paine's tactful words, "not one of Mark Twain's greatest stories." One might have expected this result from Mrs. Fiske's letter. Yet Twain himself certainly did not plan to produce a pot-boiler; on the contrary, he wrote his business agent F. A. Duneka that he was "deeply interested" in the work and "dead to everything else" during its composition. The reason for such serious attention to a minor undertaking was simple: "the heroine is my daughter, Susy, whom we lost. It was not intentional—it was a good while before I found it out." [24] For the first time in a long career, Twain was using one of his own children as the direct inspiration for a story.

Casting his own dead daughter in the heroine's role was not the chief reason for the eventual failure of "A Horse's Tale." What proved far more damaging was Twain's taking Mrs. Fiske's original hint so literally. Following to absurd lengths the pattern of his past work and perhaps influenced by the success of *Black Beauty,* he made a horse the narrator of Cathy Alison's pathetically brief life. Soldier Boy, Buffalo Bill's favorite mount, is, to say the least, an awkward successor to Simon Wheeler, Huck Finn, Louis de Conte, and Theodor Fischer. Even though the setting is a more or less realistic cavalry post on the Great Plains, a story-telling Army mount

22. Paine, 3, 1245.
23. MT to Mrs. M. M. Fiske (n.d.), in Paine, *Letters, 2,* 777–78.
24. MT to F. A. Duneka (Oct. 7, 1906), ibid., p. 779.

strains the reader's credulity to the breaking point—and beyond. For one thing, Soldier Boy is not a hard-boiled horse capable of detached commentary on human affairs. He is, rather, a rank sentimentalist and idolizes Cathy Alison, the nine-year-old niece of the Commanding General of Fort Paxton. Furthermore, his language is stilted to the point of parody, as in this typical exchange with another horse:

> [The Mexican Plug] ". . . Did you say *her* Excellency?"
> [Soldier Boy] "The same. A Spanish lady, sweet blossom of a ducal house. And truly a wonder; knowing everything, capable of everything; speaking all the languages, master of all sciences, a mind without horizons, a heart of gold, the glory of her race! On whom be peace!"
> "Amen. It is marvellous!" [27, 174]

Unfortunately, Cathy is regarded no less worshipfully by the human figures in the tale. Troopers, Indian scouts, officers, children, Negro servants—everyone is her willing slave. When the steeplechase is organized, Cathy wins the silver bugle. When the children form a play Troop, Cathy is elected Lieutenant General and takes charge of the military games with the skill of a latter-day Joan of Arc. "Yes, they are soldiers, those little people," Soldier Boy remarks, "and healthy, too, not ailing any more, the way they used to be sometimes. It's because of her drill. She's got a fort now—Fort Fanny Marsh. Major-General Tommy Drake planned it out, and the Seventh and Dragoons built it . . . she's dressed like a page, of old times, they say . . . She's lovely in it—oh, just a dream! In some ways she is just her age, but in others she's as old as her uncle, I think" (27, 177–78).

As Twain became more and more engrossed with his fantasy, he forgot the story of the horse he had promised to tell. Soldier Boy fades into the background as Cathy dominates the story. This shift necessitates a new narrator, General Alison, the doting uncle. In the process, details from Nook Farm days crop up again and again. Soldier Boy's name, for instance, was originally that of a family cat, as was "Buffalo Bill." Even the illustrations continue the long-delayed act of devotion. Cathy Alison is Susy Clemens to the life. "I am sending you her picture to use," Twain wrote his publisher, "and to reproduce with photographic exactness the unsurpassable *expression* and all. May you find an artist who has lost an idol!" [25]

Though bathed in seas of nostalgia, Cathy displays nonetheless some of the sturdy characteristics associated with Mark Twain's children. Unformed in many ways and wide-eyed, yet old in instinctive wisdom, she is an American Saint Joan. Adults naturally defer to her powers of virtue and will, for her page's costume symbolically recalls both the Maid and King Edward of England. Her initiation, too, is as sudden and wrenching as any of her predecessors. At the tale's end Cathy is in Spain —where Mrs. Fiske wanted her to be all along—looking for her lost companion, Soldier Boy, who has been stolen and sold. One day at the bull fight the inevitable reunion takes place:

> . . . two horses lay dying; the bull had scattered his persecutors for the moment, and stood raging, panting, pawing the dust in clouds over his back, when the man that had been wounded returned to the ring on a remount, a poor blindfolded wreck that had yet something ironically military about his bearing—and the next moment the bull had ripped him open and his bowels were dragging upon the ground and the bull was charging his swarm of pests again. Then came pealing through the air a bugle-call that froze my blood—"*It is I, Soldier—come!*" I turned; Cathy was flying down through the massed

25. MT to F. A. Duneka (Oct. 7, 1906), ibid., p. 779.

people; she cleared the parapet at a bound, and sped toward that riderless horse, who staggered forward towards the remembered sound; but his strength failed, and he fell at her feet, she lavishing kisses upon him and sobbing, the house rising with one impulse, and white with horror! Before help could reach her the bull was back again—

She was never conscious again in life. We bore her home, all mangled and drenched in blood, and knelt by her and listened to her broken and wandering words, and prayed for her passing spirit, and there was no comfort—nor ever will be, I think.   [27, 217–18]

As is so often the case in Twain's death scenes, General Alison's words reverberate with pathos carried almost to the point of travesty; nothing but the undeniable sincerity in the old officer's account saves it from the reader's snicker.

Only in a few final lines does "A Horse's Tale" recall Twain's earlier celebrations of childhood's short-lived moments of victory. At every other point the story betrays the sentimental hand of a mediocre magazine propagandist. Twain has taken so few pains to paint a convincing picture of fort life on the western prairies, has paid so little attention to reproducing the speech of actual men and children, that his tribute to the lost Susy finally delineates a dream-world, one as remote from reality as the Poe-like landscape of Twain's elegy "In Memoriam." In spite of a recognizably American setting, "A Horse's Tale" remains just as much a fantasy as *The Mysterious Stranger*. Neither world actually exists. But while Theodor Fischer's story emits now and then flashes of vivid action and authentic feeling before dissolving at the last minute into nightmare, "A Horse's Tale" presents precisely the opposite illusion—a papier-mâché world of talking horses and doting cavalrymen which suddenly achieves an atmosphere of emotional veracity in the last paragraphs. Both fabrications—the nostalgic mirage of false happiness and the opposite mirage of utter nihilism—demonstrate in clear outline the state of Twain's polarized mind during the last, desperately unhappy years of his life. Capable neither of belief nor of resting secure in his disbelief, he could only express his misanthropy and love through dreams.

In January 1908, in a state of depression at the dull wintry weather of New York, an old man sailed south alone, to Bermuda and a change of scene. On the first morning of his arrival, Twain came downstairs:

As I entered the breakfast-room the first object I saw in that spacious and far-reaching place was a little girl seated solitary at a table for two. I bent down over her and patted her cheek and said:

"I don't seem to remember your name; what is it?" By the sparkle in her brown eyes it amused her. She said:

"Why, you've never known it, Mr. Clemens, because you've never seen me before."

"Why, that is true, now that I come to think; it certainly is true, and it must be one of the reasons why I have forgotten your name. But I remember it now perfectly—it's Mary."

She was amused again; amused beyond smiling; amused to a chuckle, and she said:

"Oh no, it isn't; it's Margaret."

I feigned to be ashamed of my mistake and said:

"Ah, well, I couldn't have made that mistake a few years ago; but I am old, and one of age's earliest infirmities is a damaged memory; but I am clearer now—clearer-headed—it all comes back to me just as if it were yesterday. It's Margaret Holcomb."

She was surprised into a laugh this time, the rippling laugh that a happy brook makes when it breaks out of the shade into the sunshine, and she said:

"Oh, you are wrong again; you don't get anything right. It isn't Holcomb, it's Blackmer."

I was ashamed again, and confessed it; then:

"How old are you, dear?"

"Twelve, New-Year's. Twelve and a month."

We were close comrades—inseparables in fact—for eight days. Every day we made pedestrian excursions—called them that anyway, and honestly they were intended for that, and that is what they would have been but for the persistent intrusion of a gray and grave and rough-coated donkey by the name of Maud.[26]

Margaret Blackmer, the solitary child with the laugh like a brook's, is one of the last symbolic figures written into immortality by Mark Twain's pen. A living Cathy Alison, she represented one fixed and trustworthy point in the dissolving universe he inhabited. Hence, her election to the Angel Fish Club. This exclusive group of charming maidens, each possessed of a beautiful pin from Tiffany's as a badge of membership, was a small informal galaxy of innocents with Mark Twain as their doting center. To the dozen or so girls he elected to his Club (on the basis of "sincerity, good disposition, intelligence & school-girl age") the old man's last home at Stormfield was always open. Moreover the Connecticut country estate he built at Redding had a special name for them; it was to be called "Innocence at Home"; "& it is not misnamed, for I know the Fishes well, and am aware that they can furnish the innocence necessary to make the name good." [27] The Angel Fish Club institutionalized the dream world of Twain's old age.

26. Paine, *Mark Twain*, 3, 1435–36.

27. Fragment titled "The Aquarium," DV 375 (1908), pp. 2–3, in MTP. © Mark Twain Company.

On the steamship which bore him back to America—itself a symbolic act, for he had spent a lifetime moving from one place to another—the old man grew bored and restless. "It is dull & I need wholesome excitements & distractions," he wrote one day on several pieces of paper, "so I will go lightly excursioning along the primrose path of theology." There followed another of Mark Twain's numerous beginnings for a story. Only this time, it was clear, this was not even a beginning, but simply random jottings in conversational form. "Little Bessie Would Assist Providence" was the title Twain gave the brief dialogue which resulted. It involved a three-year-old and her mother discoursing upon theological issues, one of which was the Virgin Mary.

B. (eagerly) So then Mr. Hollister was right, after all. He says the Virgin Mary isn't a virgin any more, she's a Has Been. He says—

M. It is false! Oh, it was just like that godless miscreant to try to undermine an innocent child's holy belief with his foolish lies; and if I could have my way, I—

B. But mama—honest and true—*is* she a virgin—a real virgin, you know?

M. Certainly she is; and has never been anything *but* a virgin—oh, the adorable One, the pure, the spotless, the undefiled!

B. Why, mama, Mr. Hollister says she *can't* be. That's what *he* says. He says she had five children after she had the One that was begotten by absent treatment & didn't break anything & he thinks such a lot of child-bearing, spread over years & years & years, would ultimately wear a virgin's virginity so thin that even Wall Street would consider the stock too lavishly watered & you couldn't place it there at any discount you could name, because the Board would say it was wildcat & Wouldn't list it. That is what *he* says. And besides—

M. Go to the nursery, instantly! Go!

A second exchange between little Bessie and her horrified mother concerns the common housefly.

> . . . Mamma, did God make the house-fly?
> Certainly, my darling.
> What for?
> For some great & good purpose, & to display His power.
> What is the great & good purpose, mamma?
> We do not know, my child. We only know that he makes *all* things for a great & good purpose. But this is too large a subject for a dear little Bessie like you, only a trifle over three years old.
> Possibly, mamma, yet it profoundly interests me. I have been reading about the fly, in the newest science-book. In that book he is called "the most dangerous animal and the most murderous that exists upon the earth, killing hundreds of thousands of men, women & children every year, by distributing deadly diseases among them." . . . Isn't it horrible, mamma! One fly produces fifty-two billions of descendants in 60 days in June & July, & they go & crawl over sick people & wade through pus, & sputa, & foul matter exuding from sores, and gaum themselves with every kind of disease-germ, then they go to everybody's dinner table . . .[28]

"Little Bessie Would Assist Providence" was, of course, never published, nor was it intended to be. Nevertheless, as a bit of Twainian satire it is wholly characteristic of the other side of his mind from the Angel Fish Club—the side that admired Jonathan Swift, wrote Colonel Sherburn's speech and *What Is Man?*, and created Philip Traum. It was as natural for Mark Twain to imagine an improbable three-year-old like

28. Unpublished MS, "Little Bessie Would Assist Providence," written "On Shipboard, Feb. 22, 1908," in MTP. © Mark Twain Company.

Bessie and to fill her mouth with amusing blasphemies as it was for him to create Cathy Alison, the *fin-de-siècle* cross between Joan of Arc and Elsie Dinsmore.

Little Bessie herself is unlifelike, but her speech is not. It contains at least one word that marks it as unmistakably Mark Twain's—"gaum." The homely Southwestern expression takes us back more than forty years to the very beginning of Twain's career. He had, we recall, put the same word into the mouth of old Simon Wheeler to describe Jim Wolf's sticky appearance after his ignominious descent from a slippery roof in Hannibal. "Jim Wolf and the Tom-Cats" and "Little Bessie Would Assist Providence" are thus linked by the most intimate of ties. Not only do they testify to a lifetime's dedication to delineating a complex fictional world inhabited by innocents, but they demonstrate also the essentials of this writer's particular style. Yeats has defined "style" as "the unmistakable individual voice," which in the case of Mark Twain is almost always the speaking voice. This vernacular mode, epitomized in little Bessie's artless choice of "gaum" as the right word, was the source of Twain's best prose, the redeeming feature of his worst writing, and it constitutes the richest item in his legacy to American writers of succeeding generations.

But little Bessie's naively acid questions about theology were not the last pieces in the mosaic of Twain's prose, nor would it have been characteristic of him to have ceased writing about children on this biting note. More fitting as a last picture of innocence is "Marjorie Fleming, the Wonder Child." This short essay, composed in the last year of his life, celebrates the memory of a little girl who lived and wrote in the first years of the nineteenth century. "Geographically considered, the lassie was a Scot; but in fact she had no frontiers, she was the world's child, she was the human race in little" (29, 358). Marjorie, who died before her ninth birthday, kept a journal and wrote unbelievably lively letters to her friends and neighbors (one of whom was Sir Walter Scott); "during the brief moment that she enchanted this dull earth with her presence she was the bewitchingest speller and punctuator in all Christendom" (29, 361).

Marjorie Fleming and Mark Twain were kindred spirits. "She was made out of thunderstorms and sunshine," he writes, "and not even her little perfunctory pieties and shop-made holiness could squelch her spirits or put out her fires for long. Under pressure of a pestering sense of duty she heaves a shovelful of trade godliness into her journals every little while, but it does not offend; for none of it is her own; it is all borrowed, it is a convention, a custom of her environment, it is the most innocent of hypocrisies, and this tainted butter of hers soon gets to be as delicious to the reader as are the stunning and worldly sincerities she splatters around it every time her pen takes a fresh breath" (29, 360–61). Caught up in his admiration for "the world's child" as writer, he unconsciously sees her as a previous incarnation of his own life and spirit. The self-identification shines out in every passage. "For she has a faculty, has Marjorie! Indeed yes; when she sits down on her bottom to do a letter, there isn't going to be any lack of materials, nor of fluency, and neither is her letter going to be wanting in pepper, or vinegar, or vitriol, or any of the other condiments employed by genius to save a literary work of art from flatness and vapidity. And as for judgments and opinions, they are as commodiously in her line as they are in the Lord Chief Justice's" (29, 362). At another place Twain summarizes Marjorie's amazing range of interests in these doubly-revealing words:

> She reads philosophies, novels, baby books, histories, the mighty poets—reads them with burning interest, and frankly and freely criticizes them all; she revels in storms, sunsets, cloud effects, scenery of mountain, plain, ocean,

and forest, and all the other wonders of nature, and sets
down her joy in them all; she loves people, she detests
people, according to mood and circumstances, and delivers her opinion of them, sometimes seasoned with attar
of roses, sometimes with vitriol; in games, and all kinds
of childish play she is an enthusiast; she adores animals,
adores them all; none is too forlorn to fail of favor in her
friendly eyes, no creature so humble that she cannot find
something in it on which to lavish her caressing worship.
[29, 367]

Read in the light of a closing career, this elegy to Marjorie
might (with some necessary pruning) stand as Twain's own
epitaph. For, like her, Mark Twain was a devotee of phi-
losophies, novels, baby books, and histories. Nature, games,
animals were equally dear to the enthusiast whose wife for
thirty years called him "Youth." Twain, too, both loved and
detested people according to mood and circumstance. He had
seasoned his pages sometimes with attar of roses and sometimes with vitriol. Most significantly of all, he had displayed,
like Marjorie's understanding governess, "the seeing eye and
the wise head," qualities that opened to him the rich world
of childhood. Remaining true to that vision through the black
days proved Twain's salvation—both personally and, in the
case of *The Mysterious Stranger* at least, artistically. "Marjorie Fleming, the Wonder Child," in itself but a slight piece,
vindicates the essential health and vigor of his imagination,
tortured though it was at the last into nightmares and bemused into dreams. This child's story, unlike Theodor
Fischer's or Cathy Alison's, did not move off into the realm
of fantasy, and if her pathetic, premature death affirms the
pattern of all Twain's girlish figures from Laura Hawkins to
Joan of Arc, the historical fact of her life and personality
anchored Twain to reality. In this sense, "the world's child"
redeemed Mark Twain.

9.

Mark Twain's Tradition

"IT WAS A MOVING ADDRESS you made over Ward Cheney—
that fortunate youth!" Twain wrote his friend Joe Twichell
on the occasion of the funeral of a young Hartford friend of
theirs. "Like Susy, he got out of life all that was worth the
living, and got his great reward before he had crossed the
tropic frontier of dreams and entered the Sahara of fact." [1]
This is the disillusioned remark of a freshly bereaved and
cynical old man. But Mark Twain was a literary artist, and
in *The Mysterious Stranger* and "A Horse's Tale" he was able
to put into fictional form the ceaseless crossing of the frontier
of dreams into the wasteland of fact which went on in his
imagination during the last years of his life. Each of these
late works reflects in quite different ways the retreat inside
the borders of dreamland. For it was ultimately only from this
vantage point that he was able to describe the geography of
Sahara and to assess the rewards of exploration.

Like Melville's, Twain's books taken as a whole embody
the pattern of a quest or investigation. By steamboat and
stagecoach, by raft and horseback and balloon, the figures in
his stories move across visible and invisible frontiers—from
East to West, downstream from free territory into slave,
across the Atlantic, from the present into the past, from maturity backward into youth. This last search—the man for the

1. MT to Rev. J. H. Twichell (March 4, 1900), in Paine, *Letters*, 2,
697.

child—is, as I see it, the central motif of Twain's prose. *The Mysterious Stranger,* "A Horse's Tale," and "Little Bessie Would Assist Providence" are links in one chain, final testimonials to a literary lifetime spent exploring childhood. Forty years separate "A Horse's Tale" from "Those Blasted Children"; an even longer span lies between *The Mysterious Stranger* and the "Thomas Jefferson Snodgrass Papers." Nor was Twain's interest in children one that flared at a particular point in his life and then subsided. *Joan of Arc* was published twenty years after *Tom Sawyer* but itself appeared twenty years before *The Mysterious Stranger.* Other novelists of his day shared his fascination, but none of them conducted so lengthy and intensive a reportage of what Dylan Thomas called "news of the little world." There were a number of reasons for this.

The first of the factors explaining Twain's preoccupation with childhood has to do with the age in which he lived; the generation which grew up in years just prior to the Civil War. After Appomattox, the shape of their world changed drastically. As adults, these Americans tended to look back upon their village boyhoods and girlhoods as simpler times of idyllic happiness. They recollected in present turmoil the tranquil past: when personal ties were deep and trustworthy, when Nature lay close at hand, a Cardiff Hill behind every village, when existence was gloriously free from adult restraint. In those carefree days, too, the problems of money, sex, marriage, business, depressions, strikes, industrialism, religious disillusion, and old age were remote considerations. Death and violence, however, were not so remote, but if they did not add drama to the daydream, at least they could conveniently be forgotten. This world, as Twain's contemporaries affectionately recalled it, was rural, innocent, and identified not so much with infancy as with early adolescence. Its image was created visually in the illustrations and paintings of Winslow Homer. "Snap the Whip" might well have served as the frontispiece to *Tom Sawyer*.

It was part of Twain's good fortune to have experienced this village boyhood with particular intensity. He was fortunate also to have seized upon this theme early in his writing career and to have struck the responsive nostalgic note in his readers. That he was able to capitalize (quite literally in fact) upon this sentiment more successfully than his fellow writers is due, more than anything else, to the multiple audience he created for his books. In his evocations of childhood he never wrote simply to amuse children or bemuse adults. He did both—and more. In spite of Howells' advice, *Tom Sawyer* is not just a boy's adventure story; it is both a humorous and a deadly serious study of the American small town, and *a fortiori* so are *Huckleberry Finn* and *Pudd'nhead Wilson*. Twain's contemporaries neither attempted nor achieved this double audience. Aldrich, Warner, and Howells were content to appeal to one group or the other, and their reward in our twentieth-century eyes has been to circle as satellites around the central figure of Mark Twain.

Twain's bonanza took place not in Washoe but in Hartford, because his generation presented him with a large number of readers who were delighted to read stories about boyhood— stories, as it turned out, no one could tell better than he. This would not have happened, however, if a respectable and lucrative New England tradition had not already existed for writing about young people. Certain authors wearing the halo of Concord and Boston had made juvenile writing acceptable and had enlarged the audience for such stories to include the whole family. Thus when Twain immigrated to Nook Farm he became part of a second-generation literary circle already actively engaged in writing books for and about the young. They had Hartford right at hand as a publishing center, and connections in Boston and New York, where the respectable journals for adults—*The Atlantic Monthly, Harper's, Scribner's*—as well as the proper children's magazines like the *St. Nicholas* were glad to bring out their works. Mark Twain fitted naturally into this circle. *The Prince and the Pauper* testifies to his acceptance of both the assets and the liabilities of such membership.

For a commercial writer juvenile literature was a wide-open field in late nineteenth-century America. True, the crude newspaper sketches about children which Sam Clemens had dashed off in San Francisco were *infra dig* in the staider East. Even more strongly than the residents of Nob Hill, some Eastern readers felt that "God's little people" should not be handled as roughly as Twain had done in "Those Blasted Children" and "Disgraceful Persecution of a Boy." But the infectious humor, the oral realism, and the capacity for moral indignation which gave Twain his nickname "The Moralist of the Main"—all these qualities served him well when he came to write for a national and a world-wide audience. These basic ingredients, in fact—once he discovered his mother lode in a fictional return to boyhood—were sufficient for a lifetime's production of sketches, stories, and novels.

Even in the most carefully genteel of the stories, Twain's western penchant for the crudely apt word or idiomatic phrase was likely to erupt. This style of humor, by turns stinging and hilarious, was the natural expression of a literary education picked up at the hands of A. B. Longstreet, Sut Lovingood, and *The Spirit of the Times*. When curbed by a sense of his age's fundamental proprieties, such western exuberance proved exciting and exotic to readers of *The Atlantic* and *St. Nicholas* and endeared him even more to the larger public who were devotees of the dime novels. Twain's broad burlesques, western locales, his competent, clever boy heroes with their pert attitude toward adult respectability— all were features of *Tom Sawyer, Huckleberry Finn,* and the other boyhood books which help to account for his position as the first American writer to appeal widely across class, regional, and national lines. A large part of his popularity was due to his choice of childhood as theme; for, unlike Henry James' moral discovery of Europe, boyhood proved (like Mark Twain himself) appealing to every sort of reader.

Mobility, however, had its problems, both personal and literary. One way Twain's talented but somewhat unsubtle Missouri imagination was domesticated for national consumption was through his own family. Livy Clemens and Susy, Clara, and Jean shared the tastes of their day and class. By their literary enthusiasms the girls and their mother also furthered Mark Twain's education. Through them, he became aware of the possibilities in juvenile writing and he absorbed, sometimes quite casually and unconsciously as he read aloud to his daughters, some of the techniques of nursery novelists like Charlotte Yonge and Jacob Abbott. Though he spoofed their didactic mannerisms, he learned from these prolific story-tellers what would interest young readers. Furthermore, when he tried his own hand with a book like *The Prince and the Pauper,* he gladly solicited censorship and advice of both young and old among his Nook Farm circle. Thus his fiction was indelibly marked in character and in tone by the intimate presence of his own family and by the constant reception of ideas from them.

The last years of the nineteenth century were a family-centered age, both in America and abroad, especially as regards reading habits. The familiar norms, as Frank Norris ruefully remarked, were the amiable young girl and the group around the library table. In large part Twain accepted these norms and wrote for this audience. This does not mean that he never consciously ignored canons of good taste which the Victorian family demanded, or that he avoided topics deemed unsuitable for domestic consumption. But in general he came to regard himself as an integrated member of the respectable American upper class (after all, the Clemenses were from Virginia and before that linked to the Earls of Durham). Not all but some of his writings about children reflect and authenticate this social identification.

The coercive and stifling effects of Elmira and Hartford, and of the proper audience which accompanied such status, have been much emphasized by certain critics of Mark Twain's art. The attempt here has been to indicate opportunities as well as pitfalls in this social and artistic environment and to suggest how tentative and ironic Twain often felt his role to be. By now it is clear what part childhood as fictional theme played in this typically American situation. In practice, it proved the ideal strategy for a social satirist who had married well. That is, writing about Bad Boys, virginal maidens, and precocious infants was not only an American tradition and the most fruitful expression of his imagination but Twain's means of adjusting to his immediate environment and a compromise with his far-flung electorate. To the degree that he felt both a part of and at odds with society—and I believe this was his normal frame of mind—writing about children permitted him both to escape and to confront some embarrassing problems. As a result, childhood became the characteristic mask, as humor was the typical mode, for communication with his world.

What happened, therefore, was that Twain largely resisted social and family pressures on his art that might have turned him into a second Charles Dudley Warner or Thomas Bailey Aldrich, and by playing both sides of the juvenile street, so to speak, made an opportunity of what might have proved a fatal danger. As a commercial writer, he made a fortune in this fashion. As a literary artist, he put children to his private purposes. These objectives were in essence three-fold: to recreate in loving and honest detail the lost world of Hannibal before the War; to report and comment upon the money-crazed world of his own day; and, finally, to reduce to simple terms the Darwinian intellectual revolution which had made a shambles of his unsophisticated, post-Calvinist cosmology. These three concerns—all regarded by Twain as *moral* problems requiring *literary* formulation—achieved dramatic expression most typically and successfully through Mark Twain's childish figures.

The primary role his boys and girls are called upon to play is as moral commentator on adult society, and as such they function most powerfully in proportion as they embody a certain kind of innocence. All Twain's children possess it, though Huck Finn has more than Tom Sawyer, King Edward more than Tom Canty, Joan of Arc more than Theodor Fischer. Markedly different from the innocence of Aldrich's or Howells' children, this quality is an elusive naiveté, compounded not of inexperience but rather of a moral simplicity and directness that stems from the child's point in time and place in society. Poised on the brink of adolescence—the word "puberty" has virtually no meaning in this connection—and located outside of the normal class and family structure, the childish figure in Twain's fiction occupies a solitary and slippery eminence. His vision is always double. Looking backward to childish purity and ignorance and forward toward mature knowledge and involvement in corporate sin, the child also combines, albeit uneasily, instinctual and rational modes of thought. Normally the source of innocence is Nature, for Twain's child is really a refugee from the world of Rousseau and Wordsworth. Henry Thoreau could have identified with ease the particular innocence of Mark Twain's children, for in *Walden* he has described it. "They are not callow like the young of most birds," he wrote of the baby partridges he encountered in Walden woods, "but more perfectly developed and precocious even than chickens. The

270

remarkably adult yet innocent expression of their open and serene eyes is very memorable. All intelligence seems reflected in them. They suggest not merely the purity of infancy, but a wisdom clarified by experience. Such an eye was not born when the bird was, but is coeval with the sky it reflects." [2] Mark Twain was no Transcendentalist, and came, toward the end of his life, to see the universal sky as anything but pure and clear. Nevertheless, he would have assented, I think, to this description of the quality he treasured most in human beings.

As innocent outsiders endowed with a moral sense fatally fragile to the jars of time, Twain's young people normally assume passive parts in the world. That is, Tom and Huck and Theodor are principally observers; Injun Joe, the river folk, the villagers of Eseldorf are the active agents. After all, Twain realistically recognized that children are usually subject to adult control and manipulation. More fundamentally, however, this passivity was a way of expressing his conviction —common in an age whose modes of thought were being profoundly reoriented by Darwin and Spencer—that life itself is a rigidly determined affair. The row of children's bricks in *The Mysterious Stranger* is a paradigm for childhood and for the human condition.

Here, of course, is one of the many paradoxes in Twain's thought and art, because certain of his fictional children are supremely active agents in the world of adults. Tom Sawyer is continually dominating older people and demonstrating his superior cleverness. So also does Tom's British cousin from Offal Court. Most clearly of all, Joan of Arc represents childhood at the peak of its victorious power over circumstances. Just as Twain's fierce moral indignation appears incompatible with determinism, so does this vacillation between assigning

2. *Walden*, Vol. 2 of *The Writings of Henry D. Thoreau*, Walden Edition (Boston and New York, Houghton Mifflin, 1906), p. 251.

active and passive roles to his youthful characters seem a contradiction. Representing the child as victim and as victor, often in the same character, demonstrated unresolvable tensions within Mark Twain's outlook.

Indeed, if we press this writer's thought, at nearly every point it is liable to dissolve into contradiction. There is, for instance, the matter of the relationship of moral worth to social and racial background. Twain was ostensibly an ardent democrat and antiracist (except as regards the profligate French, of whom he wrote "the descent seems to be from flea, fly, louse, &c., down to human being, & then Frenchman").[3] Yet in the novels involving switched identities, it often happens that the aristocrat or the white man actually demonstrate a moral superiority over the poor person or the Negro which the novel ostensibly asserts. *The Prince and the Pauper* and *Pudd'nhead Wilson* are both examples of this ambivalence. They remind us that Mark Twain was the author not only of *A Connecticut Yankee* but also of "The Curious Republic of Gondour," a plea for aristocracy.

Or, again, take Twain's curious attitude toward family in his stories and novels. No reader has failed to notice the truncated picture he presents of domestic relationships and affections conspicuously absent or turned awry. Fathers, for instance, are usually dead (Tom Sawyer's) or die (Huck's, the Prince's) or deserve to die (the Pauper's). Mothers, however, when not replaced by aunts or maiden ladies, serve as wooden objects of distant adoration. Other members enact equally stereotyped roles. Nowhere is the essential unreality of Twain's fiction (as compared, say, with that of Howells) better demonstrated than in the abnormality of its family life. Without doubt, he was picking his way gingerly about a pitfall that was both private and public. Within his own ex-

3. Notebook 31[I] (last date Oct., 1896), typescript, p. 8, in MTP. © Mark Twain Company.

perience, family life held the domestic felicities of Nook Farm (associated with little girls and an idolized mother-wife) but also the colder memories of Hannibal, where fatherly kisses were reserved for deathbed farewells. In his career, too, Twain felt pressure from the side of Hartford and his *Atlantic* and *St. Nicholas* readership to depict family life as a happy and patriarchal affair. From an opposite quarter, that of newspaper humor and dime novel plots, he felt impelled toward anarchy and subversion of society's prime institution for coercive control. Rather than decide once for all, Twain played indiscriminately to both galleries.

Still more puzzling and unstable is his attitude toward childhood itself. In certain of his moods, youth was quite simply the memory of Paradise. "I suppose we all have a Jackson's Island somewhere, and dream of it when we are tired," he once wrote an English friend.[4] Even in *The Mysterious Stranger,* the most destructive of all his novels, this nostalgia is passionately presented. Normally for childhood to be bathed in this refulgent light, however, it must be divorced from society and united with Nature. It is no accident that Jackson's Island and Cardiff Hill are recurrent images of the happy side of boyhood, nor that the narrative movement in the typical story is away from the town into the countryside, up into the hills, across the prairie or desert, or down stream. Only under the Fairy Tree, if at all, can the truce with time be made.

Once carried backward into that simpler world, however, the reader of Mark Twain's stories is confronted not so much with carefree schoolboy pranks as with Aldrich and Shillaber, or with a father's enveloping blue cape, as in Howells, but invariably and insistently with violence, evil, and death. Childhood may have been for Twain the best part of life;

4. MT to Sir Walter Besant, Feb. 22, 1898, in Berg Collection, NYPL.

it was also a frightening nightmare. St. Petersburg and Dawson's Landing are modes of life as deceptive on their tranquil surface as Moby Dick's "mighty mildness of repose." The very earliest boyhood narrative—the "Boy's Manuscript"—is the only one he ever composed that did not directly confront children with the very presence and lineaments of bloody death. For some of them, like Huck Finn, life is a veritable succession of corpses. Greed and cupidity, too, thrust themselves into the lives of Twain's boys and girls. Moreover, such unsavory sides of life are displayed just as insistently in the genteel stories—those written for Mrs. Dodge's small readers—as in the so-called rougher narratives.

As a consequence of this ironic vision, the typical Twain story repeats the pattern of initiation rite so familiar to our modern anthropological imagination. His neophyte is typically an innocent stripling, just old enough to know what evil is but seldom evil himself. Menacing the inexperienced child is an adult environment apt to explode into violence at any moment. Such grim possibilities are always realized and the innocent is made to experience, forcibly and suddenly, the stupidity, cruelty, and destructiveness of human nature and, by extension, of the universe. At the same time, he learns that courage, resourcefulness, humility, nobility are likewise parts of the human condition; often, in this respect, he is his own tutor. In certain kinds of initiations, such as Tom Sawyer's, Tom Canty's, or Theodor Fischer's, the boy achieves by his experience of evil only a partial moral victory. In other instances the child is more unequivocally triumphant, though in the case of Prince Edward, Joan of Arc, and Cathy Alison a timely death is their reward. Huck Finn's introduction to the meaning of maturity manifests much the most complex situation of all, for his is the bloodiest immersion, the most anguished search for moral identity, his the signal triumph of boyhood, and his the most chilling lapse of moral imagination. If Joan of Arc is Mark Twain's closest approach to a genuinely tragic figure, Huck Finn is his ironic masterpiece. After his moment on the raft, Huck's fate is to serve out his fictional life in ignominious bondage to Tom Sawyer.

It is this preoccupation with an innocent's unsuccessful or fatal initiation, recounted usually in the child's own vernacular, that unites the fiction of Mark Twain with one main stream of American writing. The "end to innocence" or "the matter of Adam" has, at least since Hawthorne's "The Gentle Boy," been a major theme in our fiction. In distinctive but identifiable ways *The Marble Faun, Billy Budd, The Red Badge of Courage,* "The Pupil," "Indian Camp," *The Bear,* and *The Catcher in the Rye* are links in one chain. In that tradition *Huckleberry Finn* properly occupies a central place. Ernest Hemingway was one of the first to put it there, with assistance from Sherwood Anderson. As recently as 1956 William Faulkner, too, acknowledged Mark Twain as his generation's literary grandfather. Apart from *Huckleberry Finn,* however, Twain's contributions to the literature of innocence have gone somewhat unnoticed. I have tried to suggest some valid reasons for assigning *Tom Sawyer* and *Joan of Arc* more important places in the pantheon, and for taking more seriously such works as *Tom Sawyer, Abroad* and *The Prince and the Pauper* as rehearsals of the American Adam story.

Recognition by twentieth-century writers that Mark Twain was a vital link between their age and that of Hawthorne and Melville did not begin, of course, with *Green Hills of Africa.* In 1903, for instance, a young and unknown novelist named Samuel Merwin addressed the following prophetic remarks to the aging author of *Tom Sawyer:*

> I hope this letter is not an impertinence. I have just been turning about, with my head full of Spenser and Shakespeare and "Gil Blas," looking for something in our

own present day literature to which I could surrender myself as to those fine gripping old writings. And nothing could I find until I took up "Life on the Mississippi," and "Huckleberry Finn," and, just now, the "Connecticut Yankee" . . .

I like to think that "Tom Sawyer" and "Huckleberry Finn" will be looked upon, fifty or a hundred years from now, as the picture of buoyant, dramatic, *human* American life. I feel, deep in my heart, pretty sure that they will be. They won't be looked on then as the work of a "humorist" any more than we think of Shakespeare as a humorist now . . . But Shakespeare was a humorist and so, thank Heaven! is Mark Twain. And Shakespeare plunged deep into the deep, sad things of life; and so, in a different way (but in a way that has more than once brought tears to my eyes) has Mark Twain. But after all, it isn't because of any resemblance for anything that was ever before written that Mark Twain's books strike in so deep: it's rather because they've brought something really new into our literature—new, yet old as Adam and Eve and the Apple. And this achievement, the achievement of putting something into literature that was not there before, is, I should think, the most that any writer can ever hope to do.[5]

A minor novelist, Samuel Merwin is himself forgotten; no one today reads *Comrade John* or *Anthony the Absolute*. But other and better writers have agreed with Merwin that Mark Twain did bring something fresh into American letters. They find this freshness pre-eminently in *Tom Sawyer* and *Huckleberry Finn* and *Life on the Mississippi*, but also in the lesser books. It is, I would suggest, an angle of vision into experi-

5. Samuel Merwin to MT (Aug. 4, 1903), in Paine, *Letters*, 2, 743–**44.**

ence at once humorous and deeply in earnest. It is new and yet as old as Adam. It is "the picture of the buoyant, dramatic, *human* American life" observed through the innocent eye of childhood.

One does not have to look far in modern fiction to identify the legacy of Mark Twain. In the generation after him came Booth Tarkington's *Penrod,* the stories of O. Henry and Sherwood Anderson, and, somewhat later, Edgar Lee Master's *Mitch Miller,* all directly indebted to Twain and to the natural speech in which his stories are told. Following World War I (and thus recapitulating, in a sense, the psychological conditions of the Gilded Age), Twain's tradition was recognized and revived by Ernest Hemingway in the Nick Adams stories and by William Faulkner. The child's incomplete but harrowing perception of terror, so common a theme in all of Twain's stories, is dramatized in "That Evening Sun" and *The Sound and the Fury.* Even more palpable is the debt Faulkner owes Twain in a story like *The Bear.*

That Southern writers in particular are inheritors of Mark Twain's estate is indicated by the galaxy of short stories and novels appearing in the present generation. Katherine Anne Porter, Eudora Welty, Carson McCullers, Truman Capote, Shirley Ann Grau, Harper Lee are some of our better-known Southern writers who find in the freshness and immediacy of the child's mind an appropriate alembic for their insights. A rich complex of family, race, and history challenges the Southern writer, for whom Mark Twain stands in a peculiarly close relationship. His ear for dialect, his eye for the physical landscape and the social setting, his moral preoccupation with the central issue of Southern life, even the repudiation of industrialism implicit in the Mississippi River tales—all these are qualities of Twain's imagination that more than atone for his ignorance of Freud. Like Twain, these younger writers of our own day find it an appropriate way to express the wonder,

277

humor, and tragedy of their way of life by assuming, as Eudora Welty does in *Delta Wedding* or Carson McCullers in *A Member of the Wedding*, the point of view of a child.

From a totally different social and artistic environment, J. D. Salinger also accepts Twain as ancestor. From the moment when Holden Caulfield stands alone on the hill looking down upon the football game in which he cannot even participate as spectator, *The Catcher in the Rye* inescapably recalls *Huckleberry Finn.*[6] Salinger has Twain's same quick ear for an adolescent's crude, vigorous, unconsciously humorous talk. Holden's quest for an adult world that is not "phoney" recalls Huck's horrified reactions to the rascals he meets along the river. A final and irrevocable sense of alienation sends Holden Caulfield to an Arizona sanitarium; Huck Finn had vowed "to light out for the Territory." In spite of the years and miles that stretch between Park Avenue and the tanyard, there is an affinity between these novels which attests both to the continuing vitality of a boy's vision as the occasion for art and to Mark Twain's special utility in this enterprise.

Literature expresses both private and public values. If, as foreign observers are fond of pointing out, the United States is a child-centered society, we should expect writers to be sharing and creating this commitment, for the artist is both creature and maker of culture. Such is the case now and was in Mark Twain's world. This literary fascination with the formative, immature period of life has developed over a long period of time—over at least a century. During much of this time children as audience and children as subjects for adult fiction have been separate concerns for American writers. Thus Louisa May Alcott and Eudora Welty are only in a general sense practitioners in the same field. It was part of Mark Twain's special contribution to American letters to

6. See Edgar Branch, "Mark Twain and J. D. Salinger: A Study in Literary Continuity," *American Quarterly*, 9 (1957), 144–58.

unite these two traditions. Like Miss Alcott, he wrote pleasant and proper stories for the young. Like Miss Welty, on the other hand, he wrote about the child's world, relating it always to the larger adult sphere and to the social and moral problems that are eternal human concerns. In discharging both of these literary tasks Mark Twain spoke not only for the Gilded Age but for himself.

Index